Frommer's

Dec. '04

PORTABLE
London
2005

by Darwin Porter & Danforth Prince

D0666719

Here's what critics say about Frommer's:

"Amazingly easy to use. Very portable, very complete."

—*Booklist*

"Detailed, accurate, and easy-to-read information for all price ranges."

—*Glamour Magazine*

WILEY

Wiley Publishing, Inc.

Published by:

WILEY PUBLISHING, INC.

111 River St.
Hoboken, NJ 07030-5774

ISBN 0-7645-7363-2

Editor: Stephen Bassman
Production Editor: Donna Wright
Photo Editor: Richard Fox
Cartographer: Nick Trotter
Production by Wiley Indianapolis Composition Services

For information on our other products and services or to obtain technical
support, please contact our Customer Care Department within the U.S. at
800/762-2974, outside the U.S. at 317/572-3993 or fax 317/572-4002.

Wiley also publishes its books in a variety of electronic formats. Some con-
tent that appears in print may not be available in electronic formats.

Manufactured in the United States of America

5 4 3 2 1

Contents

List of Maps

ABOUT THE AUTHORS

As a team of veteran travel writers, **Darwin Porter** and **Danforth Prince** have produced numerous titles for Frommer's, including best-selling guides to Italy, France, the Caribbean, England, and Germany. Porter, a former bureau chief of *The Miami Herald,* is also a Hollywood biographer, his most recent releases entitled *The Secret Life of Humphrey Bogart* and *Katharine the Great.* Prince was formerly employed by the Paris bureau of the *New York Times,* and is today the president of Blood Moon Productions and other media-related firms.

AN INVITATION TO THE READER

In researching this book, we discovered many wonderful places-hotels, restaurants, shops, and more. We're sure you'll find others. Please tell us about them, so we can share the information with your fellow travelers in upcoming editions. If you were disappointed with a recommendation, we'd love to know that, too. Please write to:

Frommer's Portable London 2005
Wiley Publishing, Inc. • 111 River St. • Hoboken, NJ 07030-5774

AN ADDITIONAL NOTE

Please be advised that travel information is subject to change at any time—and this is especially true of prices. We therefore suggest that you write or call ahead for confirmation when making your travel plans. The authors, editors, and publisher cannot be held responsible for the experiences of readers while traveling. Your safety is important to us, however, so we encourage you to stay alert and be aware of your surroundings. Keep a close eye on cameras, purses, and wallets, all favorite targets of thieves and pickpockets.

FROMMER'S STAR RATINGS, ICONS & ABBREVIATIONS

Every hotel, restaurant, and attraction listing in this guide has been ranked for quality, value, service, amenities, and special features using a **star-rating system.** In country, state, and regional guides, we also rate towns and regions to help you narrow down your choices and budget your time accordingly. Hotels and restaurants are rated on a scale of zero (recommended) to three stars (exceptional). Attractions, shopping, nightlife, towns, and regions are rated according to the following scale: zero stars (recommended), one star (highly recommended), two stars (very highly recommended), and three stars (must-see).

In addition to the star-rating system, we also use **seven feature icons** that point you to the great deals, in-the-know advice, and unique experiences that separate travelers from tourists. Throughout the book, look for:

Finds	Special finds—those places only insiders know about
Fun Fact	Fun facts—details that make travelers more informed and their trips more fun
Kids	Best bets for kids and advice for the whole family
Moments	Special moments—those experiences that memories are made of
Overrated	Places or experiences not worth your time or money
Tips	Insider tips—great ways to save time and money
Value	Great values—where to get the best deals

The following **abbreviations** are used for credit cards:

AE	American Express	DISC	Discover	V	Visa
DC	Diners Club	MC	MasterCard		

FROMMERS.COM

Now that you have the guidebook to a great trip, visit our website at **www.frommers.com** for travel information on more than 3,000 destinations. With features updated regularly, we give you instant access to the most current trip-planning information available. At Frommers.com, you'll also find the best prices on airfares, accommodations, and car rentals-and you can even book travel online through our travel booking partners. At Frommers.com, you'll also find the following:

- Online updates to our most popular guidebooks
- Vacation sweepstakes and contest giveaways
- Newsletter highlighting the hottest travel trends
- Online travel message boards with featured travel discussions

Planning Your Trip to London

This chapter tackles the "hows" of your trip to London—those issues required to get your trip together and get on the road, whether you're a frequent traveler or a first-timer.

1 Visitor Information

Visit Britain maintains a website at **www.visitbritain.com**. You can also get information from **Visit Britain** offices. There's one in the **United States,** at 551 Fifth Ave., 7th Floor, New York, NY 10176-0799 (© **800/462-2748** or 212/986-2266; fax 212/986-1188). In **Australia,** the office is at Level 16, Gateway, 1 Macquarie Place, Sydney, NSW 2000 (© **02/9377-4400;** fax 02/9377-4499). In **New Zealand,** go to the Fay Richwhite Building, 17th Floor, 151 Queen St., Auckland 1 (© **09/303-1446;** fax 09/377-6965). For a full information packet on London, write to **Visit London Tourist Board,** Glen House, Stag Place, Victoria, SW1E 5LT (© **020/7932-2000**). You can call the recorded-message service, **London-line** (© **090/6866-3344**), 24 hours a day for information once you're in Britain (the number cannot be dialed outside Britain). Various topics are listed; calls cost 60p ($1) per minute.

Time Out, the most up-to-date magazine for what's happening in London, is online at **www.timeout.com/london**. You can pick up a print copy at any international newsstand.

To book accommodations with a credit card (MasterCard or Visa), call **Visit London Booking Office** at © **020/7604-2890,** or fax them at 020/7372-2068. They're available Monday to Friday from 9am to 6pm (London time). There is a £5 ($9.25) fee for booking.

WHAT'S ON THE WEB   The most useful site was created by a very knowledgeable source, the Visit Britain itself, and U.S. visitors are its target audience. A wealth of information is available at **www.visitbritain.com**, which lets you order brochures online, provides trip-planning hints, and even grants prompt answers to e-mail questions. This site covers all of Great Britain. Visit London, the official visitor organization for the city, offers even more specific information about the city on its website, **www.visitlondon.com**. Go to **www.baa.com** for a guide and terminal maps for Heathrow, Gatwick, Stansted, and other London-area airports, including flight arrival times, duty-free shops, airport restaurants, and info on getting from the airports to downtown London. Getting around London can be confusing, so you might want to visit **www.londontransport.co.uk** for up-to-the-minute info. For the latest details on London's theater scene, consult **www.officiallondontheatre.co.uk** or **www.londontheatre.co.uk**. At **www.multimap.com**, you can access detailed street maps of the whole United Kingdom. For directions to specific places in London, consult **www.streetmap.co.uk**.

2 Entry Requirements & Customs

ENTRY REQUIREMENTS

Citizens of the United States, Canada, Australia, New Zealand, and South Africa require a passport to enter the United Kingdom, but not a visa. Irish citizens and citizens of European Union countries need only an identity card. The maximum stay for non–European Union visitors is 6 months. Some Customs officials request proof that you have the means to leave the country (usually a round-trip ticket) and means of support while you're in Britain (someone in the U.K. will have to vouch that they are supporting you, or you may be asked to show documents that indicate that you have an income). If you're planning to fly on from the United Kingdom to a country that requires a visa, it's wise to secure the visa before you leave home.

Your valid driver's license and at least 1 year's experience is required to drive personal or rented cars. You must be 25 or over to rent a car.

For an up-to-date country-by-country listing of passport requirements around the world, go to the "Foreign Entry Requirements" Web page of the U.S. State Department at **http://travel.state.gov/foreignentryreqs/americansabroad.html**.

CUSTOMS REGULATIONS

WHAT YOU CAN BRING INTO LONDON

For Non–E.U. Nationals 18 Plus   You can bring in, duty-free, 200 cigarettes, 100 cigarillos, 50 cigars, or 250 grams of smoking tobacco. The amount allowed for each of these goods is doubled if you live outside Europe.

You can also bring in 2 liters of wine and either 1 liter of alcohol over 22 proof or 2 liters of wine under 22 proof. In addition, you can bring in 60cc (2.03 oz.) of perfume, a quarter liter (250ml) of eau de toilette, 500 grams (1 lb.) of coffee, and 200 grams (½ lb.) of tea. Visitors 15 and over may also bring in other goods totaling £145 ($268); the allowance for those 14 and under is £72.50 ($134). (Customs officials tend to be lenient about general merchandise, realizing the limits are unrealistically low.)

You can't bring your pet straight to England. Six months' quarantine is required before it is allowed in. An illegally imported animal may be destroyed.

For E.U. Citizens Visitors from fellow European Union countries can bring into Britain any amount of goods as long as the goods are intended for their personal use—not for resale.

The current policy for bringing pets into the U.K. from the E.U. is under review. Right now, animals or pets of any kind are forbidden from entering without a long quarantine period.

WHAT YOU CAN BRING HOME

For U.S. Citizens If you've been out of the country for 48 hours or more, you can bring $800 worth of goods (per person) back into the United States without paying a duty. On the next $1,000 worth of goods you pay a flat 4%. Beyond that, it works on an item-by-item basis. There are a few restrictions on amounts: 1 liter of alcohol (you must be over 21), 200 cigarettes, and 100 cigars. Antiques over 100 years old and works of art are exempt from the $400 limit, as is anything you mail home. Once per day, you can mail yourself $200 worth of goods duty-free; mark the package "For Personal Use." You can also mail $200 worth of goods per person per day to other people; label each package "Unsolicited Gift." Any package must state a description of the contents and their values on the exterior. You can't mail alcohol, perfume (it contains alcohol), or tobacco products.

For more details on regulations, check out the **U.S. Customs Service** website at **www.customs.gov** or contact the Customs office at P.O. Box 7407, Washington, DC 20044 (© **202/354-1000**) to request the free "Know Before You Go" pamphlet.

To prevent the spread of diseases, you can't bring in most plants, fruits, vegetables, meats, or other foodstuffs. Check out the USDA's website at **www.aphis.usda.gov** for more details.

For Canadian Citizens For a clear summary of **Canadian** rules, write for the booklet *I Declare,* issued by the **Canada Customs and Revenue Agency,** 333 Dunsmuir St., Vancouver, BC V6B 5R4 Canada (© **800/461-9999**), or check out the website at **www. ccra-adrc.gc.ca.** Canada allows its citizens a C$750 exemption if you're gone for 7 days or longer (only C$200 if you're gone between 48 hr. and 7 days), and you're allowed to bring back, duty-free, 200 cigarettes, 50 cigars, and 1.5 liters of wine *or* 1.14 liters of liquor *or* 8.5 liters of beer or ale. In addition, you're allowed to mail gifts to Canada at the rate of C$60 a day, provided they're unsolicited and aren't alcohol or tobacco (write "Unsolicited Gift, Under $60 Value" on the package).

3 Money

POUNDS & PENCE

Britain's decimal monetary system is based on the pound (£), which is made up of 100 pence (written as "p"). Pounds are also called "quid" by Britons. There are £1 and £2 coins, as well as coins of 50p, 20p, 10p, 5p, 2p, and 1p. Banknotes come in denominations of £5, £10, £20, and £50.

As a general guideline, the price conversions in this book have been computed at the rate of £1 = $1.85 (U.S.). Bear in mind, however, that exchange rates fluctuate daily.

ATMS

ATMs are easily found throughout London. ATMs are also connected to the major networks at airports such as Heathrow and Gatwick. You'll usually get a better exchange rate by withdrawing money at an ATM (currency exchange booths take a huge commission or give an unfavorable rate, or both), but your bank may charge a fee for using a foreign ATM. You may also need a different PIN to use overseas ATMs. Call your bank to check and get a new PIN if needed before you go.

The most popular ATM networks are **Cirrus** (© 800/424-7787; www.mastercard.com) and **PLUS** (© 800/843-7587; www.visa.com); check the back of your ATM card to see which network your bank belongs to. You can use the 800 numbers in the U.S. (also on your card) to locate ATMs in your destination or ask your bank for a list of overseas ATMs. You can find the locations of ATMs on www.visa.com and www.mastercard.com.

TRAVELER'S CHECKS

These days, traveler's checks are less necessary because most English cities and towns, especially London, have 24-hour ATMs, allowing you to withdraw small amounts of cash as needed. But if you prefer the security of the tried and true, you might want to stick with traveler's checks—provided that you don't mind showing an ID every time you want to cash a check.

Exchange rates are more favorable at your destination. Nevertheless, it's often helpful to exchange at least some money before going abroad (standing in line at the exchange bureau in the London airport could make you miss the next bus leaving for downtown after a long flight). Check with any of your local American Express or Thomas Cook offices or major banks. Or, order pounds in advance from the following: **American Express** (© **800/221-7282;** www. americanexpress.com), **Thomas Cook** (© **800/223-7373;** www. thomascook.com), or **Visa** (© **800/732-1322**).

It's best to exchange currency or traveler's checks at a bank, not a hotel or shop. Currency and traveler's checks (which garner a better exchange rate than cash) can be changed at all principal airports and at some travel agencies, such as American Express and Thomas Cook. Note the rates and ask about commission fees; it can sometimes pay to shop around and ask.

Keep a record of your traveler's checks' serial numbers—separate from the checks, of course—so you're ensured a refund in an emergency.

CREDIT CARDS

Credit cards are a safe way to carry money and they provide a convenient record of all your expenses. You can also withdraw cash advances from your credit cards at any bank (although you'll pay interest on the advance the moment you receive the cash, and you won't get frequent-flier miles on an airline credit card). At most banks you can get a cash advance at the ATM with your PIN. If you don't have a PIN, call your credit card company and ask for one. It usually takes 5 to 7 business days, but some banks provide the number over the phone if you pass a security clearance.

4 When to Go

CLIMATE

Charles Dudley Warner once said that the trouble with the weather is that everybody talks about it but nobody does anything about it. Well, Londoners talk about weather more than anyone, but they have also done something about it: Air-pollution control has resulted in the virtual disappearance of the pea-soup fogs that once blanketed the city.

A typical London-area weather forecast for a summer day predicts "scattered clouds with sunny periods and showers, possibly heavy at times." Summer temperatures seldom rise above 78°F (25°C), nor do they drop below 35°F (2°C) in winter. London, being in one of the mildest parts of the country, can be very pleasant in the spring and fall. Yes, it rains, but you'll rarely get a true downpour. Rains are heaviest in November, when the city averages 6⅓ cm (2½ in.).

The British consider chilliness wholesome and usually try to keep room temperatures about 10° below the American comfort level, so bring sweaters year-round if you tend to get cold.

HOLIDAYS

In England, public holidays include New Year's Day, Good Friday, Easter Monday, May Day (first Mon in May), spring and summer bank holidays (last Mon in May and Aug, respectively), Christmas Day, and Boxing Day (Dec 26).

LONDON CALENDAR OF EVENTS

January

January Sales. Most shops offer good reductions at this time. Many sales start as early as late December to beat the post-Christmas slump. Truly voracious shoppers camp overnight outside Harrods so that they have first pickings.

London Parade. Bands, floats, and carriages contribute to the merriment as the parade wends its way from Parliament Square to Berkeley Square in Mayfair. January 1. Procession starts around noon.

February

Chinese New Year. The famous Lion Dancers appear in Soho. Free. Either in late January or early February (based on the lunar calendar). Call ℂ **0891/505490** for schedule and event details.

Great Spitalfields Pancake Race, Old Spitalfields Market, Brushfield Street, E1. Teams of four run in relays, tossing pancakes. To join in, call ℂ **020/7375-0441** or visit www.alternative arts.co.uk. At noon on Shrove Tuesday (last day before Lent).

April

Easter Parade. Floats, marching bands, and a full day of Easter Sunday activities enliven Battersea Park. Free. Easter Sunday.

Flora London Marathon. Thirty thousand competitors run from Greenwich Park to Buckingham Palace. Call ℂ **020/7902-0189** or visit www.london-marathon.co.uk for more information or to register for the marathon. Mid- to late April.

The Queen's Birthday. The queen's birthday is celebrated with 21-gun salutes in Hyde Park, and by troops in parade dress on Tower Hill at noon. April 21.

National Gardens Scheme. More than 3,000 private gardens in London are open to the public on set days, and tea is sometimes served. Pick up the NGS guidebook for £8 ($15) from most bookstores, or contact the National Gardens Scheme Charitable Trust, Hatchlands Park, East Clandon, Guildford, Surrey GU4 7RT (✆ **01483/211-535;** www.ngs.org.uk). Late April to early May.

May

The Royal Windsor Horse Show, Home Park, Windsor Castle. You might spot a royal at this multiday horse-racing and horse-showing event. Call ✆ **01753/860-633** or visit www.royal-windsor-horse-show.co.uk for more details. Mid-May.

Chelsea Flower Show, Chelsea Royal Hospital. This show exhibits the best of British gardening, with displays of plants and flowers from all seasons. The show runs from 8am to 8pm; tickets are £29 ($54). On the last day, the show runs from 8am to 5:30pm, and tickets are £31 ($57). Tickets must be purchased in advance; they are available through the Royal Horticultural Society (✆ **020/7828-4125;** www.rhs.org.uk). Call ✆ **0870/906-3781** for information. Three days in May.

June

Trooping the Colour, Horse Guards Parade, Whitehall. The official birthday of the queen (as opposed to her actual birthday, which is Apr 21) is held on a designated date in June. Seated in a carriage, the monarch inspects her regiments and takes their salute as they parade their colors. It's a quintessentially British event, with exquisite pageantry and pomp. Tickets for the parade and for two reviews, held on preceding Saturdays, are allocated by ballot. Those interested in attending must apply for tickets between January 1 and the end of February, enclosing a stamped, self-addressed envelope or International Reply Coupon—exact dates and ticket prices are supplied later. The drawing is held in mid-March, and successful applicants *only* are informed in April. For details, and to apply for tickets, write to **HQ Household Division,** Horse Guards, Whitehall, London SW1X 6AA, enclosing a self-addressed envelope and International Reply Coupon (available at any post office). Call ✆ **020/7414-2479** for more information.

Lawn Tennis Championships, Wimbledon, Southwest London. Ever since players in flannels and bonnets took to the grass courts at Wimbledon in 1877, this tournament has drawn a socially prominent crowd. You'll still find an excited hush at Centre Court (where the most hotly contested championship matches are held). Savoring strawberries and cream is part of the experience. Tickets for Centre and Number One courts are handed out through a lottery; write to **All England Lawn Tennis Club,** P.O. Box 98, Church Road, Wimbledon, London SW19 5AE (*℃* **020/ 8944-1066**) between August and December. Include a self-addressed and stamped envelope with your letter. A number of tickets are set aside for visitors from abroad, so you may be able to purchase some in spring for this year's games; call to inquire. Outside court tickets are available daily, but *be prepared to wait in line.* Call *℃* **020/8971-2473** or visit www.wimbledon.org. Late June to early July.

City of London Festival. This is an annual arts celebration held throughout the city. Call *℃* **020/7377-0540** or visit www.colf. org for information about programs and venues. Late June to early July.

Shakespeare Under the Stars, Open Air Theatre, Inner Circle, Regent's Park, NW1 4NU. If you want to see *Macbeth, Hamlet,* or *Romeo and Juliet* (or any other Shakespeare play), our advice is to bring a blanket and a bottle of wine to watch the Bard's works performed at the Open Air Theatre. Performances are Monday through Saturday at 8pm; plus Wednesday, Thursday, and Saturday at 2:30pm. Call *℃* **020/7935-5756** or visit www.open-air-theatre.org.uk for more information and to buy tickets. There is an on-site box office, but it's best to purchase tickets in advance. Previews begin in late June and the season lasts until early September.

July

Kenwood Lakeside Concerts, north side of Hampstead Heath. Fireworks and laser shows enliven the excellent performances at these annual outdoor concerts on Hampstead Heath. Classical music drifts across the lake to the fans every Saturday and Sunday in summer from early July to late August. Call *℃* **020/8348-1286** for a schedule and information and to buy tickets. Tickets are popular, so buy yours in advance; they range from £16 to £24 ($30–$44). Early July to late August.

Hampton Court Palace Flower Show, East Molesey, Surrey. This 5-day international flower show is eclipsing its sister show in Chelsea; here, you can purchase the exhibits on the last day. Call *℃* **0870/906-3871** or visit www.rhs.org.uk for exact dates and details. Early to mid-July.

The Proms, Royal Albert Hall. "The Proms"—the annual Henry Wood Promenade Concerts at Royal Albert Hall—attract music aficionados from around the world. Staged almost daily (except for a few on Sun), the concerts were launched in 1895 and are the principal summer venue for the BBC Symphony Orchestra. Cheering, clapping, banners, balloons, and Union Jacks on parade contribute to the festive summer atmosphere. Call ℭ **020/7589-8212** or visit www.bbc.co.uk/proms for more information and for tickets. Tickets should be bought in advance. Mid-July to mid-September.

August

Notting Hill Carnival, Notting Hill. This is one of the largest street festivals in Europe, attracting more than a half-million people annually. You'll find live reggae and soul music combined with great Caribbean food. Free. Call ℭ **020/8964-0544;** www.portowebbo.co.uk, for information. Two days in late August (usually the last Sun and Mon).

September

Chelsea Antiques Fair, This is a gathering of England's best antiques dealers, held at Chelsea Old Town Hall, King's Road, SW3, ℭ **0870/350-2442.** Mid-September.

Raising of the Thames Barrier, Unity Way, SE18. Once a year, in September, a full test is done on the flood barrier. All 10 of the massive steel gates are raised out of the river for inspection, and you can get a close look at this miracle of modern engineering. Call ℭ **020/8854-1373** for the exact date and time (usually a Sun near the end of Sept).

The Ascot Festival, Ascot, Berkshire, SL5 7JN. This is Britain's greatest horse-racing weekend, providing the grand finale to the summer season at Ascot. The 3-day "meeting" combines some of the most valuable racing of the year with other entertainment. A highlight of the festival is the £250,000 ($462,500) Watership Down Stud Sales race restricted to 2-year-old fillies. Other racing highlights include the Queen Elizabeth II Stakes, with the winning horse crowned champion miler in Europe. To book tickets, call ℭ **01344/876876.** Last weekend in September.

November

Guy Fawkes Night. On the anniversary of the Gunpowder Plot, an attempt to blow up King James I and his Parliament, huge bonfires are lit throughout the city and Guy Fawkes, the most famous conspirator, is burned in effigy. Free. Check *Time Out* for locations. November 5th.

Lord Mayor's Procession and Show, from the Guildhall to the Royal Courts of Justice, in The City of London. This annual event marks the inauguration of the new lord mayor of The City of London. The queen must ask permission to enter the City—a right jealously guarded by London merchants during the 17th century. You can watch the procession from the street; the show is by invitation only. Call © **020/7332-1754;** www.lordmayor show.org, for more information. Second week in November.

5 Specialized Travel Resources

TRAVELERS WITH DISABILITIES

Many London hotels, museums, restaurants, and sightseeing attractions have wheelchair ramps. Persons with disabilities are often granted special discounts at attractions and, in some cases, nightclubs. These discounts are called "concessions" in Britain. It always pays to ask. Free information and advice is available from **Holiday Care Service,** Sunley House, 7th Floor, 4 Bedford Park, Croydon, Surrey CR0 2AP (© **0845/124-9972;** fax 0845/124-9972; www. holidaycare.org.uk).

Bookstores in London often carry *Access in London,* a publication listing hotels, restaurants, sights, shops, and more for persons with disabilities. It costs £7.95 ($14.70).

The transport system, cinemas, and theaters are still extremely hard for the disabled to negotiate, but **Transport for London** does publish a leaflet called *Access to the Underground,* which gives details on elevators and ramps at individual Underground stations; call © **020/7941-4500** or visit www.londontransport.co.uk. And the **London black cab** is perfectly suited for those in wheelchairs; the roomy interiors have plenty of room for maneuvering.

London's most visible organization for information about access to theaters, cinemas, galleries, museums, and restaurants is **Artsline,** 54 Chalton St., London NW1 1HS (© **020/7388-2227;** fax 020/ 7383-2653; www.artsline.org.uk). It offers free information about wheelchair access, theaters with hearing aids, easily wheelchair-accessible tourist attractions and cinemas, and sign language–interpreted tours and theater productions. Artsline will mail information to North America, but it's more helpful to contact them once you arrive in London; the line is staffed Monday through Friday from 9:30am to 5:30pm.

An organization that cooperates closely with Artsline is **Tripscope,** The Vassall Centre, Gill Avenue, Bristol B516 2QQ

(© **08457/585-6451** or 0117/939-7782; www.tripscope.org.uk), which offers advice on travel in Britain and elsewhere for persons with disabilities.

GAY & LESBIAN TRAVELERS

London has one of the most active gay and lesbian scenes in the world; we've recommended a number of the city's best gay clubs, lounges, and bars in chapter 7, "London After Dark."

One of the best places for information on what's hot in London's gay and lesbian scene is **Gay's the Word,** 66 Marchmont St., WC1N 1AB (© **020/7278-7654;** http://freespace.virgin.net/gays. theword; Tube: Russell Square), London's best gay-oriented bookstore and the largest such store in Britain. The staff is friendly and helpful and will offer advice about the ever-changing gay scene in London. It's open Monday through Saturday from 10am to 6:30pm and Sunday from 2 to 6pm. At Gay's the Word, as well as at other gay-friendly venues, you can find a number of gay publications, many free, including the popular *Boyz* and *Pink Paper* (this one has a good lesbian section). Also check out *9X,* filled with data about all the new clubs and whatever else is hot on the scene.

SENIOR TRAVEL

Many discounts are available to seniors. Be advised that in England you sometimes have to be a member of a British seniors association to get discounts. Public-transportation reductions, for example, are available only to holders of British Pension books. However, many attractions do offer discounts for seniors (Britain defines seniors as women 60 or over, and men 65 or over). Even if discounts aren't posted, ask if they're available.

If you're over 60, you're eligible for special 10% discounts on **British Airways** through its Privileged Traveler program. You also qualify for reduced restrictions on Advanced Purchases airline ticket cancellations. Discounts are also granted for British Airways' tours and for intra-Britain air tickets booked in North America. **British Rail** offers seniors discounted rates on first-class rail passes around Britain.

Don't be shy about asking for discounts, but carry some kind of identification that shows your date of birth. Also, mention that you're a senior when you make your hotel reservations. Many hotels offer seniors discounts. In most English cities, women over the age of 60 and men over the age of 65 qualify for reduced admission to theaters, museums, and other attractions.

Members of **AARP** (formerly known as the American Association of Retired Persons), 601 E St. NW, Washington, DC 20049 (*©* **800/ 424-3410** or 202/434-2277; www.aarp.org), get global discounts on hotels, airfares, and car rentals. AARP offers members a wide range of benefits, including *Modern Maturity* magazine and a monthly newsletter. Anyone over 50 can join.

6 Getting There

BY PLANE

Don't worry about which airport, Heathrow versus Gatwick, to fly into unless you are extremely pressed for time. Heathrow is closer to central London than Gatwick, but there is fast train service from both of the airports to the West End (see "Getting into Town from the Airport," below). **High season** on most airlines' routes to London is usually from June to the beginning of September. This is the most expensive and most crowded time to travel. **Shoulder season** is from April to May, early September to October, and December 15 to 24. **Low season** is from November 1 to December 14 and December 25 to March 31.

FROM THE UNITED STATES American Airlines (*©* **800/ 433-7300;** www.aa.com) offers daily nonstop flights to London's Heathrow Airport from eight U.S. gateways: New York's JFK (nine times daily), Chicago's O'Hare (once a day), Boston's Logan (once daily), Miami International (twice daily), Los Angeles International (two to three times daily), Newark and LaGuardia (three times daily), and Dallas (once daily).

British Airways (*©* **800/247-9297;** www.britishairways.com) offers mostly nonstop flights from 21 U.S. cities to Heathrow and Gatwick. With more add-on options than any other airline, British Airways can make a visit to Britain cheaper than you might expect. Of particular interest are the "Value Plus," "London on the Town," and "Europe Escorted" packages that include airfare and discounted accommodations throughout Britain.

Continental Airlines (*©* **800/231-0856;** www.continental. com) flies daily to Gatwick Airport from Newark, Houston, and Cleveland.

Depending on the day and season, **Delta Air Lines** (*©* **800/221- 1212;** www.delta.com) runs either one or two daily nonstop flights between Atlanta and Gatwick. Delta also offers nonstop daily service from Cincinnati.

Tips   **Airport Taxes**

You pay a departure tax of £12 ($22) for flights within Britain and the European Union; and £24 ($44) for flights to the U.S. and other countries. Your airline ticket may or may not include this tax. Ask in advance to avoid a surprise at the gate.

Northwest Airlines (© 800/225-2525; www.nwa.com) flies nonstop from Minneapolis and Detroit to Gatwick.

United Airlines (© 800/241-6522; www.united.com) flies nonstop from New York's JFK and Chicago's O'Hare to Heathrow two or three times a day, depending on the season. United also offers nonstop service three times a day from Dulles Airport, near Washington, D.C., to London's Gatwick, plus once-a-day service to Heathrow from Newark, Los Angeles, San Francisco, and Boston.

Virgin Atlantic Airways (© 800/862-8621; www.virgin-atlantic.com) flies daily to either Gatwick or Heathrow from Boston, Newark, New York's JFK, Los Angeles, San Francisco, Washington, D.C.'s Dulles, Miami, Orlando, and Las Vegas.

FROM CANADA   For travelers departing from Canada, **Air Canada** (© 888/247-2262 in the U.S. or 800/268-7240 in Canada; www.aircanada.com) flies daily to London Heathrow nonstop from Vancouver, Montreal, and Toronto. There are also frequent direct flights from Calgary and Ottawa.

FROM AUSTRALIA   **Qantas** (© 800/227-4500 or 612/13-13-13; www.qantas.com) flies from both Sydney and Melbourne daily. **British Airways** (© 800/247-9297; www.britishairways.com) has five to seven flights weekly from Sydney and Melbourne. Both airlines have a stop in Singapore.

FROM SOUTH AFRICA   **South African Airways** (© 011/978-1762; www.flysaa.com) schedules two daily flights from Johannesburg and two daily flights from Cape Town. From Johannesburg, both **British Airways** (© 0845/773-377; www.britishairways.com) and **Virgin Atlantic Airways** (© 011/340-3400; www.virgin-atlantic.com) have daily flights to Heathrow. British Airways flies five times weekly from Cape Town.

GETTING INTO TOWN FROM THE AIRPORT

LONDON HEATHROW AIRPORT   Located west of London in Hounslow (© 0870/000-0123 for flight information),

Heathrow is one of the world's busiest airports. It has four terminals, each relatively self-contained. Terminal 4 handles the long-haul and transatlantic operations of British Airways. Most transatlantic flights on U.S.–based airlines arrive at Terminal 3. Terminals 1 and 2 receive the intra-European flights of several European airlines.

It takes 35 to 40 minutes by the Underground (Tube) and costs £5.40 ($10) to make the 24km (15-mile) trip from Heathrow to the center of London. A taxi is likely to cost from £40 to £55 ($74–$102). For more information about Tube or bus connections, call © 020/7222-1234.

The British Airport Authority now operates **Heathrow Express** (© 0845/600-1515 or 877/677-1066; www.heathrowexpress.com), a 100-mph train service running every 15 minutes daily from 5:10am until 11:40pm between Heathrow and Paddington Station in the center of London. Trips cost £13 ($24) each way in economy class, rising to £21 ($39) in first class. Children under 15 go for free (when accompanied by an adult). You can save £1 ($1.85) by booking online or by phone. The trip takes 15 minutes each way between Paddington and Terminals 1, 2, and 3, 23 minutes from Terminal 4. The trains have special areas for wheelchairs. From Paddington, passengers can connect to other trains and the Underground, or they can hail a taxi. You can buy tickets on the train or at self-service machines at Heathrow Airport (also available from travel agents).

GATWICK AIRPORT While Heathrow still dominates, more and more scheduled flights land at relatively remote **Gatwick** (© 0870/000-2468 for flight information), located some 40km (25 miles) south of London in West Sussex but only a 30-minute train ride away. From Gatwick, the fastest way to get to London is via the **Gatwick Express trains** (© 0845/850-1530; www.gatwick express.co.uk), which leave for Victoria Station in London every

---

> ⓘ *Tips* **Getting from One London Airport to the Other**
>
> Some visitors will need to transfer from one airport to the other. One bus company offers these transfers. **Speedlink** (© 08705/747-777; www.speedlink.co.uk) buses leave from both terminals at Gatwick and Terminals 1, 3, and 4 at Heathrow. Trip time is about an hour, with a one-way fare costing £17.50 ($32).

30 minutes during the day and every hour at night. The one-way charge is £11 ($20) Express Class for adults, £18 ($33) for First Class, half price for children 5 to 15, free for children under 5. There are also Airbus **buses** from Gatwick to Victoria Coach Station (which is adjacent to Victoria Rail Station) operated by **National Express** (☎ **08705/808-080;** www.nationalexpress.com), approximately every hour from 4:15am to 9:15pm; the round-trip fare is £14 ($25) per person, and the trip takes approximately 1½ hours. A **taxi** from Gatwick to central London usually costs £50 to £105 ($93–$194). However, you must negotiate a fare with the driver before you enter the cab; the meter doesn't apply because Gatwick lies outside the Metropolitan Police District. For further transportation information, call ☎ **020/7222-1234.**

2

Getting to Know London

England's largest city is like a great wheel, with Piccadilly Circus at its hub and dozens of communities branching out from it. Since London is such a large conglomeration of neighborhoods and areas, each with its own personality, first-time visitors are sometimes intimidated until they get the hang of it. Many visitors spend all their time in the West End, where most of the attractions are, with a visit to the City (London's financial district) to see the Tower of London.

This chapter provides a brief orientation to the city's neighborhoods and tells you how to get around London by public transport or on foot. In addition, the "Fast Facts" section helps you find everything from babysitters to camera-repair shops.

1 Orientation

ARRIVING
For information on getting into London from the various airports, see "Getting into Town from the Airport" on p. 13.

BY TRAIN
Each of London's train stations is connected to the city's vast bus and Underground network, and each has phones, restaurants, pubs, luggage storage areas, and London Regional Transport Information Centres.

If you're coming from France, the fastest way to get to London is by the **HoverSpeed** connection between Calais and Dover, where you can get a BritRail train into London. For one-stop travel, you can take the Chunnel train direct from Paris to Waterloo Station in London.

BY CAR
Once you arrive on the English side of the channel, the M20 takes you directly into London. *Remember to drive on the left!* Two roadways encircle London: the A406 and A205 form the inner beltway; the M25 rings the city farther out. Determine which part of the city you want to enter and follow signposts.

We suggest you confine driving in London to the bare minimum, which means arriving and parking. Because of parking problems and heavy traffic, getting around London by car is not a viable option. Once there, leave your car in a garage and rely on public transportation or taxis. Before arrival in London, call your hotel and inquire if it has a garage (and what the charges are), or ask the staff to give you the name and address of a garage nearby.

VISITOR INFORMATION

The **British Travel Centre,** Rex House, 1 Regent St., Haymarket, London SW1 Y4XT (Tube: Piccadilly Circus), caters to walk-in visitors with information about all parts of Britain. There's no telephone service; you must go in person and there is often a wait in a lengthy line. On the premises you'll find a British Rail ticket office, travel and theater ticket agencies, a hotel-booking service, a bookshop, and a souvenir shop. It's open Monday through Friday from 9am to 6:30pm, Saturday and Sunday from 10am to 4pm, with extended hours on Saturday from June to September.

London Tourist Board's **Visit London,** 1 Warwick Row, London, SW1 E5ER (✆ **020/7932-2000;** Tube: Victoria Station), can help you with almost anything. The center deals chiefly with accommodations in all price categories and can handle most travelers' questions. It also arranges ticket sales for tours, and theater reservations, and offers a wide selection of books and souvenirs. From Easter to October, the center is open daily from 8am to 7pm; from November to Easter, it's open Monday through Saturday from 8am to 6pm and Sunday from 9am to 4pm.

CITY LAYOUT
AN OVERVIEW OF LONDON

While **Central London** doesn't formally define itself, most Londoners today would probably accept the Underground's Circle Line as a fair boundary.

"The City" (the financial district) is where London began; it's the original square mile that the Romans called *Londinium,* and it still exists as its own self-governing entity. Rich in historical, architectural, and social interest, the City is one of the world's great financial areas. Even though the City is jeweled with historic sights, it empties out in the evenings and on weekends, and there are lots of better places to stay if you are looking for a hopping nightlife scene.

The West End, where most of London's main attractions are found, is unofficially bounded by the Thames to the south, Farringdon Road/Street to the east, Marylebone Road/Euston Road to

Central London's Neighborhoods

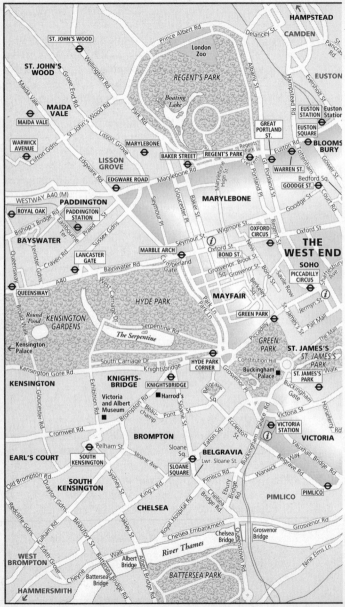

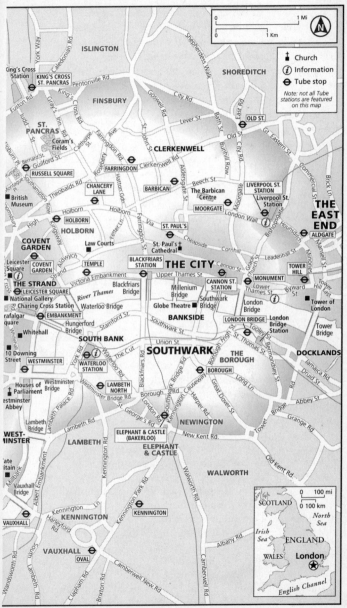

the north, and Hyde Park and Victoria Station to the west. Most visitors will spend their time in the West End, whether at Buckingham Palace, the British Museum, or the shops and theaters of Soho. You'll find the greatest concentration of hotels and restaurants in the West End. Despite attempts to extend central London's nocturnal life to the south side of the Thames—notably the ambitious South Bank Arts Centre—London's energy fades when it crosses the river. Still, the new urban development of Docklands, the tourist attraction of the new Globe Theatre, and some up-and-coming residential neighborhoods are infusing energy into the area across the river.

Farther west are the upscale neighborhoods of Belgravia, Kensington, Knightsbridge, Chelsea, Paddington and Bayswater, Earl's Court, and Notting Hill. This is also prime hotel and restaurant territory. To the east of the City is the **East End,** which forms the eastern boundary of **Inner London** (Notting Hill and Earl's Court roughly form the western boundary). Inner London is surrounded, like a donut, by the sprawling hinterland of **Outer London.**

LONDON'S NEIGHBORHOODS IN BRIEF
The City & Environs

The City When Londoners speak of "the City" (EC2, EC3), they mean the original square mile that's now the British version of Wall Street. The buildings of this district are known all over the world: the Bank of England, the London Stock Exchange, and famed insurance company Lloyd's of London. The City was the original site of *Londinium,* the first settlement of the Roman conquerors. Despite its age, the City doesn't easily reveal its past. Although it retains some of its medieval character, much of the City has been swept away by the Great Fire of 1666, the bombs of 1940, the IRA bombs of the 1990s, and the zeal of modern developers. Landmarks include Sir Christopher Wren's masterpiece, **St. Paul's Cathedral,** which stood virtually alone in the surrounding rubble after the Blitz. Some 2,000 years of history unfold at the City's **Museum of London** and at the **Barbican Centre,** opened by Queen Elizabeth in 1982.

Following the Strand eastward from Trafalgar Square, you'll come to Fleet Street. In the 19th century, this corner of London became the most concentrated newspaper district in the world. William Caxton printed the first book in English here, and the *Daily Consort,* the first daily newspaper printed in England, was launched at Ludgate Circus in 1702. In recent times, however, most London tabloids have abandoned Fleet Street for the Docklands across the river. Where the Strand becomes Fleet Street stands Temple Bar, where the actual City of London begins. The Tower of London looms at the eastern fringe of the City, shrouded in legend, blood, and history, and permanently besieged by battalions of visitors.

The average visitor will venture into the City during the day to sample its attractions or to lunch at pubs such as **Ye Olde Cheshire Cheese,** then return to the West End for evening amusement. As a hotel district, the City wasn't even on the map until recent times. The opening of the **Great Eastern Hotel** has brought a lot of business clients who prefer to stay here to avoid the traffic jams involved in getting into and out of the City. Stay in the City if you would prefer a hotel in a place like New York's Wall Street instead of a midtown address. If you can't afford the Great Eastern, consider the cheaper **Rookery** in newly fashionable Smithfield. The City lures hotel guests who prefer its quirky, quiet, offbeat flavor at night, when it's part ghost town, part movie set. There is some nightlife here, including pubs and restaurants. It's fun to wander the area when all the crowds are gone, pondering the thought that you're walking the same streets that Samuel Johnson trod so long ago.

The City of London still prefers to function on its own, separate from the rest of London. It maintains its own **Information Centre** at St. Paul's Churchyard, EC4 (© **020/7332-1456**), which is open Monday through Friday from 9:30am to 5pm and Saturday from 9:30am to 12:30pm.

The East End Traditionally, this was one of London's poorest districts, nearly bombed out of existence during World War II. In the words of one commentator at the time, Hitler created "instant urban renewal" here. The East End extends east from the City Walls, encompassing Stepney, Bow, Poplar, West Ham, Canning Town, and other districts. The East End is the home of the Cockney. To be a true Cockney, it's said that you must be born within the sound of the Bow Bells of **St. Mary-le-Bow** church, an old church rebuilt by Sir Christopher Wren in 1670.

These days, many immigrants to London make their homes in the East End. London is pushing eastward, and the East End might even become fashionable, somewhat like the Lower East Side of New York. But that day isn't quite here, and except for the Docklands area (see below), much of the East End doesn't concern the average visitor. Attractions that you may want to visit if you are in the area include St. Clements Danes church, the Temple of Mithras, and Sir Christopher Wren's Monument to the Great Fire of 1666.

Docklands In 1981, the London Docklands Development Corporation (LDDC) was formed to redevelop Wapping, the Isle of Dogs, the Royal Docks, and Surrey Docks, in the most ambitious scheme of its kind in Europe. The area is bordered roughly by Tower Bridge to the west and London City Airport and the Royal Docks to the east. Many businesses have moved here; Thames-side warehouses have been converted to Manhattan-style lofts; and museums, entertainment complexes, shops, and an ever-growing list of restaurants have popped up at this 21st-century river city in the making.

Canary Wharf, on the Isle of Dogs, is the heart of Docklands. This 28-hectare (69-acre) site is dominated by a 240m-high (787-ft.) tower, which is the tallest building in the United Kingdom, and was designed by Cesar Pelli. The Piazza of the tower is lined with shops and restaurants. On the south side of the river at Surrey Docks, Sir Terence Conran has converted the Victorian warehouses of Butler's Wharf into offices, workshops, houses, shops, and restaurants. Butler's Wharf is also home to the **Design Museum.** Chances are you'll venture here for sights and restaurants, not for lodging, unless you've got business in the area. The area is fun during the day, and you'll find some of London's finest restaurants here, offering good food and a change of pace from the West End—this is postmillennium London, whereas the West End is the essence of traditional. See our recommendations in chapter 4 "Where to Dine." To get to Docklands, take the Underground to Tower Hill and pick up the **Docklands Light Railway** (© 020/7222-1234), which operates Monday to Saturday from 5:30am to 12:30am, from 7:30am to 11:30pm Sunday.

South Bank Although not officially a district, this is where you'll find the **South Bank Arts Centre,** the largest arts center in Western Europe and still growing. Reached by Waterloo Bridge (or on foot by Hungerford Bridge), it lies across the Thames from the Victoria Embankment. Culture buffs flock to its galleries and halls, which encompass the **National Theatre, Queen Elizabeth Hall, Royal Festival Hall,** and the **Hayward Gallery.** The center also houses the National Film Theatre and the Museum of the Moving Image (MOMI).

Although its day as a top hotel district in London may come in a decade or so (since there's no room left in the West End), that hasn't happened yet. The South Bank is a destination for daytime adventures or for evening cultural attractions. You may want to dine here during a day's and evening's exploration of the area. See our recommendations in chapter 4, "Where to Dine."

Nearby are such neighborhoods as Elephant and Castle, and Southwark, home to **Southwark Cathedral.** To get here, take the Tube to Waterloo Station.

West End Neighborhoods

Bloomsbury This district, a world within itself, is bound roughly by Euston Road to the north, Gower Street to the west, and Clerkenwell to the east. It is, among other things, the academic heart of London. You'll find the **University of London,** several other colleges, and many **bookstores** here. Writers like Virginia Woolf, who lived in the area (it figured in her novel *Jacob's Room*), have fanned the neighborhood's reputation as a place devoted to liberal thinking, arts, and "sexual frankness." The novelist and her husband, Leonard, were unofficial leaders of a group of artists and writers known as "the Bloomsbury Group." However, despite its student population, Bloomsbury is a fairly staid neighborhood. The heart of Bloomsbury is **Russell Square,** whose outlying streets are lined with moderately priced to expensive hotels and B&Bs. It's a noisy but central place to stay. Most visitors come to visit the **British Museum,** one of the world's greatest repositories of treasures from around the globe. The **British Telecom Tower** (1964) on Cleveland Street is a familiar landmark.

Of all the areas described so far, this is the only one that could be called a hotel district. Hotel prices have risen dramatically in the past decade, but are nowhere near the levels of those in Mayfair and St. James's. In price, Bloomsbury's hotels are comparable to what you'll find in Marylebone to the west. But Bloomsbury is more convenient than Marylebone. At its southern doorstep lie the restaurants and nightclubs of Soho, the theater district, and the markets of Covent Garden. If you stay here, it's a 10-minute Tube ride to the heart of the action of the West End.

At the western edge of Bloomsbury you'll find **Fitzrovia,** bounded by Great Portland, Oxford, and Gower streets, and reached by the Goodge Street Tube. Goodge Street, with its many shops and pubs, forms the heart of the village. Fitzrovia was once the stamping ground for writers and artists like Ezra Pound, Wyndham Lewis, and George Orwell, among others. The bottom end of Fitzrovia is a virtual extension of Soho, with a cluster of Greek restaurants.

Holborn The old borough of Holborn (*Ho*-burn), which abuts the City southeast of Bloomsbury, encompasses the heart of legal

London—this is where you'll find the city's barristers, solicitors, and law clerks. Still Dickensian in spirit, the area preserves the Victorian author's literary footsteps in the two Inns of Court (where law students perform their apprenticeships and where barristers' chambers are located), featured in *David Copperfield,* and the Bleeding Heart Yard of *Little Dorrit* fame. **The Old Bailey** courthouse, where judges and lawyers still wear old-fashioned wigs, has stood for English justice through the years—Fagin went to the gallows from this site in *Oliver Twist.* Everything in Holborn is steeped in history. For example, as you're downing a half-pint of bitter at the **Viaduct Tavern,** 126 Newgate St. (Tube: St. Paul's), you can reflect on the fact that the pub was built over the notorious Newgate Prison. You might come here for some sightseeing, perhaps quenching your thirst in a historic pub.

Covent Garden & the Strand   The flower, fruit, and "veg" market is long gone (since 1970), but memories of Professor Higgins and his "squashed cabbage leaf," Eliza Doolittle, linger on. **Covent Garden** contains the city's liveliest group of restaurants, pubs, and cafes outside Soho, as well as some of the city's hippest shops. The restored marketplace here, with its glass and iron roofs, has been called a magnificent example of urban recycling. London's **theater district** begins in Covent Garden and spills over into Leicester Square and Soho. Inigo Jones's **St. Paul's Covent Garden** is known as the actors' church; over the years, it has attracted everybody from Ellen Terry to Vivien Leigh. The **Theatre Royal Drury Lane** was where Charles II's mistress Nell Gwynne made her debut in 1665, and was also where Irish actress Dorothea Jordan caught the eye of the Duke of Clarence, later William IV. The **Strand** forms the southern border of Covent Garden. It's packed with theaters, shops, first-class hotels, and restaurants. Old pubs, **Dr. Johnson's House,** and tearooms fragrant with brewing Twinings English tea evoke memories of the rich heyday of this district as the center of London's activity. The Strand runs parallel to the Thames River, and to walk it is to follow in the footsteps of Charles Lamb, Mark Twain, Henry Fielding, James Boswell, William Thackeray, and Sir Walter Raleigh, among others. The Strand's **Savoy Theatre** helped make Gilbert and Sullivan household names.

You'll probably come here for theater or dining rather than for a hotel room. Covent Garden has few hotels (although the ones that do exist are very nice). We recommend the best ones (p. 48). Expect to spend a lot for the privilege of staying in such a central zone. The Strand, of course, has always been known for its swank Savoy Hotel.

Piccadilly Circus & Leicester Square Piccadilly Circus, with its statue of Eros, is the heart and soul of London. The circus isn't Times Square yet, but its traffic, neon, and jostling crowds might indeed make "circus" an apt word to describe this place. Piccadilly, which was the western road out of London, was named for the "picadil," a ruffled collar created by Robert Baker, a 17th-century tailor. If you want grandeur, retreat to the Regency promenade of exclusive shops, the **Burlington Arcade,** designed in 1819. The English gentry—tired of being mud-splashed by horses and carriages along Piccadilly—came here to do their shopping. Some 35 shops, offering a treasure trove of expensive goodies, await you. A bit more tawdry is **Leicester Square,** a hub of theaters, restaurants, movie palaces, and nightlife. Leicester Square is London's equivalent of New York's Times Square. The square changed forever in the Victorian era, when four towering entertainment halls were opened. In time, the old entertainment palaces changed from stage to screen; today, three of them still show films. In another sign of the times, the old Café de Paris is no longer a chic cabaret—now it's a disco.

There are a few hotels here, although they're invariably expensive. Stay here if you'd want a hotel in Times Square in New York. It's convenient for those who want to be at the center of the action. The downside is noise, congestion, and pollution.

Soho A nightclubber's paradise, Soho is a confusing grid of streets crammed with restaurants. It's a great place to visit, but you probably won't want to stay there (there aren't many hotels, anyway). These densely packed streets in the heart of the West End are famous for their cosmopolitan mix of people and trades. A decade ago, much was heard about the decline of Soho with the influx of sex shops; even the pub where Dylan Thomas used to drink himself into oblivion became a sex cinema. Since then, non-sex-oriented businesses have returned, and fashionable restaurants and shops prosper. Soho is now the heart of London's expanding gay scene.

Soho starts at Piccadilly Circus and spreads out, more or less bordered by Regent Street to the west, Oxford Street to the north, Charing Cross Road to the east, and the **theaters along Shaftes-bury Avenue** to the south. Carnaby Street, a block from Regent Street, was the center of the universe in the Swinging '60s, but is now a schlocky tourist trap. Across Shaftesbury Avenue is London's **Chinatown,** centered on Gerrard Street. It's small, authentic, and packed with good restaurants. **Soho's** heart—featuring great delicatessens, butchers, fish stores, and wine merchants—

is farther north, on Brewer, Old Compton, and Berwick streets (Berwick St. features a wonderful open-air fresh-food market). To the north of Old Compton Street, Dean, Frith, and Greek streets have fine restaurants, pubs, and clubs. The British movie industry is centered in Wardour Street. The average visitor comes to Soho to dine because many of its restaurants are convenient to the theater district. Most travelers don't stay in Soho, but a certain action-oriented visitor prefers the *joie de vivre* of the neighborhood as compared to staid Bloomsbury or swank Mayfair. Does this sound like you? Check out Soho's accommodations starting on p. 50.

Marylebone West of Bloomsbury and Fitzrovia, Marylebone extends north from Marble Arch, at the eastern edge of Hyde Park. Most first-time visitors head here to explore **Madame Tussaud's** waxworks or walk along **Baker Street** in the footsteps of Sherlock Holmes. The streets form a near-perfect grid, with the major ones running north–south between Regent's Park and Oxford Street. Architect Robert Adam laid out **Portland Place,** one of the most characteristic squares in London, from 1776 to 1780. At **Cavendish Square,** Mrs. Horatio Nelson waited for the return of Admiral Nelson. Marylebone Lane and High Street retain a bit of small-town atmosphere, but this is otherwise a rather anonymous area. Dickens wrote nearly a dozen books while he resided here. At **Regent's Park,** you can visit Queen Mary's Gardens or, in summer, see Shakespeare performed in an open-air theater. **Marylebone** has emerged as a major "bedroom" district for London, competing with Bloomsbury to its east. It's not as convenient as Bloomsbury, but the hub of the West End's action is virtually at your doorstep if you lodge here, northwest of Piccadilly Circus and facing Mayfair to the south. Once known only for its town houses turned into B&Bs, the district now offers accommodations in all price ranges, catering to everyone from rock stars to frugal family travelers.

Mayfair Bounded by Piccadilly, Hyde Park, and Oxford and Regent streets, this is the most elegant, fashionable section of London, filled with luxury hotels, Georgian town houses, and swank shops. The area is sandwiched between Piccadilly Circus and Hyde Park. It's convenient to London's best shopping and close to the West End theaters, yet (a bit snobbily) removed from the peddlers and commerce of Covent Garden and Soho.

Grosvenor Square (pronounced *Grov*-nor) is nicknamed "Little America" because it's home to the American Embassy and a statue of Franklin D. Roosevelt. **Berkeley Square** (*Bark*-ley) was made famous by the song "A Nightingale Sang in Berkeley Square." You'll want to dip into this exclusive section at least once. One of the curiosities of Mayfair is **Shepherd Market,** a village of pubs, two-story inns, restaurants, and book and food stalls, nestled within Mayfair's grandness. The hotels of Mayfair, especially those along Park Lane, are the most expensive and grand in London. This is the place if you're seeking sophisticated, albeit expensive, accommodations that are close to the **Bond Street** shops, boutiques, and art galleries. Also, if "address" is important to you, and you're willing to pay for a good one, Mayfair has a bed waiting for you.

St. James's Often called "Royal London," St. James's basks in its associations with everybody from the "merrie monarch" Charles II to Elizabeth II, who lives at its most famous address, **Buckingham Palace.** The neighborhood begins at **Piccadilly Circus** and moves southwest, incorporating **Pall Mall, The Mall, St. James's Park,** and **Green Park.** It's "frightfully convenient," as the English say; within its confines are American Express and many of London's leading department stores. This is the neighborhood where English gentlemen seek haven at that male-only bastion of English tradition, the gentlemen's club, where poker is played, drinks are consumed, and pipes are smoked (St. James's Club is one of the most prestigious of these clubs). Be sure to stop in at **Fortnum & Mason,** 181 Piccadilly, the world's most luxurious grocery store. Launched in 1788, the store sent hams to the Duke of Wellington's army and baskets of tinned goodies to Florence Nightingale in the Crimea. Hotels in this neighborhood tend to be expensive, but if the queen should summon you to Buckingham Palace, you won't have far to go.

Westminster Westminster has been the seat of the British government since the days of Edward the Confessor (1042–66). Dominated by the **Houses of Parliament** and **Westminster Abbey,** the area runs along the Thames to the east of St. James's Park. **Trafalgar Square,** one of the city's major landmarks, is located at the area's northern end and remains a testament to England's victory over Napoleon in 1805. The square is home to the landmark National Gallery, which is filled with glorious paintings. Whitehall is the main thoroughfare, linking Trafalgar Square with **Parliament Square.** You can visit Churchill's Cabinet War Rooms and walk down **Downing Street** to see **Number 10,** home to Britain's prime minister. No visit is complete without a call at **Westminster Abbey,** one of the greatest Gothic churches in the world. It has witnessed a parade of English history, beginning when William the Conqueror was crowned here on Christmas Day 1066.

Westminster also encompasses **Victoria,** an area that takes its name from bustling Victoria Station, "the gateway to the Continent." Many B&Bs and hotels have sprouted up here because of the neighborhood's proximity to the rail station. Victoria is cheap and convenient if you don't mind the noise and crowds.

Welfare recipients occupy many hotels along Belgrave Road. If you've arrived without a hotel reservation, you'll find the pickings better on the streets off Belgrave Road. Your best bet is to walk along Ebury Street, east of Victoria Station and Buckingham Palace Road. Here you'll find some of the best moderately priced lodgings in central London. Since you're near Victoria Station, the area is convenient for day trips to Oxford, Windsor, or Canterbury.

Beyond the West End

Knightsbridge One of London's most fashionable neighborhoods, Knightsbridge is a top residential, hotel, and shopping district just south of Hyde Park. **Harrods** on Brompton Road is its chief attraction. Founded in 1901, Harrods has been called "the Notre Dame of department stores." Right nearby, **Beauchamp Place** (*Bee*-cham) is one of London's most fashionable shopping streets, a Regency-era, boutique-lined street with a scattering of restaurants. Most hotels here are deluxe or first class.

Knightsbridge is one of the most convenient areas of London; ideally located if you want to head east to the theater district or the Mayfair shops, or west to Chelsea or Kensington's restaurants and attractions. Knightsbridge is also a swank address, with many fine hotels, although none are at the level of the palaces of Mayfair.

Belgravia South of Knightsbridge, this area has long been an aristocratic quarter of London, rivaling Mayfair in grandeur. Although it reached its pinnacle of prestige during the reign of Queen Victoria, the duke and duchess of Westminster still live at **Eaton Square,** and Belgravia remains a hot area for chic hotels. The neighborhood's centerpiece is **Belgrave Square.** When town houses were built from 1825 to 1835, aristocrats followed—the duke of Connaught, the earl of Essex, and even Queen Victoria's mother.

Belgravia is a tranquil district. If you lodge here, no one will ever accuse you of staying on the "wrong side of the tracks." The neighborhood is convenient to the little restaurants and pubs of Chelsea, which is located to Belgravia's immediate west. Victoria Station is located to its immediate east, so Belgravia is convenient if you're planning to take day trips from London.

Chelsea This stylish Thames-side district lies south and to the west of Belgravia. It begins at **Sloane Square,** with **Gilbert Ledward's Venus fountain** playing watery music. The area has always been a favorite of writers and artists, including Oscar Wilde (who was arrested here), George Eliot, James Whistler, J. M. W. Turner, Henry James, and Thomas Carlyle (whose former home can be visited). Mick Jagger and Margaret Thatcher (not together) have been more recent residents, and the late Princess Diana and her "Sloane Rangers" (a term used to describe posh women, derived from Chelsea's Sloane Square) of the 1980s gave the area even more recognition. There are some swank hotels here and a scattering of modestly priced ones. The main drawback to Chelsea is inaccessibility. Except for Sloane Square, there's a dearth of Tube stops, and unless you like to take a lot of buses or expensive taxis, you may find getting around a chore.

Chelsea's major boulevard is **King's Road,** where Mary Quant launched the miniskirt in the 1960s and where the English punk look began. King's Road runs the length of Chelsea; it's at its liveliest on Saturday. The outrageous fashions of the King's Road boutiques aren't typical of otherwise upmarket Chelsea, an elegant village filled with town houses and little mews dwellings which only successful stockbrokers and solicitors can afford to occupy. On the Chelsea/Fulham border is **Chelsea Harbour,** a luxury development of apartments and restaurants with a marina. You can spot its tall tower from far away; the golden ball on top moves up and down to indicate the tide level.

Kensington This Royal Borough (W8) lies west of Kensington Gardens and Hyde Park and is traversed by two of London's major shopping streets, **Kensington High Street** and **Kensington Church Street.** Since 1689, when asthmatic William III fled Whitehall Palace for Nottingham House (where the air was fresher), the district has enjoyed royal associations. In time, Nottingham House became Kensington Palace, and the royals grabbed a chunk of Hyde Park to plant their roses. Queen Victoria was born here. Kensington Palace, or "KP," as the royals say, was home to the late Princess Margaret (who had 20 rooms with a view), and is still home to Prince and Princess Michael of Kent, and the duke and duchess of Gloucester. Kensington Gardens is now open to the public, ever since George II decreed that "respectably dressed" people would be permitted in on Saturday— providing that no servants, soldiers, or sailors came (as you might imagine, that rule is long gone). During the reign of William III, Kensington Square developed, attracting artists and writers.

Thackeray wrote *Vanity Fair* while living here. With all those royal associations, Kensington is a fashionable neighborhood. If you're a frugal traveler, head for South Kensington for moderately priced hotels and B&Bs. Southeast of Kensington Gardens and Earl's Court, primarily residential **South Kensington** is often called "museumland" because it's dominated by a complex of museums and colleges, including the **Natural History Museum,** the **Victoria and Albert Museum,** and the **Science Museum;** nearby is **Royal Albert Hall.** South Kensington boasts some zfashionable restaurants and town-house hotels. One of the neighborhood's curiosities is the **Albert Memorial,** completed in 1872 by Sir George Gilbert Scott; for sheer excess, this Victorian monument is unequaled in the world.

A hotel room in Kensington is a prestigious address. But as Princess Margaret may have told you, you're at the far stretch of the West End, lying some 20 minutes by Tube from the heart of the theater district. As for South Kensington, it was once considered the "boondocks," although with the boundaries of the West End expanding, the neighborhood is much closer to the action than it has ever been before.

Paddington & Bayswater Paddington radiates out from Paddington Station, north of Hyde Park and Kensington Gardens. It's one of the major B&B centers in London, attracting budget travelers who fill the lodgings in Sussex Gardens and Norfolk Square. After the first railway was introduced in London in 1836, a circle of sprawling railway terminals, including Paddington Station (which was built in 1838), spurred the growth of this middle-class area. Just south of Paddington, north of Hyde Park, and abutting more fashionable Notting Hill to the west is **Bayswater,** also filled with a large number of B&Bs that attract budget travelers. Inspired by Marylebone and elegant Mayfair, a relatively prosperous set of Victorian merchants built terrace houses around spacious squares in this area.

Paddington and Bayswater make up a sort of "in-between" area of London. If you've come to London to see the attractions in the east, including the British Museum, the Tower of London, and the theater district, you'll find yourself commuting a lot. Stay here for moderately priced lodgings (there are expensive hotels, too) and for convenience to transportation. Rapidly gentrifying, this area ranges from seedy to swank.

Notting Hill Increasingly fashionable Notting Hill is bounded on the east by Bayswater and on the south by Kensington. Hemmed in on the north by Westway and on the west by the

Shepherd's Bush ramp leading to the M40, it has many turn-of-the-century mansions and small houses sitting on quiet, leafy streets, plus a growing number of hot restaurants and clubs. Gentrified in recent years, it's becoming an extension of central London. Hotels are few, but increasingly chic.

Even more remote than Paddington and Bayswater, Notting Hill lies at least another 10 minutes west of those districts. In spite of that, many young professional visitors to London wouldn't stay anywhere else.

In the northern half of Notting Hill is the hip neighborhood known as **Notting Hill Gate,** home to Portobello Road, which boasts one of London's most famous street markets. The area Tube stops are Notting Hill Gate, Holland Park, and Ladbroke Grove.

Nearby **Holland Park,** an expensive residential neighborhood, promotes itself as "10 minutes by Tube from practically anywhere," a bit of an exaggeration.

2 Getting Around

BY PUBLIC TRANSPORTATION

The London Underground and the city's buses operate on the same system of six fare zones. The fare zones radiate out in rings from the central zone 1, which is where most visitors spend the majority of their time. Zone 1 covers the area from Liverpool Street in the east to Notting Hill in the west, and from Waterloo in the south to Baker Street, Euston, and King's Cross in the north. To travel beyond zone 1, you need a multizone ticket. Note that all single one-way, round-trip, and 1-day pass tickets are valid only on the day of purchase. Tube and bus maps should be available at any Underground station. You can download them before you travel from the excellent **London Transport (LT)** website: www.tfl.gov.uk/tfl. (You can also send away for a map by writing to **London Transport,** Travel Information Service, 42–50 Victoria St., London SW1H 0TL.) There are also **LT Information Centres** at several major Tube stations: Euston, King's Cross, Oxford Circus, St. James's Park, Liverpool Street Station, and Piccadilly Circus, as well as in the British Rail stations at Euston and Victoria and in each of the terminals at Heathrow Airport. Most of them are open daily (some close Sun) from at least 9am to 5pm. A 24-hour public-transportation information service is also available at ✆ **020/7222-1234.**

TRAVEL DISCOUNTS   If you plan to use public transportation a lot, investigate the range of fare discounts available. **Travelcards** offer unlimited use of buses, Underground, and British Rail services in Greater London for any period ranging from a day to a year. Travelcards are available from Underground ticket offices, LT Information Centres, main post offices in the London area, and some newsstands. You need to bring a passport-size photo to purchase a Travelcard; you can take a photo at any of the instant photo booths in London's train stations. Children under age 5 generally travel free on the Tube and buses.

The **1-Day Travelcard** allows you to go anywhere throughout Greater London. For travel anywhere within zones 1 and 2, the cost is £5.30 ($9.80) for adults or £2.60 ($4.80) for children 5 to 15. The **Off-Peak 1-Day Travelcard,** which isn't valid until after 9:30am on weekdays (or on night buses), is even cheaper. For two zones, the cost is £4.30 ($7.95) for adults and £2 ($3.70) for children 5 to 15.

Weekend Travelcards are valid for 1 weekend, plus the Monday if it's a national holiday. They're not valid on night buses; travel anywhere within zones 1 and 2 all weekend costs £6.40 ($12) for adults or £2 ($3.70) for kids 5 to 15.

1-Week Travelcards cost adults £17 ($31) and children £7 ($13) for travel in zones 1 and 2.

The 1-day **Family Travelcard** allows as many journeys as you want on the Tube, buses (excluding night buses) displaying the London Transport bus sign, and even the Docklands Light Railway or any rail service within the travel zones designated on your ticket.

Tips **Don't Leave Home Without It**

For another option for public transportation in London, make sure you buy a **London Visitor Travelcard** before you leave home. This card, which allows unlimited transport within all six zones of Greater London's Underground (as far as Heathrow) and bus network, as well as some discounts on London attractions, isn't available in the U.K. You don't even need a passport picture. A pass good for 3 consecutive days of travel is $35 for adults, $16 for children 5 to 15; for 4 consecutive days of travel, it's $46 for adults, $19 for children; and for 7 consecutive days of travel, it's $69 for adults, $29 for children. Contact **BritRail Travel International,** 44 S. Broadway, White Plains, NY 10601 (© **800/677-8585,** or 800/555-2748 in Canada; www.raileurope.com). It will take up to 2 to 3 business days for the card to reach you at home.

The family card is valid Monday through Friday after 9:30am and all day on weekends and public holidays. It's available for families as small as two (one adult and one child) to as large as six (two adults and four children). Cost is £2.80 ($5.20) per adult and 80p ($1.50) per child.

You can also buy **Carnet** tickets, a booklet of 10 single Underground tickets valid for 12 months from the issue date. Carnet tickets are valid for travel only in zone 1 (Central London) and cost £15 ($28) for adults and £5 ($9.25) for children (up to 15). A book of Carnet tickets saves you £5 ($9.25) over the cost of 10 separate single tickets.

THE UNDERGROUND

The Underground, or Tube, is the fastest and easiest way to get around. All Tube stations are clearly marked with a red circle and blue crossbar. Routes are conveniently color-coded.

If you have British coins, you can get your ticket at a vending machine. Otherwise, buy it at the ticket office. You can transfer as many times as you like as long as you stay in the Underground. The flat fare for one trip within the Central zone is £2 ($3.70). Trips from the Central zone to destinations in the suburbs range from £2.20 to £3.80 ($4.05–$7) in most cases. It's also possible to purchase weekly passes (see "Travel Discounts," above), going for £17 ($31) for adults or £7 ($13) for children in the Central zone, £38.30 ($71) for adults or £16.50 ($31) for children for all six zones.

Slide your ticket into the slot at the gate, and pick it up as it comes through on the other side and hold on to it—it must be presented when you exit the station at your destination. If you're caught without a valid ticket, you'll be fined £10 ($19) on the spot. If you owe extra money, you'll be asked to pay the difference by the attendant at the exit. The Tube runs roughly from 5am to 11:30pm. After that you must take a taxi or night bus to your destination. For information on the London Tube system, call the **London Underground** at ✆ **020/7222-1234,** but expect to stay on hold for a good while before a live person comes on the line. Information is also available on **www.londontransport.co.uk**.

The long-running saga known as the Jubilee Line Extension is beginning to reach completion. This line, which once ended at Charing Cross, has been extended eastward to serve the growing suburbs of the southeast and the Docklands area. This east–west axis helps ease traffic on some of London's most hard-pressed underground lines. The line also makes it much easier to reach Greenwich.

BY BUS

The first thing you learn about London buses is that nobody just boards them. You "queue up"—that is, form a single-file line at the bus stop.

The comparably priced bus system is almost as good as the Underground and gives you better views of the city. To find out about current routes, pick up a free bus map at one of London Transport's Travel Information Centres, listed above. The map is available in person only, not by mail. You can also obtain a map at **www.londontransport.co.uk/buses**.

As with the Underground, fares vary according to distance traveled. Generally, bus fares are £1 ($1.85), slightly less than Tube fares. If you want your stop called out, simply ask the conductor or driver. To speed up bus travel, passengers have to purchase tickets before boarding. Drivers no longer collect fares on board. Some 300 roadside ticket machines serve stops in central London—in other words, it's "pay as you board." You'll need the exact fare, however, as ticket machines don't make change. It will still be possible to pay on the double-decker red buses that continue to serve 20 of the 60 major bus routes in London, although in time these may be phased out.

Buses generally run 24 hours a day. A few night buses have special routes, running once an hour or so; most pass through Trafalgar Square. Keep in mind that night buses are often so crowded (especially on weekends) that they are unable to pick up passengers after a few stops. You may find yourself waiting a long time. Consider taking a taxi. Call the 24-hour **hot line** (© 020/7222-1234) for schedule and fare information.

BY TAXI

London cabs are among the most comfortable and best-designed in the world. You can pick one up either by heading for a cab rank or by hailing one in the street (the taxi is available if the yellow taxi sign on the roof is lit); once it has stopped for you, a taxi is obliged to take you anywhere you want to go within 9.5km (6 miles) of the pickup point, provided it's within the metropolitan area. To **call a cab,** phone © 020/7272-0272 or 020/7253-5000.

The meter starts at £3.80 ($7.05), with increments of £3.40 ($6.30) per mile thereafter, based on distance or time. Each additional passenger is charged 40p (75¢). Passengers pay 10p (20¢) for each piece of luggage in the driver's compartment and any other item more than .6m (2 ft.) long. Surcharges are imposed after 8pm and on weekends and public holidays. All these tariffs include VAT.

Fares usually increase annually. It's recommended that you tip 10% to 15% of the fare.

If you call for a cab, the meter starts running when the taxi receives instructions from the dispatcher, so you could find that the meter already reads a few pounds more than the initial drop of £3.60 ($6.70) when you step inside.

Minicabs are also available, and they're often useful when regular taxis are scarce or when the Tube stops running. These cabs are meterless, so you must negotiate the fare in advance. Unlike regular cabs, minicabs are forbidden by law to cruise for fares. They operate from sidewalk kiosks, such as those around Leicester Square. If you need to call one, try **Brunswick Chauffeurs/Abbey Cars** (© 020/8969-2555) in west London; **London Cabs, Ltd.** (© 020/8778-3000) in east London; or **Newname Minicars** (© 020/8472-1400) in south London. Minicab kiosks can be found near many Tube or BritRail stops, especially in outlying areas.

If you have a complaint about taxi service or if you leave something in a cab, contact the **Public Carriage Office,** 15 Penton St., N1 9PU (Tube: Angel Station). If it's a complaint, you must have the cab number, which is displayed in the passenger compartment. Call © 020/7918-2000 with complaints.

Cab sharing is permitted in London, as British law allows cabbies to carry two to five persons. Taxis accepting such riders display a notice on yellow plastic, with the words "Shared Taxi." Each of two riders sharing is charged 65% of the fare a lone passenger would be charged. Three persons pay 55%, four pay 45%, and five (the seating capacity of all new London cabs) pay 40% of the single-passenger fare.

FAST FACTS: London

American Express The main Amex office is at 30–31 Haymarket, SW1 (© 020/7484-9600; Tube: Piccadilly Circus). Full services are available Monday to Saturday from 9am to 6pm. On Sundays from 10am to 5pm, only the foreign-exchange bureau is open.

Business Hours Banks are usually open Monday through Friday from 9:30am to 3:30pm. Business offices are open Monday through Friday from 9am to 5pm; the lunch break lasts an hour, but most places stay open during that time. Pubs and bars stay open from 11am to 11pm Monday through Saturday and from noon to 10:30pm on Sunday. Stores generally open at 9am and close at 5:30pm, staying open until 7pm on Wednesday or Thursday. Most central shops close on Saturday around 1pm. In a recent change, some stores are now open for 6 hours on Sunday, usually from 11am to 5pm.

Dentists For dental emergencies, call **Eastman Dental Hospital** (℅ 020/7915-1000; Tube: King's Cross or Chancery Lane).

Doctors Call ℅ **999** in a medical emergency. Some hotels have physicians on call for emergencies. For nonemergencies, try **Medical Express,** 117A Harley St., W1 (℅ **020/7499-1991**; Tube: Regent's Park). A private British clinic, it's not part of the free British medical establishment. For filling the British equivalent of a U.S. prescription, there's sometimes a surcharge of £20 ($37) on top of the cost of the medications. The clinic is open Monday through Friday from 9am to 5:30pm and Saturday from 9:30am to 2pm.

Drugstores In Britain they're called chemists. Every police station has a list of emergency chemists (dial 0 and ask the operator for the local police). One of the most centrally located, keeping long hours, is **Bliss the Chemist,** 5 Marble Arch, W1 (℅ 020/7723-6116; Tube: Marble Arch), open daily from 9am to midnight. Every London neighborhood has a branch of **Boots the Chemist,** Britain's leading pharmacy, which is also open until midnight.

Electricity British current is 240 volts, AC, so you'll need a converter or transformer for U.S.-made electrical appliances, as well as an adapter that allows the plug to match British outlets. Some (but not all) hotels supply them for guests. If you've forgotten one, you can buy a transformer/adapter at most branches of **Boots the Chemist.**

Embassies & High Commissions The **U.S. Embassy** is at 24 Grosvenor Sq., W1 (℅ **020/7499-9000**; Tube: Bond St.). Hours are Monday through Friday from 8:30am to 5:30pm. However, for passport and visa information, go to the **U.S. Passport and Citizenship Unit,** 55–56 Upper Brook St., London, W1 (℅ **020/ 7499-9000,** ext. 2563 or 2564; Tube: Marble Arch or Bond St.). Passport and Citizenship Unit hours are Monday through Friday from 8:30 to 11:30am and Monday and Friday from 2 to 4pm.

The **Canadian High Commission,** MacDonald House, 38 Grosvenor Sq., W1 (℅ **020/7258-6600**; Tube: Bond St.), handles visas for Canada. Hours are Monday through Friday from 8am to 4pm; 8 to 11am for immigration services.

The **Australian High Commission** is at Australia House, the Strand, WC2 (© **020/7379-4334**; Tube: Charing Cross or Aldwych). Hours are Monday through Friday from 9am to 5:20pm; 9 to 11am for immigration services; passports 9:30am to 3:30pm.

The **New Zealand High Commission** is at New Zealand House, 80 Haymarket at Pall Mall, SW1 (© **020/7930-8422**; Tube: Charing Cross or Piccadilly Circus). Hours are Monday through Friday from 10am to 4pm.

The **Irish Embassy** is at 17 Grosvenor Place, SW1 (© **020/ 7235-2171**; Tube: Hyde Park Corner). Hours are Monday through Friday from 9:30am to 1pm and 2 to 5pm.

Emergencies For police, fire, or an ambulance, dial © **999**.

Hospitals The following offer emergency care in London, 24 hours a day, with the first treatment free under the National Health Service: **Royal Free Hospital**, Pond Street (© **020/7794- 0500**; Tube: Belsize Park), and **University College Hospital**, Grafton Way (© **020/7387-9300**; Tube: Warren St.). Many other London hospitals also have accident and emergency departments.

Hot Lines If you're in some sort of legal emergency, call **Release** (© **020/7729-9904**), open from 10am to 5:30pm. The **Rape Crisis Line** (© **0845/1232-324**) accepts calls after 6pm. **Samaritans,** 46 Marshall St. (© **020/7734-2800**), maintains a crisis hot line that helps with all kinds of trouble, even threatened suicides. From 9am to 9pm daily, a live attendant is on duty to handle emergencies; the rest of the time, a series of recorded messages tells callers other phone numbers and addresses where they can turn to for help. **Alcoholics Anonymous** (© **020/7833-0022**) answers its hot line daily from 10am to 10pm. The **AIDS** 24-hour hot line is © **0800/567-123**.

Legal Aid In every case where legal aid is required by a foreign national within Britain, the British Tourist Authority advises visitors to contact their embassy.

Liquor Laws No alcohol is served to anyone under 18. Children under 16 aren't allowed in pubs, except in certain rooms, and then only when accompanied by a parent or guardian. Pubs are open Monday through Saturday from 11am to 11pm and Sunday from noon to 10:30pm. Restaurants are allowed to serve liquor during the same hours as pubs; however, only people eating a meal on the premises can be served. You can buy beer, wine, and liquor in supermarkets, liquor stores (called off-licenses), and many local grocery stores during any hour that pubs are open. In hotels, liquor may be served from 11am to 11pm to both residents and nonresidents; after 11pm, only residents may be served. Any nightclub that charges admission is allowed to serve alcohol until 3am or so. Don't drink and drive; penalties are stiff.

Lost & Found Be sure to tell all of your credit card companies the minute you discover your wallet has been lost or stolen, and file a report at the nearest police precinct. Your credit card company or insurer may require a police report number or record of the loss. Most credit card companies have an emergency toll-free number to call if your card is lost or stolen; they may be able to wire you a cash advance immediately or deliver an emergency credit card in a day or two. Visa's U.S. emergency number is ✆ **800/847-2911** or 410/581-9994. American Express cardholders and traveler's check holders should call ✆ **800/221-7282.** MasterCard holders should call ✆ **800/307-7309** or 636/722-7111. For other credit cards, call the toll-free number directory at ✆ **800/555-1212.**

In Britain, for Amex issues call ✆ **0208/551-1111;** for Visa and MasterCard issues, call ✆ **0870/242-4240.**

If you need emergency cash over the weekend when all banks and American Express offices are closed, you can have money wired to you via **Western Union** (✆ 800/325-6000; www.westernunion.com).

Identity theft and fraud are potential complications of losing your wallet, especially if you've lost your driver's license along with your cash and credit cards. Notify the major credit-reporting bureaus immediately; placing a fraud alert on your records may protect you against liability for criminal activity. The three major U.S. credit-reporting agencies are **Equifax** (✆ **888/766-0008;** www.equifax.com), **Experian** (✆ **888/397-3742;** www.experian.com), and **TransUnion** (✆ **800/680-7289;** www.transunion.com). Finally, if you've lost all forms of photo ID, call your airline and explain the situation; they might allow you to board the plane if you have a copy of your passport or birth certificate and a copy of the police report you've filed.

Newspapers & Magazines The *Times, Daily Telegraph, Daily Mail,* and *Guardian* are dailies carrying the latest news.

The *International Herald Tribune,* published in Paris, and an international edition of *USA Today,* beamed via satellite, are available daily (*USA Today* will be printed as a newsletter). Copies of *Time* and *Newsweek* are sold at most newsstands. Magazines such as *Time Out, City Limits,* and *Where* contain useful information about the latest happenings in London.

Police   In an emergency, dial ℂ **999** (no coins required).

Post Offices   The **main post office** is at 24–28 William IV St. (ℂ **020/7484-9307;** Tube: Charing Cross). It operates as three separate businesses: inland and international postal service and banking (Mon–Fri 8:30am–6:30pm and Sat 9am–5:30pm); philatelic postage-stamp sales (Mon–Fri 8:30am–6:30pm and Sat 9am–5:30pm) for collectors; and the post shop, selling greeting cards and stationery (Mon–Sat 8:30am–6:30pm). Other post offices and post-office branches are open Monday to Friday from 9am to 5:30pm and Saturday from 9am to 12:30pm. Many post-office branches and some main post offices close for an hour at lunchtime.

Restrooms   They're marked by PUBLIC TOILETS signs in streets, parks, and Tube stations; many are automatically sterilized after each use. The English often call toilets "loos." You'll also find well-maintained lavatories in all larger public buildings, such as museums and art galleries, large department stores, and railway stations. It's not really acceptable to use the lavatories in hotels, restaurants, and pubs if you're not a customer, but we can't say that we always stick to this rule. Public lavatories are usually free, but you may need a small coin to get in or to use a proper washroom.

Taxes   There is a 17.5% national **value-added tax (VAT)** added to all hotel and restaurant bills and included in the price of many items you purchase. It can be refunded if you shop at stores that participate in Global Refund Tax-Free Shopping (signs are posted in the window). See the "How to Get Your VAT Refund" box, p. 158.

You also pay a departure tax of £10 ($19) for flights within Britain and the European Union; it's £20 ($37) for flights to the U.S. and other countries. Your airline ticket may or may not include this tax. Ask in advance to avoid a surprise at the gate.

To encourage energy conservation, the British government levies a 25% tax on gasoline (petrol). If you've read our warnings about driving in London, this will be of no importance to you whatsoever.

Telephone **To call London:** If you're calling London from the United States:

1. Dial the international access code: 011.
2. Dial the country code 44.
3. Dial the city code 20 and then the number. (London's official city code is 020, but you will dial 20 because you always have to omit the zero from the area code when calling London from outside of England.) So the whole number you'd dial would be 011-44-20-0000-0000.

To make international calls: To make international calls from London, first dial 00 and then the country code (U.S. or Canada, 1; U.K., 44; Ireland, 353; Australia, 61; New Zealand, 64). Next you dial the area code and number. For example, if you wanted to call the British Embassy in Washington, D.C., you would dial 00-1-202-588-7800.

Or call through one of the following long-distance access codes: **AT&T USA Direct** (© 0800/890-011), **Canada Direct** (© 0800/890-016), **Australia** (© 0800/890-061), or **New Zealand** (© 0800/890-064). Common country codes are **U.S. and Canada,** 1; **Australia,** 61; **New Zealand,** 64; **South Africa,** 27.

For directory assistance: Dial © 118212 for a full range of services; for the rest of Britain, dial © 118118.

For operator assistance: If you need operator assistance in making a call, dial © 100 if you're trying to make an international call and © 192 if you want to call a number in England.

Toll-free numbers: Numbers beginning with 0800 within London are toll-free, but calling a 1-800 number in the U.S. from England is not toll-free. In fact, it costs the same as an overseas call.

To call within London: Dial the local seven- or eight-digit number.

To call within Britain (outside of London): Phone numbers outside the major cities consist of an exchange code plus telephone number. To dial the number, you need to dial the exchange code first. Information sheets on call-box walls give the codes in most instances. If your code isn't there, call the operator by dialing © 100.

There are three types of public pay phones: those taking only coins, those accepting only phone cards (called Cardphones), and those taking both phone cards and credit cards. At coin-operated phones, insert your coins before dialing. The minimum charge is 10p (19¢).

Phone cards are available in four values £2 ($3.70), £5 ($9.25), £10 ($19), and £20 ($37)—and are reusable until the total value has expired. Cards can be purchased from newsstands and post offices. You can also use credit cards—Access (MasterCard), Visa, American Express, and Diners Club—at credit-call pay phones, commonly found at airports and large railway stations.

Tipping In restaurants, service charges in the 15% to 20% range are usually added to the bill. Sometimes this is clearly marked; at other times, it isn't. When in doubt, ask. If service isn't included, it's customary to add 15% to the bill. Sommeliers get about £1.95 ($3.60) per bottle of wine served. You can leave small change if the service is good. There's no tipping in pubs. In cocktail bars, the server usually gets about 75p ($1.40) per round of drinks.

Hotels, like restaurants, often add a service charge of 10% to 15% to most bills. In smaller B&Bs, the tip isn't likely to be included. Therefore, tip people who performed special services, such as for the person who served you breakfast. If several persons have served you in a B&B, many guests ask that 10% or 15% be added to the bill and divided among the staff. Tip chambermaids £1 ($1.85) per day for cleaning up (more if you've made their job extra difficult).

It's standard to tip taxi drivers 10% to 15% of the fare, although a tip for a taxi driver should never be less than 30p (55¢), even for a short run. Barbers and hairdressers expect 10% to 15%. Tour guides expect £3 ($5.55), although it's not mandatory. Theater ushers don't expect tips.

3

Where to Stay

The good news is that more than 10,000 hotel rooms have opened in London post-millennium, relieving the overcrowding that existed at peak travel months. The downside is that most of these hotels are in districts far from the city center and are of the no-frills budget-chain variety.

Some hoteliers have decided to adapt former public or institutional buildings rather than start from scratch. The imposing County Hall building in the S1 district now boasts two chains: a luxurious Marriott and a leaner, meaner Travel Inn. Another trend is a shift away from the West End to such respectable sections as Greenwich (now a virtual suburb of London), Docklands, and even the City (London's financial district).

With all the vast improvements and upgrades made at the turn of the 21st century, chances are you'll like your room. What you won't like is the price. Even if a hotel remains scruffy, London hoteliers have little embarrassment about jacking up prices. Hotels in all categories remain overpriced.

London boasts some of the most famous hotels in the world—temples of luxury like Claridge's and The Dorchester and more recent rivals like the Four Seasons. The problem is that there are too many of these high-priced hotels (and now there are many budget options) and not enough moderately priced options.

Even at the luxury level, you might be surprised at what you don't get. Many of the stately Victorian and Edwardian gems are so steeped in tradition that they lack many modern conveniences that are standard in other luxury hotels around the world. Some have modernized with a vengeance, but others retain amenities from the Boer War era. London does have some cutting-edge, chintz-free hotels that seem to have been flown in straight from Los Angeles—complete with high-end sound systems and gadget-filled marble bathrooms. However, these cutting-edge hotels are not necessarily superior; though they're streamlined and convenient, they frequently lack the personal service and spaciousness that characterize the grand old hotels.

Since the late 1990s, new boutique hotels have been generating lots of excitement. With their charm, intimacy, and attention to detail, they're an attractive alternative to the larger, stuffier establishments. The "boutiquing" of the hotel scene continues postmillennium. The city offers more personally run and privately operated hotels than ever. We've surveyed the best of them, concentrating on the reasonably priced choices.

If you're looking for budget options, don't despair. London has some good-value places in the lower price ranges, and we've included the best of these. An affordable option is a bed-and-breakfast. At their best, B&Bs are clean, comfortable, and friendly. Good B&Bs are in short supply, so don't reserve a room at one without a recommendation you can trust. The following reliable services will recommend and arrange a B&B room for you: **London Bed & Breakfast Association** (© 800/852-2632 in the U.S., fax 020/ 8749-7084; fax from U.S. 619/531-1686). **The London Bed and Breakfast Agency Limited** (© 020/7586-2768; fax 020/7586-6567; www.londonbb.com) is another reputable agency that can provide inexpensive accommodations in selected private homes for £22 to £44 ($41–$81) per person per night, based on double occupancy (although some accommodations will cost a lot more). **London B&B** (© 800/872-2632 in the U.S.; fax 619/531-1686; www.londonbandb.com) offers B&B accommodations in private family residences or unhosted apartments. Homes are inspected for quality and comfort, amenities, and convenience.

A NOTE ABOUT PRICES   Unless otherwise noted, published prices are rack rates for rooms with a private bathroom. Many include breakfast (usually continental) and a 10% to 15% service charge. The British government also imposes a VAT (value-added tax) that adds 17.5% to your bill. This is not included in the prices quoted in the guide. Always ask for a better rate, particularly at the first-class and deluxe hotels (B&Bs generally charge a fixed rate). Parking rates are per night.

1 The West End

BLOOMSBURY

EXPENSIVE

The Academy Hotel ⋆   The Academy is in the heart of London's publishing district. If you look out your window, you see where Virginia Woolf and other literary members of the Bloomsbury Group passed by every day. Many original architectural details were preserved

Where to Stay in London

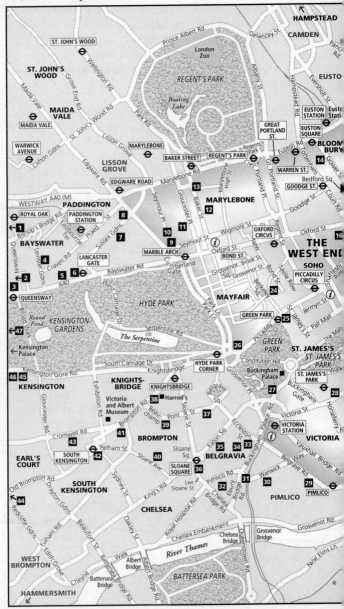

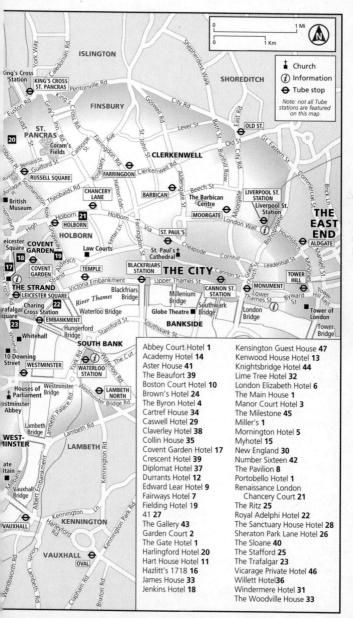

Abbey Court Hotel **1**
Academy Hotel **14**
Aster House **41**
The Beaufort **39**
Boston Court Hotel **10**
Brown's Hotel **24**
The Byron Hotel **4**
Cartref House **34**
Caswell Hotel **29**
Claverley Hotel **38**
Collin House **35**
Covent Garden Hotel **17**
Crescent Hotel **39**
Diplomat Hotel **37**
Durrants Hotel **12**
Edward Lear Hotel **9**
Fairways Hotel **7**
Fielding Hotel **19**
41 **27**
The Gallery **43**
Garden Court **2**
The Gate Hotel **1**
Harlingford Hotel **20**
Hart House Hotel **11**
Hazlitt's 1718 **16**
James House **33**
Jenkins Hotel **18**

Kensington Guest House **47**
Kenwood House Hotel **13**
Knightsbridge Hotel **44**
Lime Tree Hotel **32**
London Elizabeth Hotel **6**
The Main House **1**
Manor Court Hotel **3**
The Milestone **45**
Miller's **1**
Mornington Hotel **5**
Myhotel **15**
New England **30**
Number Sixteen **42**
The Pavilion **8**
Portobello Hotel **1**
Renaissance London
   Chancery Court **21**
The Ritz **25**
Royal Adelphi Hotel **22**
The Sanctuary House Hotel **28**
Sheraton Park Lane Hotel **26**
The Sloane **40**
The Stafford **25**
The Trafalgar **23**
Vicarage Private Hotel **46**
Willett Hotel **36**
Windermere Hotel **31**
The Woodville House **33**

when these three 1776 Georgian row houses were joined. The hotel was substantially upgraded in the 1990s, with a bathroom added to every bedroom (whether there was space or not). Fourteen have a shower/tub combination; the rest have showers only. The beds, so they say, were built to "American specifications." True or not, they promise you a restful night's sleep. Grace notes include glass panels, colonnades, and intricate plasterwork on the facade. With over-stuffed armchairs and half-canopied beds, rooms sometimes evoke English country-house living, but that of the poorer relations. Guests who have been here before always request rooms opening on the garden in back and not those in front with ducted fresh air, though the front units have double-glazing to cut down on the noise. The theater district and Covent Garden are within walking distance. *Warning:* If you have a problem with stairs, know that no elevators rise to the four floors.

21 Gower St., London WC1E 6HG. © 020/7631-4115. Fax 020/7636-3442. www. etontownhouse.com. 49 units. £163–£189 ($302–$350) double; £215 ($398) suite. AE, DC, MC, V. Tube: Tottenham Court Rd., Goodge St., or Russell Sq. **Amenities:** Bar; limited room service; laundry service; same-day dry cleaning; nonsmoking rooms. *In room:* A/C, TV, dataport, minibar, hair dryer, iron/ironing board, safe, beverage maker, trouser press.

Myhotel ★ *(finds* Creating shock waves among staid Bloomsbury hoteliers, Myhotel is a London row house on the outside with an Asian *moderne*-style interior. It is designed according to feng shui principles—the ancient Chinese art of placement that analyzes the flow of energy in a space. The rooms have mirrors, but they're positioned so you don't see yourself when you first wake up—feng shui rule no. 1 (probably a good rule, feng shui or no feng shui). Rooms are havens of comfort, taste, and tranquillity. Excellent sleep-inducing beds are found in all rooms, along with a small bathroom with a tub. Tipping is discouraged, and each guest is assigned a personal assistant responsible for that guest's happiness. Aimed at today's young, hip traveler, Myhotel lies within a short walk of Covent Garden and the British Museum.

11–13 Bayley St., Bedford Sq., London WC1B 3HD. © 020/7667-6000. Fax 020/ 7667-6001. www.myhotels.co.uk. 78 units. £185–£250 ($342–$463) double; from £330 ($611) suite. AE, DC, MC, V. Tube: Tottenham Court Rd. **Amenities:** Restaurant; bar; exercise room; spa; car at discounted rate; 24-hr. room service; massage; babysitting; laundry service; same-day dry cleaning; nonsmoking rooms. *In room:* A/C, TV w/pay movies, dataport, hair dryer, safe, beverage maker, trouser press (in some).

Renaissance London Chancery Court ★★★ The *London Times* may have gotten carried away with the hype, proclaiming this "one of the most exciting hotels in the world," but this landmark 1914 building in the financial district has been stunningly transformed into a government-rated five-star hotel, retaining the grandeur of the past but boasting all the comforts and conveniences of today. The surprise hit of 2003, this is a seven-floor Edwardian monument with a marble staircase. The building has been used as a backdrop for such films as *Howard's End* and *The Saint* because filmmakers were drawn to its soaring archways and classical central courtyard. The interior of the hotel encases you in womblike luxury. The glamorous and exceedingly comfortable rooms are all furnished with fine linens and decorated in different hues of cream, red, and blue. The bathrooms are about the most spacious in London, clad in Italian marble with lavish shower/tub combinations. The best accommodations are on the sixth floor, opening onto a cozy interior courtyard hidden from the busy world outside.

252 High Holborn, WC1V 7EN. © **800/468-3571** in the U.S. or Canada, or 020/7829-9888. Fax 020/7829-9889. www.renaissancehotels.com. 356 units. £180–£240 ($333–$444) double; £285–£465 ($527–$860) suite. AE, DC, MC, V. Tube: Holborn. **Amenities:** 2 restaurants; 2 bars; cocktail lounge; luxurious spa; business center; 24-hr. room service; massage; babysitting; sauna; laundry service/dry cleaning; nonsmoking rooms; rooms for those w/limited mobility. *In room:* A/C, TV w/pay movies, dataport, kitchenette, minibar, coffeemaker, hair dryer, iron, safe.

MODERATE

Crescent Hotel   Although Ruskin and Shelley no longer pass by, the Crescent still stands in the heart of academic London. The private square is owned by the City Guild of Skinners (who are furriers, as you might have guessed) and guarded by the University of London, whose student residential halls are across the street. You have access to the gardens and private tennis courts belonging to the City Guild of Skinners. The hotel owners view Crescent as an extension of their home and welcome you to its comfortably elegant Georgian surroundings, which date from 1810. Some guests have been returning for 4 decades. Bedrooms range from small singles with shared bathrooms to more spacious twin and double rooms with private showers. All have extras such as alarm clocks. Twins and doubles have private plumbing, with tiny bathrooms. Many rooms are singles, ranging in price from £46 to £83 ($85–$154), depending on the plumbing.

49–50 Cartwright Gardens, London WC1H 9EL. © **020/7387-1515.** Fax 020/7383-2054. www.crescenthoteloflondon.com. 27 units, 18 with bathroom (some with shower only, some with tub and shower). £89 ($165) double with bathroom. Rates include English breakfast. MC, V. Tube: Russell Sq., King's Cross, or Euston. **Amenities:** Use of tennis courts in Cartwright Gardens; babysitting. *In room:* TV, coffeemaker.

Harlingford Hotel *Value*　This hotel is comprised of three town houses built in the 1820s and joined together around 1900 with a bewildering array of staircases and meandering hallways. Set in the heart of Bloomsbury, it's run by a management that seems genuinely concerned about the welfare of its guests, unlike the management at many of the neighboring hotel rivals. (They even distribute little mincemeat pies to their guests during the Christmas holidays.) Double-glazed windows cut down on the street noise, and all the bedrooms are comfortable and inviting. Shower-only bathrooms are small, however, since the house wasn't originally designed for them. The most comfortable rooms are on the second and third levels, but expect to climb some steep English stairs (there's no elevator). Avoid the rooms on ground level, as they are darker and have less security. You'll have use of the tennis courts in Cartwright Gardens.

61–63 Cartwright Gardens, London WC1H 9EL. ⓒ 020/7387-1551. Fax 020/7387-4616. www.harlingfordhotel.com. 44 units. £95 ($175) double; £105 ($194) triple; £110 ($204) quad. Rates include English breakfast. AE, DC, MC, V. Tube: Russell Sq., King's Cross, or Euston. **Amenities:** Use of tennis courts in Cartwright Gardens. *In room:* TV, coffeemaker, hair dryer.

The Jenkins Hotel *Value*　Followers of the Agatha Christie TV series *Poirot* will recognize this Cartwright Gardens residence—it was featured in the series. The antiques are gone and the rooms are small, but some of the original charm of the Georgian house remains—enough so that the London *Mail on Sunday* proclaimed it one of the "10 best hotel values" in the city. All the rooms have been redecorated in traditional Georgian style, and many have been completely refurbished with new beds and upholstery. All but one room has a private bathroom. Most have shower-only bathrooms. The location is great, near the British Museum, theaters, and antiquarian bookshops. There are some drawbacks: no lift and no reception or sitting room. But this is a place where you can settle in and feel at home.

45 Cartwright Gardens, London WC1H 9EH. ⓒ 020/7387-2067. Fax 020/7383-3139. www.jenkinshotel.demon.co.uk. 13 units. £85 ($157) double; £105 ($194) triple. Rates include English breakfast. MC, V. Tube: Russell Sq., King's Cross, or Euston. **Amenities:** Use of washer/dryer; all nonsmoking rooms. *In room:* TV, dataport, minibar, fridge, coffeemaker, hair dryer, iron, safe.

COVENT GARDEN & THE STRAND
VERY EXPENSIVE

Covent Garden Hotel *Value*　This former hospital building lay neglected for years until it was reconfigured in 1996 by hot hoteliers

Tim and Kit Kemp—whose flair for interior design is legendary—into one of London's most charming boutique hotels in one of the West End's hippest shopping neighborhoods. *Travel and Leisure* called this hotel 1 of the 25 hottest places to stay in the *world*. It remains so. Behind a bottle-green facade reminiscent of a 19th-century storefront, the hotel has a welcoming lobby outfitted with elaborate inlaid furniture and elegant draperies, plus two charming restaurants. Upstairs, accessible via a dramatic stone staircase, soundproof bedrooms are furnished in English style with Asian fabrics, many adorned with hand-embroidered designs. The hotel has a decorative trademark—each room has a clothier's mannequin, a female form draped in the fabric that decorates that particular room. Each room comes with luxurious amenities including full marble bathrooms with double vanities and deep soaking tubs. Some guests prefer the attic rooms with their sloping ceilings and small arched windows.

10 Monmouth St., London WC2H 9HB. ⓒ 800/553-6674 in the U.S., or 020/7806-1000. Fax 020/7806-1100. www.firmdale.com. 58 units. £245–£295 ($453–$546) double; £350–£795 ($648–$1,471) suite. AE, MC, V. Tube: Covent Garden or Leicester Sq. **Amenities:** Restaurant; bar; small exercise room; concierge; tour desk; business services; 24-hr. room service; massage; babysitting; laundry service; same-day dry cleaning; video library; nonsmoking rooms. *In room:* A/C, TV/VCR, dataport, minibar, hair dryer, safe.

MODERATE

The Fielding Hotel ⓡ *Finds*   One of London's more eccentric hotels, the Fielding is cramped, quirky, and quaint, and an enduring favorite. Luring media types, the hotel is named after novelist Henry Fielding of *Tom Jones* fame, who lived in Broad Court. It lies on a pedestrian street still lined with 19th-century gas lamps. The Royal Opera House is across the street, and the pubs, shops, and restaurants of lively Covent Garden are just beyond the front door. Rooms are small but charmingly old-fashioned and traditional. Some units are redecorated or at least "touched up" every year, though floors dip and sway, and the furnishings and fabrics, though clean, have known better times. The bathrooms, some with antiquated plumbing, are equipped with showers. But with a location like this, in the heart of London, the Fielding keeps guests coming back; in fact, many love the hotel's rickety charm. Children under 13 are not welcome.

4 Broad Court, Bow St., London WC2B 5QZ. ⓒ 020/7836-8305. Fax 020/7497-0064. www.the-fielding-hotel.co.uk. 24 units. £100–£115 ($185–$213) double; £130 ($241) suite. AE, DC, MC, V. Tube: Covent Garden. **Amenities:** Bar; laundry service; nonsmoking rooms. *In room:* TV, dataport, coffeemaker.

INEXPENSIVE

Royal Adelphi Hotel   If you care most about being in a central location, consider the Royal Adelphi. Close to Covent Garden, the theater district, and Trafalgar Square, it's an unorthodox choice away from the typical B&B stamping grounds. London has far better B&Bs, but not in this part of town. Although the bedrooms call to mind London's swinging 1960s heyday, accommodations are decently maintained and comfortable, with good beds. Plumbing, however, is a bit creaky, and the lack of air-conditioning can make London feel like summer in the Australian outback during the city's few hot days.

21 Villiers St., London WC2N 6ND. ℂ 020/7930-8764. Fax 020/7930-8735. www. royaladelphi.co.uk. 47 units, 34 with bathroom. £70 ($130) double without bathroom; £92 ($170) double with bathroom. AE, DC, MC, V. Tube: Charing Cross or Embankment. *In room:* TV, coffeemaker, hair dryer.

TRAFALGAR SQUARE
EXPENSIVE

The Trafalgar 𝔊𝔊   In the heart of landmark Trafalgar Square, this is Hilton's first boutique hotel in London. The facade of this 19th-century structure was preserved, while the guest rooms inside were refitted to modern standards. Because of the original architecture, many of the rooms are uniquely shaped and sometimes offer split-level layouts. Large windows open onto panoramic views of Trafalgar Square. The decor in the rooms is minimalist, and comfort is combined with simple luxury, including the deluxe tiled bathrooms with shower/tub combinations. The greatest view of London's cityscape is from the Hilton's rooftop garden.

Unusual for London, the bar, Rockwell, specializes in bourbon, with more than 100 brands. Jago is the hotel's organic-produce restaurant, serving comfort food.

2 Spring Gardens, Trafalgar Sq., London SW1A 2TS. ℂ 800/774-1500 in the U.S., or 020/7870-2900. Fax 020/7870-2911. www.hilton.com. 129 units. £159–£229 ($294–$424) double; from £289 ($535) suite. AE, DC, MC, V. Tube: Charing Cross. **Amenities:** Restaurant; bar; concierge; sauna; courtesy car; business services; 24-hr. room service; laundry service; same-day dry cleaning; nonsmoking rooms; rooms for those w/limited mobility. *In room:* A/C, TV w/pay movies, dataport, minibar, hair dryer, safe, beverage maker.

SOHO
EXPENSIVE

Hazlitt's 1718 𝔊𝔊 (Finds)   This gem, housed in three historic homes on Soho Square, is one of London's best small hotels. Built in 1718, the hotel is named for William Hazlitt, who founded the

Unitarian church in Boston and wrote four volumes on the life of his hero, Napoleon.

Hazlitt's is a favorite with artists, actors, and models. It's eclectic and filled with odds and ends picked up around the country at estate auctions. Some find its Georgian decor a bit spartan, but the 2,000 original prints hanging on the walls brighten it considerably. Many bedrooms have four-poster beds, and some bathrooms have their original claw-foot tubs (only two units have a shower). Some of the floors dip and sway, and there's no elevator, but it's all part of the charm. It has just as much character as The Fielding Hotel (p. 49) but is a lot more comfortable. Some rooms are a bit small, but most are spacious, all with state-of-the-art appointments. Most bathrooms have 19th-century styling but up-to-date plumbing, with oversize tubs and old brass fittings; the showers, however, are mostly hand-held. Accommodations in the back are quieter but perhaps too dark, and only those on the top floor have air-conditioning.

6 Frith St., London W1V 5TZ. © **020/7434-1771**. Fax 020/7439-1524. www.hazlittshotel.com. 23 units. £205–£255 ($379–$472) double; £300 ($555) suite. AE, DC, MC, V. Tube: Leicester Sq. or Tottenham Court Rd. **Amenities:** 24-hr. room service; babysitting; laundry service; same-day dry cleaning; nonsmoking rooms. *In room:* A/C (some rooms), TV/VCR, dataport, minibar, hair dryer, safe.

MAYFAIR
VERY EXPENSIVE

Brown's Hotel 🏨🏨   Almost every year a hotel sprouts up trying to evoke an English country-house ambience with Chippendale and chintz; this quintessential town-house hotel watches these competitors come and go, and it always comes out on top. Brown's was founded by James Brown, a former manservant to Lord Byron, who knew the tastes of well-bred gentlemen and wanted to create a dignified, clublike place for them. He opened its doors in 1837, the same year Queen Victoria took the throne.

Brown's occupies 14 historic houses just off Berkeley Square and its guest rooms vary considerably in decor, but all show restrained taste in decoration and appointments; even the wash basins are antiques. Accommodations range in size from small to extra spacious; some suites have four-poster beds. Bathrooms come in a variety of sizes, but they are beautifully equipped with robes, luxurious cosmetics, tubs, and showers.

30 Albemarle St., London W1S 4BP. © **020/7493-6020**. Fax 020/7493-9381. www.brownshotel.com. 118 units. £239–£345 ($442–$638) double; from £403 ($746) suite. AE, DC, MC, V. Off-site parking £40 ($74). Tube: Green Park. **Amenities:** Restaurant; bar; health club; concierge; business center; 24-hr. room service; laundry

service; same-day dry cleaning; nonsmoking rooms. *In room:* A/C, TV/VCR w/pay movies, dataport, minibar, hair dryer, safe.

Sheraton Park Lane Hotel *ⓡⓡ* Since 1924, this has been the most traditional of the Park Lane mansions, even more so than The Dorchester. The hotel was sold in 1996 to the Sheraton Corporation, which continues to upgrade it but maintains its quintessential British style. Its Silver Entrance remains an Art Deco marvel that has been used as a backdrop in many films, including the classic BBC miniseries *Brideshead Revisited.*

Overlooking Green Park, the hotel offers luxurious accommodations that are a good deal—well, at least for pricey Park Lane, where anything under $500 a night is a bargain. Many suites have marble fireplaces and original marble bathrooms. The rooms have all benefited from impressive refurbishment. All have double-glazed windows to block out noise. The most tranquil rooms open onto a street in the rear. Rooms opening onto the court are dark. In the more deluxe rooms, you get trouser presses and better views. Bathrooms are generally spacious and well equipped with shower/tub combos; many also have robes.

Piccadilly, London W1J 7BX. ⓒ **800/325-3535** in the U.S., or 020/7499-6321. Fax 020/7499-1965. www.starwood.com/sheraton. 307 units. £270–£310 ($500–$574) double; from £429 ($794) suite. AE, DC, MC, V. Parking £35 ($65). Tube: Hyde Park Corner or Green Park. **Amenities:** 2 restaurants; fabled 1920s palm court; bar; health club; concierge; business center; 24-hr. room service, laundry service; same-day dry cleaning; nonsmoking rooms; rooms for those w/limited mobility. *In room:* A/C (in most rooms), TV w/pay movies, dataport, minibar, hair dryer, iron, safe.

ST. JAMES'S
VERY EXPENSIVE

The Ritz *ⓡⓡⓡ* Built in French Renaissance style and opened by César Ritz in 1906, this hotel overlooking Green Park is synonymous with luxury. Gold-leafed molding, marble columns, and potted palms abound, and a gold-leafed statue, *La Source,* adorns the fountain of the oval-shaped Palm Court. After a major restoration, the hotel is better than ever: New carpeting and air-conditioning have been installed in the guest rooms, and an overall polishing has recaptured much of The Ritz's original splendor. Still, this Ritz lags far behind the much grander one in Paris (with which it is not affiliated). The Belle Epoque guest rooms, each with its own character, are spacious and comfortable. Many have marble fireplaces, elaborate gilded plasterwork, and a decor of soft pastel hues. A few rooms have their original brass beds and marble fireplaces. Bathrooms are elegantly appointed in either tile or marble and filled with deep tubs with showers, robes, phones, and deluxe toiletries. Corner rooms are grander and more spacious.

150 Piccadilly, London W1J 9BR. ℂ 877/748-9536 in the U.S. or 020/7493-8181. Fax 020/7493-2687. www.theritzlondon.com. 133 units. £310–£405 ($574–$749) double; from £785 ($1,452) suite. Children under 12 stay free in parent's room. AE, DC, MC, V. Parking £54 ($100). Tube: Green Park. **Amenities:** 2 restaurants (including the Palm Court); bar; exercise room; concierge; business services; 2 salons; 24-hr. room service; massage; babysitting; laundry service; same-day dry cleaning; nonsmoking rooms; rooms for those w/limited mobility. *In room:* A/C, TV/VCR w/pay movies, fax, dataport, minibar, hair dryer, safe.

The Stafford Hotel 🏵🏵🏵 Famous for its American Bar, its clubby St. James's address, and the warmth of its Edwardian decor, The Stafford is in a cul-de-sac off one of London's most centrally located and busiest neighborhoods. The recently refurbished late-19th-century hotel has retained a country-house atmosphere, with antique charm and modern amenities. The Stafford competes well with Dukes and 22 Jermyn Street for a tasteful, discerning clientele, and seems to maintain a slight edge in attracting an upmarket clientele.

All the guest rooms are individually decorated, reflecting the hotel's origins as a private home. Many singles contain queen-size beds. Some of the deluxe units offer four-posters that will make you feel like Henry VIII. Nearly all the bathrooms are clad in marble with tubs and stall showers, toiletries, and chrome fixtures. A few of the hotel's more modern accommodations, boasting king-size beds, are located in the restored stable mews across the yard. Much has been done to preserve the original style of these rooms, including preservation of the original A-beams on the upper floors. You can bet that no 18th-century horse ever slept with the electronic safes, stereo systems, and quality furnishings (mostly antique reproductions) that these rooms feature. Units on the top floor are small.

16–18 St. James's Place, London SW1A 1NJ. ℂ 800/525-4800 in the U.S., or 020/7493-0111. Fax 020/7493-7121. www.thestaffordhotel.co.uk. 81 units. £225–£250 ($416–$463) double; from £270 ($500) suite. AE, DC, MC, V. Tube: Green Park. **Amenities:** Restaurant; famous American bar; health club privileges nearby; concierge; business services; 24-hr. room service; babysitting; laundry service; same-day dry cleaning; all nonsmoking rooms. *In room:* A/C, TV/VCR, fax, dataport, hair dryer, safe.

2 Westminster & Victoria

EXPENSIVE

41 🏵🏵🏵 *Finds* This relatively unknown but well-placed gem is a treasure worth seeking out, especially if you're looking for a touch of class. The property offers the intimate atmosphere of a private club combined with a level of personal service that's impossible to achieve at larger hotels. It's best suited to couples or those traveling alone—especially women, who will be made to feel comfortable. The cordial staff goes the extra mile to fulfill a guest's every wish. The surroundings match the stellar service. Public areas feature an abundance of mahogany, antiques, fresh flowers, and rich fabrics. Read, relax, or watch TV in the library-style lounge, where a complimentary continental breakfast, afternoon snacks, and evening canapés (all included in the room rate) are served each day.

Guest rooms are individually sized, but all feature elegant black-and-white color schemes, magnificent beds with Egyptian-cotton linens, and "AV centers" that offer free Internet access and DVD/CD players. Most rooms have working fireplaces. The spotless marble bathrooms sport separate tubs and power showers (only one room has a shower/tub combo) and feature Penhaligon toiletries. The bi-level junior suites toss in a separate seating area (good for families looking for extra space) and Jacuzzi tubs.

41 Buckingham Palace Rd., London SW1W OPS. ⓒ **877/955-1515** in the U.S. or Canada, or 020/7300-0041. Fax 020/7300-0141. www.41hotel.com. 18 units. £200 ($370) double; £400–£500 ($740–$925) suite. Rates include continental breakfast, afternoon snacks, and evening canapés. Extra person £45 ($83). Special Internet packages and discounts available. AE, DC, MC, V. Tube: Victoria. **Amenities:** Lounge; bar; access to nearby health club; concierge; business center; 24-hr. room service; laundry service/dry cleaning; nonsmoking rooms; 1 room for those w/limited mobility. *In room:* A/C, TV, minibar, tea/coffeemaker, hair dryer, iron/ironing board, safe.

MODERATE

Lime Tree Hotel   The Wales-born Davies family, longtime veterans of London's B&B business, have transformed a run-down guesthouse into a cost-conscious, cozy hotel for budget travelers. The simply furnished bedrooms are scattered over four floors of a brick town house; each has been recently refitted with new curtains and cupboards. The front rooms have small balconies overlooking Ebury Street; units in the back don't have balconies, but are quieter and feature views over the hotel's small rose garden. The Lime Tree's rooms tend to be larger than other hotel rooms offered at similar prices, and breakfasts are generous. Six rooms come with a shower/tub combo, the rest with shower only. Buckingham Palace, Westminster Abbey, and the Houses of Parliament are within easy reach, as is Harrods. Nearby is the popular Ebury Wine Bar.

135–137 Ebury St., London SW1W 9RA. ⓒ **020/7730-8191.** Fax 020/7730-7865. www.limetreehotel.co.uk. 29 units. £84–£125 ($155–$231) double. Rates include

English breakfast. AE, DC, MC, V. No children under 5. Tube: Victoria. **Amenities:** All nonsmoking rooms. *In room:* TV, coffeemaker, hair dryer, safe.

New England   A family-run business, going strong for nearly a quarter of a century, this hotel shut down at the millennium for a complete overhaul. Today, it's better than ever and charges an affordable price. Its elegant 19th-century exterior conceals a completely bright and modern interior. The hotel is justly proud of its clientele of "repeats." On a corner in the Pimlico area, which forms part of the City of Westminster, the hotel is neat and clean and one of the most welcoming in the area. It's also one of the few hotels in the area with an elevator. All the bathrooms have power showers.

20 Saint George's Dr., London SW1V 4BN. © 020/7834-1595. Fax 020/7834-9000. www.newenglandhotel.com. 25 units. £95–£99 ($176–$183) double; £119 ($220) triple; £139 ($257) quad. Rates include breakfast. AE, MC, V. Tube: Victoria. **Amenities:** Nonsmoking rooms; rooms for those w/limited mobility. *In room:* TV, dataport, hair dryer.

The Sanctuary House Hotel ⋒   Only in the new London, where hotels are bursting into bloom like daffodils, would you find a hotel so close to Westminster Abbey. And a pub hotel, no less, with rooms on the upper floors above the tavern. The building was converted by Fuller Smith and Turner, a traditional brewery in Britain. Accommodations have a rustic feel, but they have first-rate beds, along with restored bathrooms with shower/tub combinations. Downstairs, a pub/restaurant, part of The Sanctuary, offers old-style British meals that have ignored changing culinary fashions. "We like tradition," one of the perky staff members told us. "Why must everything be trendy? Some people come to England nostalgic for the old. Let others be trendy." Actually, the food is excellent if you appreciate the roast beef, Welsh lamb, and Dover sole that pleased the palates of Churchill and his contemporaries. Naturally, there's always plenty of brew on tap.

33 Tothill St., London SW1H 9LA. © 020/7799-4044. Fax 020/7799-3657. www. fullershotels.com. 34 units. £85–£130 ($157–$241) double. AE, DC, MC, V. Parking £25 ($46). Tube: St. James's Park. **Amenities:** Restaurant; pub; limited room service; laundry service/dry cleaning; nonsmoking rooms; rooms for those w/limited mobility. *In room:* A/C, TV, dataport, coffeemaker, hair dryer, trouser press.

Windermere Hotel ⋒ *Value*   This award-winning small hotel is an excellent choice near Victoria Station. The Windermere was built in 1857 as a pair of private dwellings on the site of the old Abbot's Lane. The lane linked Westminster Abbey to its abbot's residence— so all the kings of medieval England trod here. A fine example of early Victorian classical design, the hotel has lots of English character. Most rooms have a small bathroom equipped with a shower, and the public bathrooms are adequate and well maintained. Rooms come in a wide range of sizes, some accommodating three or four lodgers. The cheaper ones are somewhat cramped. The ground-floor rooms facing the street tend to be noisy at night, so stay away from those if you're a light sleeper.

142–144 Warwick Way, London SW1V 4JE. 📞 **020/7834-5163.** Fax 020/7630-8831. www.windermere-hotel.co.uk. 22 units, 20 with bathroom. £89 ($165) double without bathroom; £109 ($202) double with bathroom; £145 ($268) triple with bathroom; £149 ($276) quad with bathroom. Rates include English breakfast. AE, MC, V. Tube: Victoria. **Amenities:** Restaurant; bar; limited room service; nonsmoking rooms. *In room:* TV, dataport, coffeemaker, hair dryer, safe.

INEXPENSIVE

Caswell Hotel   Thoughtfully run by Mr. and Mrs. Hare, Caswell is on a cul-de-sac, a calm oasis in a busy area. Mozart lived nearby while he completed his first symphony, as did that "notorious couple" of the literati, Harold Nicholson and Victoria Sackville-West. Beyond the chintz-filled lobby, the decor is understated. There are four floors of well-furnished but not spectacular bedrooms. Both the private bathrooms (small units with shower stalls) and the corridor bathrooms are adequate and well maintained. How does the Caswell explain its success? One staff member said, "This year's guest is next year's business."

25 Gloucester St., London SW1V 2DB. 📞 **020/7834-6345.** www.hotellondon.co.uk. 19 units, 8 with bathroom. £58 ($107) double without bathroom; £78 ($144) double with bathroom. Rates include English breakfast. MC, V. Tube: Victoria. *In room:* TV, minibar, hair dryer, safe, beverage maker, no phone.

Collin House 🎇   This B&B emerges as a winner on a street lined with the finest Victoria Station–area B&Bs. William IV had just begun his reign when this house was constructed in 1830. Private, shower-only bathrooms have been discreetly installed, and everything works efficiently. For rooms without bathrooms, there are adequate hallway facilities, some of which are shared by only two rooms. Traffic in this area of London is heavy outside, and the front windows are not soundproof, so be warned if you're a light sleeper. Year after year, the owners continually make improvements in the furnishings and carpets. All bedrooms, which vary in size, are comfortably furnished and well maintained. Two rooms are large enough for families. A generous breakfast awaits you each morning in the basement of this nonsmoking facility.

104 Ebury St., London SW1W 9QD. ℂ and fax **020/7730-8031**. www.collinhouse. co.uk. 12 units, 8 with bathroom (shower only). £68 ($126) double without bathroom; £82 ($152) double with bathroom; £95 ($176) triple without bathroom. Rates include English breakfast. MC, V. Tube: Victoria. *In room:* TV, hair dryer available, safe, no phone.

James House/Cartref House *Kids*   Hailed by many publications, including the *Los Angeles Times,* as one of the top 10 B&B choices in London, James House and Cartref House (across the street from each other) deserve their accolades. Each room is individually designed. Some of the large rooms have bunk beds that make them suitable for families. Clients in rooms with a private shower-only bathroom will find somewhat cramped quarters; corridor bathrooms are adequate and frequently refurbished. The English breakfast is so generous that you might end up skipping lunch. There's no elevator, but guests don't seem to mind. Both houses are nonsmoking. You're just a stone's throw from Buckingham Palace should the queen invite you over for tea. **Warning:** Whether or not you like this hotel will depend on your room assignment. Some accommodations are fine but several rooms (often when the other units are full) are hardly large enough to move around in. This is especially true of some third-floor units. Some "bathrooms" reminded us of those found on small ocean-going freighters. Ask before booking and request a larger room.

108 and 129 Ebury St., London SW1W 9QU. James House ℂ **020/7730-7338;** Cartref House ℂ **020/7730-6176.** Fax 020/7730-7338. www.jamesandcartref.co.uk. 19 units, 12 with bathroom. £70 ($130) double without bathroom; £85 ($157) double with bathroom; £135 ($250) quad with bathroom. Rates include English breakfast. AE, MC, V. Tube: Victoria. **Amenities:** All nonsmoking rooms. *In room:* TV, hair dryer, beverage maker, no phone.

3 Hotels from Knightsbridge to South Kensington

KNIGHTSBRIDGE
VERY EXPENSIVE

The Beaufort *★★*   If you'd like to stay at one of London's finest boutique hotels, offering personal service in an elegant, tranquil town-house atmosphere, head here. The Beaufort, only 180m (590 ft.) from Harrods, sits in a cul-de-sac behind two Victorian porticoes and an iron fence. Owner Diana Wallis, a television producer, combined a pair of adjacent houses from the 1870s, ripped out the old decor, and created a graceful and stylish hotel that has the feeling of a private house. You register at a small desk extending off a bay-windowed parlor, and then climb the stairway used by the queen of Sweden during her stay. Each guest room is tasteful and bright, individually decorated in a modern color scheme and adorned with well-chosen paintings by London artists. Rooms come with earphone radios, flowers, and a selection of books. Most bedrooms are exceedingly small, but they're efficiently organized. The most deluxe and spacious rooms are in the front. Those in the back are smaller and darker. Included in the rates are a 24-hour free bar, continental breakfast, and light meals from room service, plus English cream teas each afternoon, and brandy, chocolates, and shortbread in each room. The junior suites offer a personal fax/answering machine, dataport, and use of a mobile phone. Bathrooms are adequate and tidily maintained, with shower/tub combinations.

33 Beaufort Gardens, London SW3 1PP. ℂ **020/7584-5252**. Fax 020/7589-2834. www.thebeaufort.co.uk. 28 units. £165–£260 ($305–$481) double; £300 ($555) junior suite. Rates include continental breakfast, bar, light meals, and afternoon tea. AE, DC, MC, V. Tube: Knightsbridge. **Amenities:** Bar; access to nearby health club; junior suites include complimentary limo to or from the airport; 24-hr. room service; babysitting; laundry service; same-day dry cleaning; nonsmoking rooms. *In room:* A/C, TV, dataport, hair dryer, iron/ironing board.

The Berkeley 𝕽𝕽𝕽   One of London's most appealing hotels, The Berkeley is housed in a travertine-faced French Regency–inspired building in Knightsbridge near Hyde Park, a premise it has occupied since it was built in 1972. This newer version replaced a hotel, built in the late 19th century, that was frequently visited and widely praised by Noel Coward, and from which were salvaged some of the original architectural embellishments, including what is now the popular Blue Bar. Inside, you'll find an understated environment inspired by Art Deco and French classical precedents, all with a contemporary edge. Adjacent to the small lobby is the newly redesigned Caramel Room where tea, drinks, informal dining, and even a doughnut menu are served. Each of the accommodations offers high-end style, but most elegant of all are the suites, many of which contain elegant paneling and luxurious, marble-and-tile-trimmed baths. The Berkeley offers two world-class restaurants, both of them established by celebrity chefs. They include Marcus Wareing's Petrus, and Gordon Ramsay's somewhat less grand and more whimsical Boxwood Cafe. The rooftop swimming pool with its associations to ancient Rome is one of many highlights within this extraordinary hotel.

Wilton Place, London SW1X 7RL. ℂ **800-63-SAVOY (72869)** or 020/7950-5490. Fax 020/7950-5484. www.savoygroup.com or www.the-berkeley.com. 157 units. £279–£395 ($516–$731) double; £490–£3,100 ($907–$5,735) suite. AE, DC, MC, V. Tube: Knightsbridge or Hyde Park Corner. **Amenities:** 2 restaurants; 2 bars; rooftop swimming pool; health club w/sauna; spa; 24-hr. room service; babysitting; laundry service/dry cleaning. *In room:* A/C, TV w/rental movies, dataport, minibar, hair dryer, safe, beverage maker, trouser press, films on demand.

EXPENSIVE

Aster House ★★★ *Value*   This is the winner of the 2002 London Tourism Award for best B&B in London. It's just as good now as it was then. Within an easy walk of Kensington Palace, the late Princess Diana's home, and the museums of South Kensington, it is a friendly, inviting, and well-decorated lodging on a tree-lined street. The area surrounding the hotel, Sumner Place, looks like a Hollywood set depicting Victorian London. Aster House guests eat breakfast in a sunlit conservatory and can feed the ducks in the pond outside. Since the B&B is a Victorian building spread across five floors, each unit is unique in size and shape. Rooms range from spacious, with a four-poster bed, to a Lilliputian special with a single bed. Some beds are draped with fabric tents for extra drama, and each room is individually decorated in the style of an English manor-house bedroom. The small bathrooms are beautifully kept with showers ("the best in Europe," wrote one guest) or tubs and showers.

3 Sumner Place, London SW7 3EE. ② 020/7581-5888. Fax 020/7584-4925. www. asterhouse.com. 14 units. £130–£175 ($241–$324) double. Rates include buffet breakfast. MC, V. Tube: South Kensington. **Amenities:** Laundry service; same-day dry cleaning. *In room:* A/C, TV, dataport, coffeemaker, hair dryer, safe.

Claverley Hotel ★   Located on a quiet cul-de-sac, this tasteful hotel, one of the neighborhood's very best (and winner of the Spencer Trophy for the Best Bed & Breakfast Hotel in Central London), is just a few blocks from Harrods. It's a small, cozy place accented with Georgian-era accessories. The lounge has the atmosphere of a country house, and complimentary tea, coffee, and biscuits are served all day in the Reading Room. Most rooms have wall-to-wall carpeting and comfortably upholstered armchairs, and each has a tidy bathroom with a shower stall. Recently refurbished rooms have a marble bathroom and "power shower." Rooms are individually decorated, some with four-poster beds.

13–14 Beaufort Gardens, London SW3 1PS. ② 800/747-0398 in the U.S., or 020/ 7589-8541. Fax 020/7584-3410. www.claverleyhotel.co.uk. 33 units. £120–£190 ($222–$352) double; £190–£215 ($352–$398) junior suite. Rates include English breakfast. AE, DC, MC, V. Parking £3 ($6) per hour on the street. Tube: Knightsbridge. **Amenities:** Same-day dry cleaning; all nonsmoking rooms. *In room:* TV, dataport, hair dryer, safe.

Knightsbridge Hotel ★★ *Value*   The Knightsbridge Hotel attracts visitors from all over the world seeking a small, comfortable hotel in a high-rent district. It's fabulously located, sandwiched between fashionable Beauchamp Place and Harrods, with many of the city's top theaters and museums close at hand. Built in the early 1800s as a private town house, this place sits on a tranquil, tree-lined square, free from traffic. Two of London's premier hoteliers, Kit and Tim Kemp, who have been celebrated for their upmarket boutique hotels, have gone more affordable with a revamp of this hotel in the heart of the shopping district. All the Kemp "cult classics" are found here including such *luxe* touches as granite-and-oak bathrooms, the Kemps' famed honor bar, and Frette linens. The hotel has become an instant hit. All the beautifully furnished rooms have shower-only private bathrooms clad in marble or tile. Most bedrooms are spacious and furnished with traditional English fabrics. The best rooms are nos. 311 and 312 at the rear, each with a pitched ceiling and a small sitting area.

10 Beaufort Gardens, London SW3 1PT. ℭ 020/7584-6300. Fax 020/7584-6355. www.firmdalehotels.com. 44 units. £155–£285 ($287–$527) double; from £335 ($620) suite. Rates include English or continental breakfast. AE, MC, V. Tube: Knightsbridge. **Amenities:** Bar; concierge; courtesy car; 24-hr. room service; babysitting; laundry service; same-day dry cleaning. *In room:* TV w/pay movies (DVD in most rooms), dataport, minibar, hair dryer, safe.

KENSINGTON
VERY EXPENSIVE

The Milestone ⭐⭐⭐   This outstanding boutique hotel, conveniently located in a Victorian town house across the street from Kensington Palace, offers modern luxury in an intimate, traditional setting. The Milestone's beautiful public rooms are awash with fresh flowers, dark woods, antique furnishings, and fabric wall coverings, creating the cozy atmosphere of a private manor house. The staff is gracious, and guests aren't just pampered—they're spoiled rotten. There's a small but well-equipped health club, which is a real rarity in London hotels of this size.

Guest rooms and suites are spread over six floors and vary in size and shape (a few rooms are a bit small). They feature a full range of amenities, luxurious beds, and marble bathrooms, some of which have Jacuzzis. All accommodations are individually and creatively decorated, though some are more theme-intensive than others. The masculine Savile Row Room is "papered" in pinstriped material and sports a tailor's dummy and books on men's fashion; the serene Royal Studio has a small balcony and a sleigh bed; and the bi-level Club Suite offers an English library–style lounge, complete with an antique billiards table. You can request a room overlooking the palace and Kensington Gardens, but be advised that these have original leaded windows, which look wonderful but can't be double-glazed, so traffic noise does leak through. Suites come with 24-hour butler service. *Note:* This hotel often offers special deals on its website, so it's possible to stay here for a princely rather than a kingly sum.

1 Kensington Court, London W8 5DL. (C) **877/955-1515** in the U.S. and Canada, or 020/7917-1000. Fax 020/7917-1010. www.redcarnationhotels.com. 57 units. £175–£335 ($324–$620) double; £440–£810 ($814–$1,499) suite. AE, DC, MC, V. Tube: High St. Kensington. **Amenities:** 3 restaurants; bar; health club; Jacuzzi; sauna; concierge; 24-hr. room service; babysitting; laundry service; same-day dry cleaning; nonsmoking rooms. *In room:* A/C, TV/VCR w/pay movies, CD/DVD player, fax, dataport, minibar, coffeemaker, hair dryer, iron/ironing board, safe.

INEXPENSIVE

Ashburn Hotel *Value*   In the Royal Borough of Kensington, this discovery lies within walking distance of the major shopping areas and such attractions as Kensington Palace and the Victoria and Albert Museum. The hotel is imbued with an old-fashioned but cozy aura, with comfortably furnished bedrooms. Housekeeping is immaculate, and the welcome is friendly. Rooms come in a wide range of configurations, and can be suitable for many different travelers—singles, twins, doubles, triples, or family accommodations. It's not the most glamorous address in the area, but is known for its good value.

111 Cromwell Rd., London SW7 4DP. (C) 020/7370-3321. www.ashburn-hotel.co.uk/prices/asp. 41 units. MC, V. £95 ($176) double; £105 ($194) triple; £115 ($213) quad; £28 ($52) per person in family unit. Tube: Gloucester Rd. **Amenities:** Secretarial services; lounge; Internet in lobby. *In room:* TV, hair dryer, beverage maker.

BELGRAVIA
EXPENSIVE

The Diplomat Hotel *Finds*   Part of The Diplomat's charm is that it is a small and reasonably priced hotel located in an otherwise prohibitively expensive neighborhood. Only minutes from Harrods Department Store, it was built in 1882 as a private residence by noted architect Thomas Cubbitt. It's very well appointed and was completely overhauled in 2002 and 2003. The registration desk is framed by the sweep of a partially gilded circular staircase; above it, cherubs gaze down from a Regency-era chandelier. The staff is helpful, well mannered, and discreet. The high-ceilinged guest rooms are tastefully done in Victorian style. You get good—not grand—comfort here. Rooms are a bit small and usually furnished with twin beds. Bathrooms, with shower stalls, are also small but well maintained.

2 Chesham St., London SW1X 8DT. ℂ 020/7235-1544. Fax 020/7259-6153. www. btinternet.com/~diplomat.hotel. 26 units. £125–£170 ($231–$315) double. Rates include English buffet breakfast. AE, DC, MC, V. Tube: Sloane Sq. or Knightsbridge. **Amenities:** Snack bar; nearby health club; business services; babysitting; laundry service; same-day dry cleaning; rooms for those w/limited mobility. *In room:* TV, dataport, coffeemaker, hair dryer, safe (in some), trouser press.

CHELSEA
EXPENSIVE

The Sloane Hotel 🏵🏵   This "toff" (dandy) address, a redbrick Victorian-era town house that has been tastefully renovated in recent years, is located in Chelsea near Sloane Square. It combines valuable 19th-century antiques with modern comforts. Our favorite spot here is the rooftop terrace; with views opening onto Chelsea, it's ideal for a relaxing breakfast or drink. Bedrooms come in varying sizes, ranging from small to spacious, but all are opulently furnished with flouncy draperies, tasteful fabrics, and sumptuous beds. Many rooms have draped four-poster or canopied beds and, of course, antiques. The deluxe bathrooms have shower/tub combinations, with chrome power showers, wall-width mirrors (in most rooms), and luxurious toiletries.

29 Draycott Place, London SW3 2SH. ℂ 800/324-9960 in the U.S., or 020/7581-5757. Fax 020/7584-1348. www.sloanehotel.com. 22 units. £215–£250 ($398–$463) double; from £250 ($463) suite. AE, DC, MC, V. Tube: Sloane Sq. **Amenities:** Airport transportation (w/prior arrangement); business services; 24-hr. room service; babysitting; laundry service; same-day dry cleaning. *In room:* A/C, TV/VCR w/pay movies, dataport, hair dryer.

MODERATE

Willett Hotel 🏵 *Value*   On a tree-lined street leading off Sloane Square, this dignified Victorian town house lies in the heart of Chelsea. Named for the famous London architect William Willett, its stained glass and chandeliers reflect the opulence of the days when Prince Edward was on the throne. Under a mansard roof with bay windows, the hotel is a 5-minute walk from the shopping mecca of King's Road and close to such stores as Peter Jones, Harrods, and Harvey Nichols. Individually decorated bedrooms come in a wide range of sizes. All rooms have well-kept bathrooms, equipped with shower/tub combinations. Some rooms are first class, with swagged draperies, matching armchairs, and canopied beds. But a few of the twins are best left for Lilliputians.

32 Sloane Gardens, London SW1 8DJ. ℂ 020/7824-8415. Fax 020/7730-4830. www.eeh.co.uk. 19 units. £100–£170 ($185–$315) double. Rates include English breakfast. AE, DC, MC, V. Tube: Sloane Sq. **Amenities:** Concierge; limited room

service; babysitting; laundry service; same-day dry cleaning; nonsmoking rooms. *In room:* A/C in most rooms, TV/VCR, dataport, fridge (in some), coffeemaker, hair dryer, iron, safe.

SOUTH KENSINGTON
EXPENSIVE

Number Sixteen ⊛   This luxurious pension is composed of four early-Victorian town houses linked together. The scrupulously maintained front and rear gardens make this one of the most idyllic spots on the street. The rooms are decorated with an eclectic mix of English antiques and modern paintings, although some of the decor looks a little faded. Accommodations range from small to spacious and have themes such as tartan or maritime. The beds are comfortable, and bathrooms are tiled and outfitted with vanity mirrors, heated towel racks, and hand-held showers over small tubs. There's an honor-system bar in the library. On chilly days, a fire roars in the fireplace of the flowery drawing room, although some prefer the more masculine library. Breakfast can be served in your bedroom, in the conservatory, or if the weather's good, in the garden, with its bubbling fountain and fishpond.

16 Sumner Place, London SW7 3EG. ⓒ **800/592-5387** in the U.S., or 020/7589-5232. Fax 020/7584-8615. www.numbersixteenhotel.co.uk. 42 units. £170–£195 ($315–$361) double; £250 ($463) suite. Rates include continental breakfast. AE, DC, MC, V. Parking £25 ($46). Tube: South Kensington. **Amenities:** Access to nearby health club; 24-hr. room service; babysitting; laundry service; same-day dry cleaning; nonsmoking rooms. *In room:* TV/VCR, dataport, minibar, hair dryer, safe.

MODERATE

The Gallery ⊛ *Finds*   This is the place to go if you want to stay in an exclusive little town-house hotel but don't want to pay £300 ($555) a night for the privilege. Two splendid Georgian residences have been restored and converted into this remarkable hotel, which remains relatively unknown. The location is ideal, near the Victoria and Albert Museum, Royal Albert Hall, Harrods, Knightsbridge, and King's Road. Bedrooms are individually designed and decorated in Laura Ashley style, with half-canopied beds and marble-tiled bathrooms with brass fittings and shower/tub combos. The junior suites have private roof terraces, minibars, Jacuzzis, and air-conditioning. A team of butlers takes care of everything. The lounge, with its mahogany paneling, moldings, and deep colors, has the ambience of a private club. The drawing room beckons you to relax and read in a quiet corner. The Gallery Room displays works by known and unknown artists for sale.

8–10 Queensberry Place, London SW7 2EA. ℂ **800/270-9206** in the U.S., or 020/ 7915-0000. Fax 020/7915-4400. www.eeh.co.uk. 36 units. £130–£160 ($241–$296) double; from £250 ($463) junior suite. Rates include buffet English breakfast. AE, DC, MC, V. Tube: South Kensington. **Amenities:** Bar; access to nearby health club; courtesy car; business center; 24-hr. room service; babysitting; laundry service; same-day dry cleaning; 24-hr. butler service; nonsmoking rooms. *In room:* A/C (in most rooms), TV, dataport, coffeemaker, hair dryer, safe.

INEXPENSIVE

The Vicarage Hotel 🐾 (Kids) Owners Eileen and Martin Diviney enjoy a host of admirers on all continents. Their much-improved hotel is tops for old-fashioned English charm, affordable prices, and hospitality. On a residential garden square close to Kensington High Street, not far from Portobello Road Market, this Victorian town house retains many original features. Individually furnished in country-house style, the bedrooms can accommodate up to four, making it a great place for families. If you want a little nest to hide away in, opt for the very private top-floor aerie (no. 19). Guests find the corridor shower-only bathrooms adequate and well maintained. Guests meet in a cozy sitting room for conversation and to watch the telly. As a thoughtful extra, hot drinks are available 24 hours a day. In the morning, a hearty English breakfast awaits.

10 Vicarage Gate, London W8 4AG. ℂ **020/7229-4030**. Fax 020/7792-5989. www. londonvicaragehotel.com. 17 units, 8 with bathroom. £46 ($85) single without bathroom; £102 ($189) double with bathroom; £78 ($144) double without bathroom; £95 ($176) triple without bathroom; £102 ($189) family room for 4 without bathroom. Rates include English breakfast. No credit cards. Tube: High St. Kensington or Notting Hill Gate. *In room:* TV, hair dryer, beverage maker, no phone.

4 Hotels from Marylebone to Holland Park

MARYLEBONE
EXPENSIVE

Durrants Hotel 🐾 This historic hotel off Manchester Square (established in 1789) with its Georgian-detailed facade is snug, cozy, and traditional—almost like a poor man's Brown's (p. 51). We find it to be one of the most quintessentially English of all London hotels. You could invite the queen to Durrants for tea. Over the 100 years that they have owned the hotel, the Miller family has incorporated several neighboring houses into the original structure. A walk through the pine-and-mahogany-paneled public rooms is like stepping back in time: You'll even find an 18th-century letter-writing room. The rooms are rather bland but for elaborate cove moldings and comfortable furnishings, including good beds. Some are air-conditioned, and some are, alas, small. Bathrooms are tiny, with shower/tub combinations but little room to maneuver.

26–32 George St., London W1H 6BJ. $\textcircled{C}$ **020/7935-8131.** Fax 020/7487-3510. www.durrantshotel.co.uk. 92 units. £145–£165 ($268–$305) double; £180 ($333) family room for 3; from £285 ($527) suite. AE, MC, V. Tube: Bond St. or Baker St. **Amenities:** Restaurant; pub; concierge; 24-hr. room service; babysitting; laundry service; same-day dry cleaning; rooms for those w/limited mobility. *In room:* A/C, TV, dataport, hair dryer, safe.

MODERATE

Hart House Hotel $\textcircled{R}$ *Kids* Hart House is a long-enduring favorite with Frommer's readers. In the heart of the West End, this well-preserved historic building (one of a group of Georgian mansions occupied by exiled French nobles during the French Revolution) lies within easy walking distance of many theaters. The rooms—done in a combination of furnishings, ranging from Portobello antique to modern—are spic-and-span, each one with a different character. Favorites include no. 7, a triple with a big bathroom and shower. Ask for no. 11, on the top floor, if you'd like a brightly lit aerie. Housekeeping rates high marks here, and the bedrooms are comfortably appointed with chairs, an armoire, a desk, and a large chest of drawers. The shower-only bathrooms, although small, are efficiently organized. Hart House has long been known as a good, safe place for traveling families. Many of its rooms are triples. Larger families can avail themselves of special family accommodations with connecting rooms.

51 Gloucester Place, Portman Sq., London W1U 8JF. $\textcircled{C}$ **020/7935-2288.** Fax 020/ 7935-8516. www.harthouse.co.uk. 15 units. £105 ($194) double; £130 ($241) triple; £150 ($278) quad. Rates include English breakfast. AE, MC, V. Tube: Marble Arch or Baker St. **Amenities:** Babysitting; laundry service/dry cleaning; all nonsmoking rooms; rooms for those w/limited mobility. *In room:* TV, dataport, coffeemaker, hair dryer.

INEXPENSIVE

Boston Court Hotel Upper Berkeley is a classic street of B&Bs; in days of yore, it was home to Elizabeth Montagu (1720–1800), "queen of the bluestockings," who defended Shakespeare against attacks by Voltaire. Today, it's a good, safe, respectable retreat at an affordable price. This unfrilly hotel offers accommodations in a centrally located Victorian-era building within walking distance of Oxford Street shopping and Hyde Park. The small, basic rooms have been refurbished and redecorated with a no-nonsense decor and have well-kept bathrooms with private showers.

26 Upper Berkeley St., Marble Arch, London W1H 7PF. ⓒ **020/7723-1445.** Fax 020/7262-8823. www.bostoncourthotel.co.uk. 15 units (7 with shower only). £69 ($128) double with shower only; £75–£79 ($139–$146) double with bathroom; £85–£89 ($157–$165) triple with bathroom. Rates include continental breakfast. MC, V. Tube: Marble Arch. **Amenities:** Laundry service; nonsmoking rooms. *In room:* TV w/pay movies, dataport, fridge, coffeemaker, hair dryer.

Edward Lear Hotel   This popular hotel, situated 1 block from Marble Arch, is made all the more desirable by the bouquets of fresh flowers in its public rooms. It occupies a pair of brick town houses dating from 1780. The western house was the London home of 19th-century artist and poet Edward Lear, famous for his nonsense verse, and his illustrated limericks adorn the walls of one of the sitting rooms. Steep stairs lead up to cozy rooms which range from spacious to broom-closet size. Many bedrooms have been redecorated but still look a bit drab. Few can complain, as this is an area of £400 ($740) a-night mammoths. If you're looking for classiness, know that the bacon on your plate came from the same butcher used by the queen. One major drawback to the hotel: This is a very noisy part of town. Rear rooms are quieter. Bathrooms are well maintained, most with a shower and tub.

28–30 Seymour St., London W1H 5WD. ⓒ **020/7402-5401.** Fax 020/7706-3766. www.edlear.com. 31 units, 12 with bathroom. £67 ($124) double without bathroom; £74 ($137) double with bathroom; £79 ($146) suite. Rates include English breakfast. MC, V. Tube: Marble Arch. *In room:* TV w/pay movies, dataport, coffeemaker.

PADDINGTON & BAYSWATER
EXPENSIVE

London Elizabeth Hotel ⚐   This elegant Victorian town house is ideally situated, overlooking Hyde Park. Amid the buzz and excitement of central London, the hotel's atmosphere is an oasis of charm and refinement. Even before the hotel's recent £3 million ($5.6 million) restoration, it oozed character. Individually decorated rooms range from executive to deluxe and remind us of staying in an English country house. Deluxe rooms are fully air-conditioned, and some contain four-poster beds. Executive units usually contain one double or twin bed. Some rooms have special features such as Victorian antique fireplaces, and all contain first-rate bathrooms with showers and tubs. Suites are pictures of grand comfort and luxury— the Conservatory Suite boasts its own veranda, part of the house's original 1850 conservatory.

Lancaster Terrace, Hyde Park, London W2 3PF. ⓒ **020/7402-6641.** Fax 020/7224-8900. www.londonelizabethhotel.co.uk. 49 units. £115–£150 ($213–$278) double;

£180–£250 ($333–$463) suite. AE, DC, MC, V. Parking £10 ($19). Tube: Lancaster Gate or Paddington. **Amenities:** Restaurant; bar; 24-hr. room service; laundry service; same-day dry cleaning; nonsmoking rooms. *In room:* A/C, TV, dataport, hair dryer, iron.

Miller's Residence *Finds* Staying here is like spending a night in Charles Dickens' Old Curiosity Shop. Others say that the little hotel looks like the set of *La Traviata*. Miller's calls itself an 18th-century rooming house, and there's nothing quite like it in London. A roaring log fire blazes in the large book-lined drawing room in winter. The individually designed rooms are named after romantic poets. They vary in shape and size, but all are luxuriously furnished with antiques, prints, and tasteful curios. Each room contains a small bathroom with a shower and tub. In addition to its double rooms, Miller's offers two sumptuous suites with multiple bedrooms, a drawing room, and a fully equipped kitchen.

111A Westbourne Grove, London W2 4UW. ⓒ **020/7243-1024.** Fax 020/7243-1064. www.millersuk.com. 6 units. £150 ($278) double; £230 ($426) suite. Rates include continental breakfast. AE, DISC, MC, V. Tube: Bayswater or Notting Hill Gate. **Amenities:** Limited business services; babysitting; laundry service; same-day dry cleaning. *In room:* TV/VCR, dataport, kitchen in suites.

MODERATE

Mornington Hotel Affiliated with Best Western, the Mornington brings a touch of northern European hospitality to the center of London. Just north of Hyde Park and Kensington Gardens, the hotel has a Victorian exterior and a Scandinavian-inspired decor. The area isn't London's most fashionable, but it's close to Hyde Park and convenient to Marble Arch, Oxford Street shopping, and the ethnic restaurants of Queensway. Recently renovated guest rooms are tasteful and comfortable, all with pay movies. Bathrooms are small but tidy, with showers and tubs. Every year we get our annual Christmas card from "the gang," as we refer to the hotel staff—and what a helpful crew they are.

12 Lancaster Gate, London W2 3LG. ⓒ **800/528-1234** in the U.S., or 020/7262-7361. Fax 020/7706-1028. www.mornington.com. 66 units. £135–£160 ($250–$296) double; £145 ($268) triple. Rates include Scandinavian and English cooked breakfast. AE, DC, MC, V. Tube: Lancaster Gate. **Amenities:** Bar; courtesy car; business center; laundry service; same-day dry cleaning. *In room:* TV w/pay movies, coffeemaker.

The Pavilion *Finds* Until the early 1990s, this was a rather ordinary-looking B&B. Then a team of entrepreneurs with ties to the fashion industry took over and redecorated the rooms with sometimes wacky themes, turning it into an idiosyncratic little hotel. The result is a theatrical and often outrageous decor that's appreciated by the many fashion models and music-industry folks who regularly make this their temporary home in London. Rooms are, regrettably, rather small, but each has a distinctive style. Examples include a kitschy 1970s room ("Honky-Tonk Afro"), an Oriental bordello–themed room ("Enter the Dragon"), and even rooms with 19th-century ancestral themes. One Edwardian-style room, a gem of emerald brocade and velvet, is called "Green with Envy." Each contains tea-making facilities and small bathrooms with excellent showers.

34–36 Sussex Gardens, London W2 1UL. ℂ 020/7262-0905. Fax 020/7262-1324. www.pavilionhoteluk.com. 29 units. £100 ($185) double; £120 ($222) triple. Rates include continental breakfast. AE, DC, MC, V. Parking £5 ($9.25). Tube: Edgeware Rd. **Amenities:** Laundry service; same-day dry cleaning. *In room:* TV, dataport, beverage maker.

INEXPENSIVE

Fairways Hotel   A small hotel near Hyde Park, and a favorite of bargain hunters, this welcoming, well-run B&B is the domain of Jenny and Steve Adams. The black-and-white town house is easily recognizable: Just look for its colonnaded front entrance with a wrought-iron balustrade stretching across the second floor. Scorning the modern, the Adamses opt for traditional charm and character. They call their breakfast room "homely" (Americans might say homey)—it's decorated with photos of the family and a collection of china. Bedrooms are attractive and comfortably furnished, with hot and cold running water and intercoms. Bathrooms are small but tidy, and some have showers and tubs. Those who share the corridor bathrooms will find them clean and well maintained. The home-cooked breakfast is plenty of fortification for a full day of sightseeing.

186 Sussex Gardens, London W2 1TU. ℂ and fax **020/7723-4871.** www.fairways-hotel.co.uk. 18 units, 10 with bathroom. £60 ($111) double without bathroom; £70 ($130) double with bathroom. Rates include English breakfast. MC, V. Tube: Paddington or Lancaster Gate. *In room:* TV, coffeemaker, hair dryer (on request), safe.

Garden Court   You'll find this hotel on a tranquil Victorian garden square in the heart of the city. Two private houses (dating from 1870) were combined to form one efficiently run hotel, located near such attractions as Kensington Palace, Hyde Park, and the Portobello Antiques Market. Each year, rooms are redecorated and refurbished, although an overall renovation plan seems to be lacking. Most accommodations are spacious, with good lighting, generous shelf and closet space, and comfortable furnishings. If you're in a room without a bathroom, you'll generally have to share with the occupants of only one other room. There are many homelike touches throughout the hotel, including ancestral portraits and silky flowers. Each room is individually decorated and "comfy"; it's like visiting your great-aunt. Rooms open onto the square in front or the gardens in the rear. Shower-and-tub bathrooms are installed in areas never intended for plumbing, so they tend to be very cramped.

30–31 Kensington Gardens Sq., London W2 4BG. ℭ 020/7229-2553. Fax 020/ 7727-2749. www.gardencourthotel.co.uk. 34 units, 16 with bathroom. £58 ($107) double without bathroom; £88 ($163) double with bathroom; £72 ($133) triple without bathroom; £99 ($183) triple with bathroom. Rates include English breakfast. MC, V. Tube: Bayswater. **Amenities:** Coin-op washers and dryers. *In room:* TV, dataport, hair dryer.

NOTTING HILL GATE
EXPENSIVE

The Portobello Hotel 🏵   On an elegant Victorian terrace near Portobello Road, two 1850s-era town houses have been combined to form a quirky property that has its devotees. We remember these rooms when they looked better, but they still have plenty of character. Who knows what will show up in what nook? Perhaps a Chippendale, a claw-foot tub, or a round bed tucked under a gauze canopy. Try for no. 16, with a full-tester bed facing the garden. Some of the cheaper rooms are so tiny that they're basically garrets, but others have been combined into large doubles. Most of the small bathrooms have showers but no tubs. An elevator goes to the third floor; after that, it's the stairs. Since windows are not double-glazed, request a room in the quiet rear. Some rooms are air-conditioned. Service is erratic at best, but this is still a good choice.

22 Stanley Gardens, London W11 2NG. ℭ 020/7727-2777. Fax 020/7792-9641. www.portobello-hotel.co.uk. 24 units. £160–£180 ($296–$333) double; £200–£275 ($370–$509) suite. Rates include continental breakfast. AE, MC, V. Tube: Notting Hill Gate or Holland Park. **Amenities:** 24-hr. bar and restaurant in basement; business services; 24-hr. room service; laundry service; same-day dry cleaning; nearby gym. *In room:* A/C (some rooms), TV/VCR, dataport, minibar, hair dryer, beverage maker.

MODERATE

The Gate Hotel   This antiques-hunters' favorite is the only hotel along the length of Portobello Road—and because of rigid zoning restrictions, it will probably remain the only one for years to come. It was built in the 1820s as housing for farmhands at the now-defunct Portobello Farms and has functioned as a hotel since 1932. It has two cramped but cozy bedrooms on each of its three floors.

Be prepared for some *very* steep English stairs. Rooms are color-coordinated, with a bit of style, and have such extras as full-length mirrors and built-in wardrobes. Bathrooms are small, with tiled shower stalls (there is a shower/tub combo in one room). House-keeping is excellent. Especially intriguing are the wall paintings that show what the Portobello Market used to look like: Every character looks like it is straight from a Dickens novel. The on-site manager can direct you to the attractions of Notting Hill Gate and nearby Kensington Gardens, both within a 5-minute walk.

6 Portobello Rd., London W11 3DG. ⓒ **020/7221-0707.** Fax 020/7221-9128. www.gatehotel.com. 7 units. £75–£99 ($139–$183) double. Rates include conti-nental breakfast. AE, MC, V. Tube: Notting Hill Gate. **Amenities:** 24-hr. room serv-ice; laundry service; rooms for those w/limited mobility. *In room:* TV, dataport, fridge, hair dryer, iron, beverage maker.

The Main House 🐸🐸 *Finds* Each beautifully appointed room takes up a whole floor of this Victorian town house in Notting Hill, close to Portobello Road, the antiques markets, art galleries, and designer shops. Such attractions as Kensington Palace and Albert Hall are within walking distance. Russian princesses, Japanese pop stars, and Los Angeles film producers have already discovered this spot. Owner and creator Caroline Main is a former African explorer, Mayfair nightclub owner, and DJ. To furnish the house, she shopped "quirky" on Portobello Road, picking up gilded mirrors, watercolors of elegantly dressed 1930s women, and similar antiques. The ceilings are dramatically high, and the gleaming wood floors are swathed in animal skins. All rooms have freshly renewed private bathrooms with showers.

6 Colville Rd., London W11 2BP. ⓒ **020/7221-9691.** www.themainhouse.co.uk. 4 suites. £130 ($241) suite. MC, V. Tube: Notting Hill Gate. Parking: £4 ($7.40). Bus: 23, 27, 52, 94, or 328. **Amenities:** Reduced rate at nearby health club and spa; bike rental; courtesy car to and from point of arrival; limited room service (breakfast only); laundry service; same-day dry cleaning. *In room:* TV, dataport, hair dryer, safe.

INEXPENSIVE

Manor Court Hotel This B&B lies on a cul-de-sac at the edge of Kensington Gardens. Still slightly run-down, the neighborhood is improving, and real-estate prices are soaring as young professionals seek town houses here. A Victorian home, Manor Court lies only a 15-minute stroll from antiques mecca Portobello Road. A family favorite, it offers simple decor with basic—not stylish—furnishings, comfortable beds, and generous space. If you look carefully, you'll see elements that need restoration, but the comfort level is high and the housekeeping is immaculate. Bedrooms come in a variety of shapes and sizes, with the smaller units on the top floors. Those units that have a private bathroom come with shower stalls.

7 Clanricarde Gardens, London W2 4JJ. ⓒ **020/7792-3361**. Fax 020/7229-2875. 20 units, 16 with bathroom. £50–£55 ($93–$102) double with bathroom; £65 ($120) triple with bathroom; £75 ($139) family room with bathroom. 10% discount for any stay over 4 nights. Rates include continental breakfast. AE, MC, V. Tube: Notting Hill Gate. *In room:* TV, hair dryer.

4

Where to Dine

London has emerged as one of the great food capitals of the world. Both its veteran and upstart chefs have fanned out around the globe for culinary inspiration and returned with innovative dishes, flavors, and ideas that London diners have never seen before. These chefs are pioneering a style called "Modern British," which is forever changing and innovative, yet familiar in many ways.

Traditional British cooking has made a comeback, too. The dishes that British mums have been forever feeding their families are fashionable again. Yes, we're talking British soul food: bangers and mash, Norfolk dumplings, nursery puddings, cottage pie. This may be a rebellion against the minimalism of the nouvelle cuisine of the 1980s, but maybe it's just plain nostalgia. Pig's nose with parsley-and-onion sauce may not be your idea of cutting-edge cuisine, but Simpson's-in-the-Strand is serving it for breakfast.

These days, many famous chefs spend more time writing cookbooks and on TV than in their own kitchens. That chef you've read about in *Condé Nast Traveler* or *Travel & Leisure* may not be in the kitchen when you get here. But don't worry: The cuisine isn't suffering. An up-and-coming new chef, perhaps even better than the one you heard about, has probably taken over the kitchen.

1 In & Around the City

THE CITY
EXPENSIVE

Prism ✫✫ MODERN BRITISH   In the financial district, called the City, this restaurant attracts London's movers and shakers, at least those with demanding palates. In the former Bank of New York, Harvey Nichols—known for his chic department store in Knightsbridge—took this 1920s neo-Grecian hall and installed Mies van der Rohe chairs in chrome and lipstick-red leather. In this setting, traditional English dishes from the north are given a light touch—try the tempura of Whitby cod, or cream of Jerusalem artichoke soup with roasted scallops and truffle oil. For a first course, you may opt for a small, seared calves' liver with a mushroom risotto, or try a salad composed of flecks of Parmesan cheese seasoning a savoy cabbage salad and Parma ham. The menu reveals the chef has traveled a bit—note such dishes as Moroccan spiced chicken livers, lemon and parsley couscous, and a zesty chile sauce.

147 Leadenhall St., EC3. © 020/7256-3888. Reservations required. Main courses £16–£25 ($30–$46). AE, DC, DISC, MC, V. Mon–Fri noon–3pm and 6–10pm. Tube: Bank or Monument.

MODERATE

The Bridge 🖈🖈 INTERNATIONAL/MODERN BRITISH As far as restaurants go, the most panoramic view of the new riverside architecture is from the terrace of this glass-walled restaurant next to the Millennium Bridge. It looks out across the Thames to Shakespeare's Globe Theatre and the Tate Modern. Peter Gladwin, the executive chef, roams the world for inspiration—perhaps a velvety smooth gazpacho from Spain. For appetizers, try such delights as the tiger prawns with red grapefruit, avocado, and ginger; the smoked trout; the delectable French onion soup. For something really English, opt for the thinly sliced and quickly seared calves' liver, served with smoky bacon and mashed potatoes laced with sage. If you want to drop in for a drink and a look at that view, you can order dim sum at the bar. The house wine, Nutbourne Sussex Reserve, comes from Gladwin's own Sussex vineyard, and has won several awards. Desserts feature the chef's own homemade ice cream and iced lemon vodka parfait.

1 Paul's Walk, EC4. © 020/7236-0000. Reservations required. Main courses £12–£14 ($22–$26). AE, MC, V. Mon–Fri 11am–10pm. Tube: St. Paul's.

Club Gascon 🖈🖈 *Finds* FRENCH This slice of southwestern France serves such tasty treats as foie gras, Armagnac, and duck confit. Chef Pascal Aussignac is all the rage in London, ever since he opened his bistro next to the meat market in Smithfield. He dedicates his bistro to his favorite ingredient: foie gras. Foie gras appears in at least nine different incarnations on the menu, and most of the first-class ingredients are imported from France. His menu is uniquely divided into these categories—"The Salt Route," "Ocean," and "Kitchen Garden." The best way to dine here is to arrive in a party of four or five and share the small dishes, each harmoniously balanced and full of flavor. Each dish is accompanied by a carefully selected glass of wine. After a foie gras pig-out, proceed to such main courses as a heavenly quail served with pear and rosemary honey. A

Where to Dine in London

74

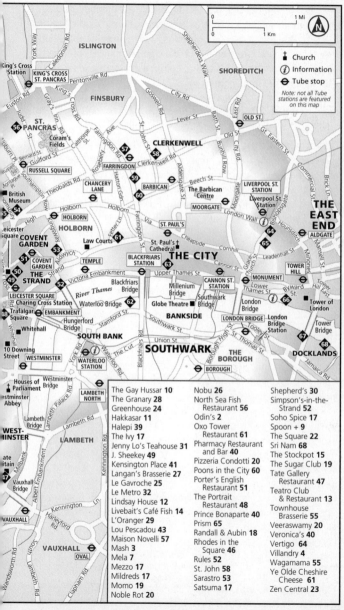

The Gay Hussar 10
The Granary 28
Greenhouse 24
Hakkasar 11
Halepi 39
The Ivy 17
Jenny Lo's Teahouse 31
J. Sheekey 49
Kensington Place 41
Langan's Brasserie 27
Le Gavroche 25
Le Metro 32
Lindsay House 12
Livebait's Café Fish 14
L'Oranger 29
Lou Pescadou 43
Maison Novelli 57
Mash 3
Mela 7
Mezzo 17
Mildreds 17
Momo 19
Noble Rot 20

Nobu 26
North Sea Fish
  Restaurant 56
Odin's 2
Oxo Tower
  Restaurant 61
Pharmacy Restaurant
  and Bar 40
Pizzeria Condotti 20
Poons in the City 60
Porter's English
  Restaurant 51
The Portrait
  Restaurant 48
Prince Bonaparte 40
Prism 65
Randall & Aubin 18
Rhodes in the
  Square 46
Rules 52
St. John 58
Sarastro 53
Satsuma 17

Shepherd's 30
Simpson's-in-the-
  Strand 52
Soho Spice 17
Spoon + 9
The Square 22
Sri Nam 68
The Stockpot 15
The Sugar Club 19
Tate Gallery
  Restaurant 47
Teatro Club
  & Restaurant 13
Townhouse
  Brasserie 55
Veeraswamy 20
Veronica's 40
Vertigo 64
Villandry 4
Wagamama 55
Ye Olde Cheshire
  Cheese 61
Zen Central 23

cassoulet of morels and truffles transforms a plain but perfectly cooked steak. To finish an absolutely elegant repast—dare we call it too rich—there is a selection of "puds," as the British say, ranging from strawberries with basil sorbet to a confit of rhubarb and sherry vinegar. If those don't interest you, opt for a moist almond tart with a biting shot of Granny Smith juice.

57 W. Smithfield, EC1. © **020/7796-0600.** Reservations required. Fixed-price 5-course menu £38 ($70). Main courses £7–£16 ($13–$30). AE, MC, V. Mon–Fri noon–2pm; Mon–Thurs 7–10pm; Sat 7–10:30pm. Tube: Barbican.

Poons in the City ⍟ CHINESE   Since 1992, Poons has operated this branch in the City, less than a 5-minute walk from the Tower of London. The restaurant is modeled on the Luk Yew Tree House in Hong Kong. Main courses feature crispy aromatic duck, prawns with cashew nuts, and barbecued pork. Poons's famous *lap yuk soom* (like Cantonese tacos) includes finely chopped wind-dried bacon. Special dishes can be ordered on 24 hours' notice. At the end of the L-shaped restaurant is an 80-seat fast-food area and takeout counter that's accessible from Mark Lane. The menu changes every 2 weeks.

2 Minster Pavement, Minster Court, Mincing Lane, EC3. © **020/7626-0126.** Reservations recommended for lunch. Fixed-price lunch and dinner £15–£31 ($28–$57); a la carte main courses £6–£10 ($11–$19); fast-food main dishes £5.50–£7 ($10–$13). AE, DC, MC, V. Mon–Fri noon–10:30pm. Tube: Tower Hill or Monument.

INEXPENSIVE

Fox and Anchor ⍟ *Finds* TRADITIONAL BRITISH   For British breakfast at its best, try this place, which has been serving traders from the nearby Smithfield meat market since 1898. Breakfasts are gargantuan, especially if you order the "Full House"—a plate with at least eight items, including sausage, bacon, kidneys, eggs, beans, black pudding, and fried bread, along with unlimited tea or coffee, toast, and jam. Add a Black Velvet (champagne with Guinness), or the more fashionable Bucks Fizz (orange juice and champagne, known in the U.S. as a mimosa). The Fox and Anchor is noted for its fine English ales, which are all available at breakfast. Butchers from the market, spotted with blood, still appear, as do nurses getting off their shifts, and clerks and City tycoons who've been making millions all night.

115 Charterhouse St., EC1. © **020/7253-5075.** Reservations recommended. "Full house" breakfast £7.50 ($14). Main courses £7.50–£15 ($14–$28). AE, MC, V. Mon–Fri from 7am, closing time varies from 8–10pm. Tube: Barbican or Farringdon.

The George & Vulture TRADITIONAL BRITISH   Dickens enthusiasts seek out this Pickwickian place. Founded in 1660, it claims that it's "probably" the world's oldest tavern, referring to an inn that operated on this spot in 1175. While they no longer put up overnight guests here, The George & Vulture does serve English lunches (but no dinners) in a warren of small dining rooms scattered over the tavern's three floors. Besides the daily specials, the menu includes a mixed grill, a loin chop, a lamb-based hot pot, and a grilled Dover-sole filet with tartar sauce. Potatoes and buttered cabbage are the standard vegetables, and the apple tart is always reliable. The system is to arrive and give your name, then retire to any of the three different pubs on the same narrow street for a drink (Simpson's Bar, the Cross Key's Pub, or the Jamaican pub across the way); you're "fetched" when your table is ready. After, be sure to explore the mazes of pubs, shops, wine houses, and other old buildings near the tavern. The Pickwick Club, a private literary group, meets here four times a year for reunion dinners. Cedric Dickens, the octogenarian great-great-grandson of Charles Dickens, heads the literary club.

3 Castle Court, Cornhill, EC3. (C) 020/7626-9710. Reservations accepted before 12:45pm. Main courses £8–£15 ($15–$28). AE, DC, MC, V. Mon–Fri noon–2:45pm. Tube: Bank.

Vertigo 42 (F) (finds) CONTINENTAL/SEAFOOD/TAPAS   This is a relatively unknown little spot, on the 42nd floor of Tower 42 in the heart of the City, that offers one of London's most spectacular views. After securing a special security pass downstairs, you're taken to Vertigo 42 in a high-speed elevator. Dining here is like being on top of the world, as you take in the views of London that eagles enjoy, from the Canada Tower to the Law Courts. We prefer to come here as the sun sets on London and the city lights begin to twinkle. Blue binoculars are provided if you want a more intimate view of the cityscape. Six champagnes are served by the glass, and there's an array of well-presented, very tasty food, ranging from lobster to Iranian fresh caviar to excellent sushi. The organic smoked salmon in salsa verde is a delight, and the fresh Cornish crab arrives from the West Country of England. You must be 18 to patronize this restaurant.

Tower 42, Old Broad St., EC2. (C) 020/7877-7842. Reservations required. Main courses £9.50–£17 ($18–$31); tapas £7.50–£12 ($14–$22); fixed-price lunch menu £15 ($28). AE, DC, MC, V. Mon–Fri 11:45am–3pm and 5–10pm. Closed weekends. Tube: Liverpool St.

Ye Olde Cheshire Cheese (Kids) TRADITIONAL BRITISH   The foundation of this carefully preserved building was laid in the 13th century, and it holds the most famous of the old City chophouses and pubs. Established in 1667, it claims to be the spot where Dr. Samuel Johnson (who lived nearby) entertained admirers with his acerbic wit. Charles Dickens and other literary lions also patronized the place. Later, many of the ink-stained journalists and scandal-mongers of 19th- and early-20th-century Fleet Street made it their watering hole. You'll find five bars and two dining rooms here. The house specialties include "Ye Famous Pudding" (steak, kidney, mush-rooms, and game) and Scottish roast beef with Yorkshire pudding and horseradish sauce. Sandwiches, salads, and standby favorites such as steak and kidney pie are also available, as are dishes such as Dover sole. The Cheshire is the best and safest venue to introduce your children to a British pub.

Wine Office Court, 145 Fleet St., EC4. ✆ 020/7353-6170. Main courses £7.50–£10 ($14–$19). AE, DC, MC, V. Meals: Mon–Fri noon–9:30pm; Sat noon–2:30pm and 6–9:30pm; Sun noon–2:30pm. Drinks and bar snacks: Mon–Fri 11:30am–11pm. Tube: St. Paul's or Blackfriars.

CLERKENWELL
MODERATE

St. John 🕸🕸 MODERN BRITISH   Located in a former smoke-house just north of Smithfield Market, this air-conditioned, can-teenlike dining room is the restaurant of choice for carnivores. It is a showcase for the talents of owner/chef Fergus Henderson, a leader in the offal movement, which advocates the use of all animal parts in cuisine. In true British tradition, he uses the entire animal—we're talking neck, trotters, tail, liver, heart, the works. It's called nose-to-tail cookery.

Don't think you'll be served warmed-over haggis: The food is excellent and flavor-packed. There's an earthiness and simplicity to this cuisine that's unequaled in London. The grilled lamb chops, garnished with sliced pig's tongue, bacon, salsify, and dandelion, are matchless. Roast bone marrow appears with a parsley salad, and pork chops are called pig chops. It's hard these days to find an eel, bacon, and clam stew, but you'll discover one here. French wines wash it all down. Desserts run to puddings such as vanilla-rice or dates and walnuts with butterscotch. Dessert oddity? Where else can you get a good goat curd, marc (the product of grapes and their seeds after pressing), and rhubarb concoction these days? The breads served here can also be purchased in an on-site bakery.

26 St. John St., EC1. ✆ 020/7251-0848. Reservations required. Main courses £15–£19 ($27–$35). AE, DC, DISC, MC, V. Mon–Fri noon–3pm; Mon–Sat 6pm–mid-night. Tube: Farringdon.

SHOREDITCH
EXPENSIVE

Fifteen 🅐🅐 MODERN BRITISH   When James Oliver, author of *The Naked Chef*, opened this restaurant, it created a media blitz. Oliver chronicled his trials and tribulations on a six-part TV show on the Food Network called "Jamie's Kitchen." Oliver takes "disadvantaged" young people and trains them from scratch in just 4 months before turning them loose as your chef for the day, with all the profits going to charity. In a redbrick Victorian building, convenient for touring the trendy Hoxton Square art galleries, the decor is contemporary and clean cut, not unduly gussied up.

What to expect in the way of food? Although a bit hyped in the media, it's quite sumptuous, and has won the praise of London's battle-toughened food critics such as Fay Maschier on *The Evening Standard*, who felt that Jamie should be "knighted" for his efforts. She claimed that Fifteen serves some of the best dishes she's sampled in a long time. Even Michelin-starred chefs have shown up here, raving about the dishes, especially the succulent pastas. Our party recently delighted in such dishes as scallop crudo with Japanese yuzu lime, pomegranates, crispy ginger, fresh coconut, and herb shoots. The filet of McDuff beef poached in a Barossa Merlot is one of the most gorgeous filets you are likely to encounter in London. You can even drop in for breakfast, which is about the only time you're guaranteed a seat; dinner reservations must be made well in advance.

15 Westland Place, N1. ✆ 020/7251-1515. Breakfast £2–£10 ($4–$19); main courses £11–£32 ($20–$59). Mon–Sat 8–10:30am, noon–2:15pm, and 6:30–9:30pm; bar Mon–Sat 11am–11pm. AE, MC, V. Tube: Old Street.

DOCKLANDS
EXPENSIVE

Butler's Wharf Chop House 🅐 TRADITIONAL BRITISH   Of the four restaurants housed in Butler's Wharf (another Butler's Wharf restaurant is listed below), this one is the closest to Tower Bridge. It maintains its commitment to moderate prices. The Chop House was modeled after a large boathouse, with banquettes, lots of exposed wood, flowers, candles, and windows overlooking Tower Bridge and the Thames. Lunchtime crowds include workers from the city's financial district; evening crowds are made up of friends dining together leisurely.

Dishes are largely adaptations of British recipes: fish and chips with mushy peas; steak-and-kidney-pudding with oysters; roast rump of lamb with garlic mash and rosemary; and grilled pork filet with apples, chestnuts, and cider sauce. After, there might be a chocolate and caramel tart. The bar offers such choices as Theakston's best bitter, several English wines, and a half-dozen French clarets by the jug.

36E Shad Thames, SE1. ✆ 020/7403-3403. Reservations recommended. Fixed-price 2-course lunch £20 ($37); fixed-price 3-course lunch £24 ($44); dinner main courses £13–£25 ($23–$46). AE, DC, MC, V. Mon–Sun noon–3pm; Mon–Sat 6–11pm. Tube: Tower Hill or London Bridge.

MODERATE
The Bengal Clipper ⟡ INDIAN   This former spice warehouse
by the Thames serves what it calls "India's most remarkable dishes." The likable and often animated restaurant is outfitted with cream-colored walls, tall columns, and modern artwork inspired by the Moghul Dynasty's depictions of royal figures, soaring trees, and well-trained elephants. Seven windows afford sweeping views over the industrialized Thames-side neighborhood, and live piano music plays in the background. The cuisine includes many vegetarian choices derived from the former Portuguese colony of Goa and the once-English colony of Bengal. There is a zestiness and spice to the cuisine, but it's never overpowering. The chefs keep the menu fairly short so that all ingredients can be purchased fresh every day.

A tasty specialty is stuffed *murgh masala,* a tender breast of chicken with potatoes, onions, apricots, and almonds, cooked with yogurt and served with a delectable curry sauce. The perfectly cooked duckling (off the bone) comes in a tangy sauce with a citrus bite. One of the finest dishes we tasted in North India is served here and has lost nothing in the transfer: marinated lamb simmered in cream with cashew nuts, seasoned with fresh ginger. One of the best offerings from the Goan repertoire is the *karkra chop,* a spicy patty of minced crab blended with mashed potatoes and peppered with Goan spices.

Shad Thames, Butler's Wharf, SE1. ✆ 020/7357-9001. Reservations recommended. Main courses £10–£25 ($19–$46); set menu from £10 ($19); Sunday buffet £7.75 ($14). AE, DC, MC, V. Daily noon–2:30pm and 6–11:30pm. Tube: Tower Hill.

CANARY WHARF
MODERATE
Sri Nam ⟡ *(Finds)* THAI   Celebrity chef Ken Hom is the chief
exponent of Thai cookery in London, and even the Thai community agrees that he's the best. Some of his culinary secrets are revealed in his book, *Foolproof Thai Cookery.* At Canary Wharf, Sri

Nam brings an authentic and very spicy (read: hot) cuisine to foodies who like to dine on the Thames. There's a buzz-filled cafe-bar on
the ground floor and a more formal restaurant upstairs. The Thai
cuisine served here is a fusion of modern with traditional, the latter
in theory the type served to the "King of Siam." The Asian bar on
the ground floor serves drinks from the Far East, plus beers and
wines. The ground-floor bar also caters to those seeking speedy
lunches or an early supper.

Climb the sweeping staircase for more serious dishes served
against a backdrop of rich, dark woods, lush silks, and bright
lanterns. The classic star of the menu is *pad thai,* a delightful stir-fry
of noodles with eggs, vegetables, and bean sprouts, garnished with
ground peanuts and fresh coriander. Served here (and rarely seen on
other London menus) is lamb masaman, a curry from south Thailand, featuring lamb flavored with peanuts and potatoes. The signature dish—and is it ever good—is Bangkok's hot green curry with
chiles, coconut milk, bamboo shoots, baby eggplant, and lime leaves.

N. Colonnade, 10 Cabot Sq., Canary Wharf, E14. ℂ 020/7715-9515. Reservations
required. Main courses £8–£18 ($15–$33). AE, DC, MC, V. Mon–Sat 11:30am–3pm
and 6–10pm; Sat noon–9pm. Tube: Canary Wharf.

SOUTH BANK
EXPENSIVE

Oxo Tower Restaurant ℛ ASIAN/INTERNATIONAL   In the
South Bank complex, on the eighth floor of the Art Deco Oxo
Tower Wharf, you'll find this dining sensation. It's operated by the
department store Harvey Nichols. Down the street from the newly
rebuilt Globe Theatre this 140-seat restaurant could be visited for its
view alone, but the cuisine is also stellar. You'll enjoy a sweeping
view of St. Paul's Cathedral and the City, all the way to the Houses
of Parliament. The decor is chic 1930s style.

The cuisine, under chef David Sharland, is rich and prepared with
finesse. Menu items change based on the season and the market.
Count on a modern interpretation of British cookery, as well as the
English classics. The fish is incredibly fresh here. The whole sea bass
for two is delectable, as is the roast rump of lamb with split pea, mint
purée, and balsamic vinegar sauce. Recently, we were impressed with
the roast filet of plaice with olive oil, and truffle cabbage cream, and
the roast squab with buttered cabbage and a foie-gras sauce.

Barge House St., South Bank, SE1. ℂ 020/7803-3888. Main courses £10–£18
($19–$33); fixed-price lunch £20 ($37). AE, DC, MC, V. Mon–Fri noon–3pm;
Mon–Sat 6–11:30pm; Sat–Sun noon–2:30pm; Sun 6–10:30pm. Tube: Blackfriars or
Waterloo.

MODERATE

Cantina Vinopolis 𝕽𝕽 *Finds* CONTINENTAL   Not far from the re-created Globe Theatre of Shakespeare's heyday, this place has been called a "Walk-Through Wine Atlas." In the revitalized Bankside area, south of the Thames near Southwark Cathedral, this bricked, walled, and high-vaulted brasserie was converted from long-abandoned Victorian railway arches. Inside you can visit both the Vinopolis Wine Gallery and the Cantina Restaurant. Although many come here just to drink the wine, the food is prepared with quality ingredients (very fresh), and the menu is sensibly priced. Start with a bit of heaven like the pea and ham soup. Dishes are full of flavor and never overcooked. Pan-fried snapper, with crushed new potatoes and salsa verde, won us over. A rump of lamb was tender and perfectly flavored and served with a polenta cake. Many of the dishes have the good country taste of a trattoria you'd find in the countryside of southern Italy. Naturally, the wine list is the biggest in the U.K.

1 Bank End, London Bridge, SE1. ℭ 020/7940-8333. Reservations required. Main courses £14–£16 ($26–$30). AE, DC, MC, V. Mon–Sat noon–3pm and 6–10:45pm; Sun noon–3:45pm. Tube: London Bridge.

2 The West End

BLOOMSBURY
VERY EXPENSIVE

Pied-à-Terre 𝕽 FRENCH   This foodie heaven understates its decor in favor of an intense focus on its subtle, sophisticated cuisine. You'll dine in a strictly minimalist room, where gray-and-pale-pink walls complement metal furniture and focused lighting that reveals a collection of modern art. France is the inspiration for the impressive wine list and some of the cuisine. The menu changes with the seasons but might include halibut filets with queen scallops and caramelized endive; roasted partridge with pear; and the house specialty, a ballotine (stuffed and rolled into a bundle) of duck confit. If you're not dining with a vegetarian, braised pigs' head is another specialty. Our favorite item on the menu? Sea bass with vichyssoise (a thick soup of potatoes, leeks, and cream) and caviar sauce. The food is beautifully presented on hand-painted plates with lush patterns. Prix-fixe menus only.

34 Charlotte St., W1. ℭ 020/7636-1178. Reservations recommended. Fixed-price 3-course lunch £22–£35 ($40–$65), 3-course dinner £45–£60 ($83–$111); 8-course tasting menu £65 ($120). AE, MC, V. Tues–Fri noon–2:30pm (last order); Mon–Sat 7–11pm. Closed last week of Dec and 1st week of Jan. Tube: Goodge St.

EXPENSIVE

Archipelago *R* FRENCH/THAI   This cozy restaurant is a celebrity favorite, attracting the likes of Madonna and Hugh Hefner when they are in town. Archipelago is definitely on the see-and-be-seen circuit. Media darling Michael Von Hruschka has decorated the restaurant in a whimsical style, with everything from birdcages to a Buddha serving as props. There are precious touches, such as the drink list written on delicate paper and inserted in an ostrich eggshell. Everything is presented in exquisite boxes, and even the bill comes in a "book." Amazingly, with all the attention paid to the environment, the cuisine does not suffer in ingredients or preparation. Launch your repast with a coconut-and-lemon-grass soup or the most delectable small-carrot spring rolls. Vegetable couscous and fish-and-banana risotto are delectable, and tiramisu is given an original touch with the addition of ginger wine.

110 Whitfield St., W1. © 020/7383-3346. Reservations required as far in advance as possible. Main courses £13–£20 ($24–$37); fixed-price 3-course lunch menu £50 ($93). MC, V. Mon–Fri noon–2:30pm; Mon–Sat 6–10:30pm. Tube: Goodge St.

MODERATE

Back to Basics *RR* SEAFOOD   Ursula Higgs's bistro draws discerning palates seeking some of the freshest seafood in London. When the weather's fair, you can dine outside. Otherwise, retreat inside to a vaguely Parisian setting with a blackboard menu and checked tablecloths. The fish is served in large portions, and you can safely forgo an appetizer unless you're ravenous. More than a dozen seafood dishes are offered; the fish can be broiled, grilled, baked, or poached, but frying is not permitted. In other words, this is no fish and chippie. Start with a bowl of tasty, plump mussels or sea bass flavored with fresh basil and chili oil. Brill appears with green peppercorn butter, and plaice is jazzed up with fresh ginger and soy sauce. For the meat eater, there is a T-bone steak or roast chicken. Also try the pastas and the vegetarian dishes. Freshly made salads accompany most meals, and an excellent fish soup is offered daily. For dessert, try the bread pudding or the freshly made apple pie.

21A Foley St., W1. © 020/7436-2181. Reservations recommended. Main courses £10–£16 ($19–$30). AE, DC, MC, V. Daily noon–3pm and 6–10pm. Tube: Oxford Circus or Goodge St.

INEXPENSIVE

The Court Restaurant *R* *Value* CONTINENTAL   Nothing in London brings culture and cuisine together quite as much as this gem of a restaurant on the sixth floor of the British Museum, with views opening onto Norman Fester's millennium development, the Great Court. The restaurant overlooks the famous round Reading Room and nestles close to the spectacular glass-and-steel roof. For museum buffs, it's the perfect venue for morning coffee, hot or cold lunches, afternoon tea, or a dinner.

The chef, Mandula Sachdev, turns out a succulent menu of familiar favorites such as coq au vin (chicken casserole in red wine), sesame-seed-coated Scottish salmon, or savory lamb and mint sausages with a "mash" of parsnips. You can watch the cooks as they prepare the market-fresh dishes for the day. The most blissful ending to a meal here is the chocolate truffle cake, which is really pure cocoa. The museum even serves its own beer, and it can compete with the product of any brewery.

The British Museum, Great Russell St., WC1. ✆ 020/7323-8978. Reservations required. Main courses £9.50–£13 ($18–$24); fixed-price 2-course menu £11–£12 ($19–$21). AE, MC, V. Mon–Wed 11am–5pm; Thurs–Sat 11am–9pm; Sun 11am–5pm. Tube: Holborn, Tottenham Court Rd., or Russell Sq.

Wagamama JAPANESE   This noodle joint, in a basement just off New Oxford Street, is noisy and overcrowded, and you'll have to wait in line for a table. It calls itself a "non-destination food station" and caters to some 1,200 customers a day. Many dishes are built around ramen noodles with your choice of chicken, beef, or salmon. Try the tasty gyoza, light dumplings filled with vegetables or chicken. Vegetarian dishes are available, but skip the so-called Korean-style dishes.

4 Streatham St., WC1. ✆ 020/7323-9223. Reservations not accepted. Main courses £5.50–£11 ($10–$20). AE, MC, V. Mon–Sat noon–11pm; Sun 12:30–10pm. Tube: Tottenham Court Rd.

COVENT GARDEN & THE STRAND

The restaurants in and around Covent Garden and the Strand are the most convenient choices when you're attending theaters in the West End.

EXPENSIVE

Rules 🍴 TRADITIONAL BRITISH   If you're looking for London's most quintessentially British restaurant, eat here. London's oldest restaurant was established in 1798 as an oyster bar; today, the antler-filled Edwardian dining rooms exude nostalgia. You can order such classic dishes as Irish or Scottish oysters, jugged hare, and mussels. Game dishes are offered from mid-August to February or March, including wild Scottish salmon; wild sea trout; wild Highland red deer; and game birds like grouse, snipe, partridge, pheasant, and woodcock. As a finale, the "great puddings" continue to impress.

35 Maiden Lane, WC2. ☎ **020/7836-5314**. Reservations recommended. Main courses £15–£21 ($28–$39). AE, DC, MC, V. Daily noon–11:30pm. Tube: Covent Garden.

Simpson's-in-the-Strand ★★ *Kids* TRADITIONAL AND MODERN BRITISH   Simpson's is more of an institution than a restaurant. Long a family favorite with lots of large tables, it has been in business since 1828, and as a result of a recent £2 million ($3.7 million) renovation, it's now better than ever with its Adam paneling, crystal, and an army of grandly formal waiters (to whom nouvelle cuisine means anything after Henry VIII) serving traditional British fare.

Most diners agree that Simpson's serves the best roasts in London, an array that includes roast sirloin of beef, roast saddle of mutton with red-currant jelly, roast Aylesbury duckling, and steak, kidney, and mushroom pie. (Remember to tip the tailcoated carver.) For a pudding, you might order the treacle roll and custard or Stilton with vintage port. Simpson's also serves traditional breakfasts. The most popular one is "The Ten Deadly Sins": a plate of sausage; fried egg; streaky and back bacon; black pudding; lambs' kidneys; bubble-and-squeak; baked beans; lambs' liver; and fried bread, mushrooms, and tomatoes. That will certainly fortify you for the day.

100 the Strand (next to the Savoy Hotel), WC2. ☎ **020/7836-9112**. Reservations required. Breakfast from £16 ($30); main courses £15–£25 ($28–$46); fixed-price pre-theater dinner £17–£21 ($31–$39). AE, DC, MC, V. Mon–Fri 7:15–10:30am; Mon–Sat 12:15–2:30pm and 5:30–10:45pm; Sun 6–8:30pm. Tube: Charing Cross or Embankment.

MODERATE

Porter's English Restaurant ★★ *Kids* TRADITIONAL BRITISH   The seventh earl of Bradford serves "real English food at affordable prices." He succeeds notably—and not just because Lady Bradford turned over her carefully guarded recipe for banana-and-ginger steamed pudding. This comfortable, two-storied restaurant is family friendly, informal, and lively. Porter's specializes in classic English pies, including Old English fish pie; lamb and apricot; and, of course, bangers and mash. Main courses are so generous—and accompanied by vegetables and side dishes—that you hardly need appetizers. They have also added grilled English fare to the menu, with sirloin and lamb steaks and marinated chicken. The puddings, including bread-and-butter pudding or steamed syrup sponge, are served hot or cold, with whipped cream or custard. The bar does quite a few exotic cocktails, as well as beers, wine, or English mead. A traditional English tea is also served from 2:30 to 5:30pm for £4.75 ($8.80) per person. Who knows? You may even bump into his Lordship.

17 Henrietta St., WC2. ℂ 020/7836-6466. Reservations recommended. Main courses £8.95–£13 ($17–$24); fixed-price menu £20 ($37). AE, DC, MC, V. Mon–Sat noon–11:30pm; Sun noon–10:30pm. Tube: Covent Garden or Leicester Sq.

INEXPENSIVE

Sarastro 𝕉 CYPRIOT/TURKISH   The setting here makes you feel like you're in the prop room of an opera house. As the manager says, "We're the show after the show." The decor is sort of neo-Ottoman, and the cuisine celebrates the bounty of the Mediterranean, especially Turkey and Cyprus. In a Victorian building behind the Theatre Royal, the restaurant is decorated with battered urns, old lamps, fading lampshades, and knickknacks—an old Turkish curiosity-shop look. Ten opera boxes adorn three sides of the restaurant; the royal box is the most desired. The restaurant takes its name from a character in Mozart's *The Magic Flute*. Live opera performances are staged from time to time. Launch your meal with delights like asparagus in red-wine sauce or fresh grilled sardines. Fresh fish is the way to go for your main course, especially river trout or grilled halibut. A zesty favorite is lamb Anatolian style with carrots, zucchini, and shallots. We're also fond of the well-seasoned lamb meatballs. A good-tasting specialty is chicken Sarastro, made with walnuts and raisins.

126 Drury Lane, WC2. ℂ 020/7836-0101. Reservations required. Main courses £8.50–£15 ($16–$28); fixed-price menu £18–£24 ($32–$43); pre-theater menu £10 ($19). AE, DC, MC, V. Daily noon–midnight. Tube: Covent Garden.

PICCADILLY CIRCUS & LEICESTER SQUARE

Piccadilly Circus and Leicester Square lie at the doorstep of the West End theaters. All the choices below (along with those in the "Covent Garden & the Strand" and "Soho" sections) are good candidates for dining before or after a show.

EXPENSIVE

Fung Shing 𝕉𝕉 CANTONESE   In a city where the competition is stiff, Fung Shing emerges as London's finest Cantonese restaurant. Firmly established as a culinary landmark, it dazzles with classic and nouvelle Cantonese dishes. Look for the seasonal specials. Some of the dishes may be a bit experimental, notably stir-fried fresh milk with scrambled egg white, but you'll feel right at home with the soft-shell crab sautéed in a light batter and served with tiny rings of red-hot chile and deep-fried garlic. Chinese gourmets come here for the fried intestines; you may prefer the hotpot of stewed duck with yam. The spicy sea bass and the stir-fried crispy chicken are worthy choices. There are more than 150 dishes from which to choose and most are moderate in price.

15 Lisle St., WC2. ℭ 020/7437-1539. Reservations required. Main courses £10–£26 ($19–$48); fixed-price menus £17–£34 ($31–$63). AE, DC, MC, V. Daily noon–11:30pm. Tube: Leicester Sq.

J. Sheekey ℱ SEAFOOD   British culinary tradition lives on at this fish joint, long a favorite of West End actors. The jellied eels that delighted Laurence Olivier and Vivien Leigh are still here, along with an array of fresh oysters from the coasts of Ireland and Brittany, plus that Victorian favorite, fried whitebait. Sheekey's fish pie is still on the menu, as is Dover sole. The old "mushy" peas still appear, but the chefs also offer the likes of steamed organic sea beet. Opt for the traditional dishes or specials based on the fresh catch of the day. The double chocolate pudding soufflé is a delight, and many favorite puddings remain.

28–32 St. Martin's Court, WC2. ℭ 020/7240-2565. Reservations recommended. Main courses £10–£31 ($19–$57). AE, DC, MC, V. Mon–Sat noon–3pm and 5:30pm–midnight; Sun noon–3:30pm and 6pm–midnight. Tube: Leicester Sq.

MODERATE

Dumpling Inn CHINESE   Despite its cutesy name, this cool, elegant restaurant serves a delectable style of Peking Mandarin cuisine that dates back almost 3,000 years. The cooking owes some of its piquancy to various Mongolian ingredients, which are well represented in the restaurant's savory stew, called "hotpot." Regulars come for the shark-fin soup; the beef in oyster sauce; the seaweed; the sesame-seed prawns on toast; the duck with chile and black-bean sauce; and the fried, sliced fish. The specialty is dumplings, and you can make a meal from the dim sum list. Portions aren't large, so order as many dishes as you'd like to sample. Chinese tea is extra. Service is leisurely, so don't dine here before a theater date.

15a Gerrard St., W1. ℭ 020/7437-2567. Reservations recommended. Main courses £8–£18 ($15–$33); fixed-price lunch or dinner £15–£30 ($28–$56). AE, MC, V. Sun–Thurs noon–11:30pm; Fri–Sat 11:30am–10:30pm. Tube: Leicester Sq.

The Ivy ℱℱ MODERN BRITISH/INTERNATIONAL   Effervescent and sophisticated, The Ivy is the dining choice of visiting theatrical luminaries and has been intimately associated with the theater district ever since it opened in 1911. With its ersatz 1930s look and tiny bar near the entrance, this place is fun, and hums with the energy of London's glamour scene. The kitchen has a solid appreciation for fresh ingredients and a talent for preparation. Favorite dishes include white asparagus with sea kale and truffle butter; seared scallops with spinach, sorrel, and bacon; and salmon fish cakes. You'll also find such English desserts as sticky toffee (sponge cake soaked in a thick caramelized syrup) and caramelized bread-and-butter pudding. Meals are served quite late to accommodate the post-theater crowd.

1 West St., WC2. ⓒ 020/7836-4751. Reservations required. Main courses £9–£35 ($17–$65); Sat–Sun fixed-price 3-course lunch £20 ($36). AE, DC, MC, V. Mon–Sat noon–3pm; daily 5:30pm–midnight (last order); Sun noon–3:30pm. Tube: Leicester Sq.

Livebait's Café Fish ⓡ SEAFOOD Don't you love the name? The catch of the day can be chargrilled or pan-fried as you desire. We know of no better place in London to sample seafood favorites enjoyed by Brits back in the days of Sir Winston Churchill—we're talking smoked haddock kedgeree (a mixture of fish, rice, and hard-boiled eggs), cockles, steamed mussels, smoky grilled sardines, and the like. We like to go when the Dover sole is brought in. This eclectic menu includes fish flown all the way from the U.S. Unlike some of the soggy chips (fries) at nearby dives, the ones here are crisp and fluffy. Our moist-fleshed sea bream, served with a crisp skin, made us want to "hasten ye back" to the restaurant the next night. From grandma's pantry comes Bailey's cheesecake or sticky toffee pudding to finish off the meal.

36–40 Rupert St., W1. ⓒ 020/7287-8989. Reservations required. Main courses £10–£18 ($19–$33); set dinner £10 ($19). AE, MC, V. Mon–Sat noon–11pm; Sun noon–9pm. Tube: Piccadilly Circus.

Randall & Aubin ⓡ *Finds* SEAFOOD Past the sex boutiques of Soho you stumble upon this real discovery, whose consultant is TV chef Ed Baines, an ex-Armani model who turned this butcher shop into a cool, hip champagne-and-oyster bar. It's an ideal place to take a lover for a *Sex in the City* type of meal and some champagne or a bottle of wine. You're never rushed here. The impressive shellfish display of the night's goodies is the "bait" used to lure you inside. Chances are you won't be disappointed. Loch Fyne oysters, lobster with chips, pan-fried fresh scallops—the parade of seafood we've sampled here has in each case been genuinely excellent. The *soupe de* *poisson* (fish soup) is the best in Soho, or else you might want one of the hors d'oeuvres such as delightful Japanese-style fish cakes or fresh Cornish crab. Yes, they still have Sevruga caviar for lotto winners. For the rare meat-only eater, there is a limited array of dishes such as a perfectly roasted chicken on the spit that has been flavored with fresh herbs. The lemon tart with crème fraîche rounds off a perfect meal.

16 Brewer St., W1. ✆ 020/7287-4447. Reservations not accepted. Main courses £11–£19 ($19–$34). AE, DC, MC, V. Mon–Sat noon–11pm; Sun 4–10:30pm. Tube: Piccadilly Circus.

INEXPENSIVE

Brown's CONTINENTAL/TRADITIONAL BRITISH The decor of this popular restaurant is reminiscent of an Edwardian brasserie, with mirrors, dark-wood trim, and cream-colored walls. The staff is attentive, hysterically busy, and high spirited. The most amazing thing about the restaurant is its size. It's a cavernous labyrinth of tables complemented by a bar whose (often single) clients tend to be good-looking, happy-go-lucky, and usually up for a chat. Expect well-prepared cuisine here, hauled out through the stand-up crowds to battered tables and bentwood chairs by an army of well-intentioned European staff. Menu items include traditional British favorites (salmon and fish cakes; or steak, mushroom, and Guinness pies); as well as continental dishes like confit of duck on a bed of lentils with pancetta, or chicken filet in red pesto served with linguine and rocket (arugula). The site of the restaurant was originally conceived in 1787 as a magistrate's court. Today, the somber overtones of the court are gone, as the restaurant is usually awash with bubbly theatergoers either headed to or coming from a West End play.

82–94 St. Martins Lane, WC2. ✆ 020/7497-5050. Reservations recommended. 2-course fixed-price menu £11 ($20), available noon–6:30pm Mon–Sat. Main courses £10–£16 ($19–$29). AE, DC, MC, V. Daily noon–11:30pm. Tube: Leicester Sq. or Covent Garden.

Cork & Bottle Wine Bar 🐸🐸 *Value* INTERNATIONAL Don Hewitson, a connoisseur of fine wines for more than 30 years, presides over this trove of blissful fermentation. The ever-changing wine list features an excellent selection of Beaujolais Crus from Alsace, 30 selections from Australia, 30 champagnes, and a good selection of California labels. If you want something to wash down, the most successful dish is a raised cheese-and-ham pie, with a cream cheese–like filling and crisp well-buttered pastry—not your typical quiche. There's also chicken and apple salad, black pudding,

Mediterranean prawns with garlic and asparagus, lamb in ale, and tandoori chicken.

44–46 Cranbourn St., WC2. © 020/7734-7807. Reservations not accepted after 6:30pm. Main courses £6.50–£12 ($12–$22); glass of wine from £3.50 ($6.50). AE, DC, MC, V. Mon–Sat 11am–11pm; Sun noon–11pm. Tube: Leicester Sq.

The Stockpot (Value) CONTINENTAL/TRADITIONAL BRITISH Pound for pound (British pounds, that is), we'd hazard a guess that this cozy little restaurant offers one of the best dining bargains in London. Meals might include a bowl of minestrone, spaghetti Bolognese, a plate of braised lamb, and apple crumble (or another dessert), among other items. At these prices, the food is hardly refined, but it's filling and satisfying nonetheless. During peak hours, The Stockpot has a share-the-table policy in its two-level dining room.

38 Panton St. (off Haymarket, opposite the Comedy Theatre), SW1. © 020/7839-5142. Reservations accepted for dinner. Main courses £2.70–£6.10 ($5–$11); fixed-price 2-course lunch £3.90 ($7.20); fixed-price 3-course dinner £6.40 ($12). No credit cards. Mon–Sat 7am–11pm; Sun 7am–10pm. Tube: Piccadilly Circus or Leicester Sq.

SOHO

The restaurants of Soho are conveniently located for those rushing to have dinner and then an evening at one of the West End theaters.

VERY EXPENSIVE

Spoon+ (R) AMERICAN In Ian Schrager's hot new Sanderson Hotel, this is a branch of the Spoon+ that master chef Alain Ducasse lures *tout Paris* to. Like its Parisian namesake, this is Monsieur Ducasse's take on "American fusion" cuisine. This is the only place you can go in London to eat a Frenchman's take on that American favorite—macaroni and cheese. Although some menu items seem designed more to shock, much of what is offered here is really good, especially the crab ceviche (crab marinated in lime juice) or the iced tomato soup (great choice) offered at the beginning. Spoon+'s chefs allow you to compose your own meal or at least pair up ingredients—perhaps a beautiful sole with a crushed lemon confit, or do you prefer it with satay sauce? You make the choices. You choose from a trio of columns: main course, sauce, and accompanying side dish. On our last visit, we found the restaurant ridiculously overpriced but then reconsidered when the entertainment of the evening arrived. Our fellow diners turned out to be none other than Madonna and her husband, Guy Ritchie.

50 Berners St., W1. ℂ 020/7300-1400. Reservations imperative. Main courses £21–£30 ($39–$56). AE, DC, MC, V. Daily noon–3pm; Mon–Sat 6–11:30pm; Sun 6–10:30pm.

EXPENSIVE

Lindsay House 𝒶𝒶 MODERN BRITISH Irish-born chef Richard Corrigan is one of our all-time favorites in London. As in an old-fashioned speakeasy, you ring the doorbell for admittance to a Regency town house deep in Soho. Unfolding before you are gilded mirrors and bare wooden floors. The staircase delivers you to one of two floors. Corrigan is one of the most inventive chefs in London, with creative offerings changing daily based on market availability. What inspires Corrigan at the market is what will end up on your plate at night. You might start with a cured foie gras rolled in spicy gingerbread, or else ravioli of rabbit in its own consommé. For your main choice, expect such delightful courses as pan-roasted filet of red mullet, or squab served with fried cabbage and bacon. An excellent poached rump of veal might also rest on your plate. Desserts are a delight—always unexpected, always a delightful surprise, such as marinated pumpkin with pistachio and chocolate sorbet.

21 Romilly St., W1. ℂ 020/7439-0450. Reservations recommended. Lunch £20–£25 ($37–$46); fixed-price 3-course dinner £48 ($89). AE, DC, MC, V. Mon–Fri noon–2:30pm; Mon–Sat 6–11pm. Tube: Leicester Sq.

Quo Vadis 𝒶 ITALIAN This hyper-trendy restaurant occupies the former apartment house of Communist patriarch Karl Marx, who would never recognize it. It was an Italian restaurant (also called Quo Vadis) from 1926 until the mid-1990s, when its interior was ripped apart and reconfigured into the stylish, postmodern place you'll find today. The stark street-level dining room is a museum-style showcase for dozens of modern paintings by the controversial Damien Hirst and other contemporary artists. But many bypass the restaurant altogether for the upstairs bar, where Hirst has put a severed cow head and a severed bull's head on display in separate aquariums. Why? They're catalysts to conversation and satirical odes to the destructive effects of Mad Cow Disease.

Quo Vadis is associated with Marco Pierre White, but don't expect to see the temperamental culinary superstar; as executive chef, he only functions as a consultant. Also, don't expect that the harassed and overburdened staff will have the time to pamper you. And the food? It's appealingly presented and very good, but not nearly as artful or innovative as the setting might lead you to believe. You might begin with one of the fresh pastas created daily, our favorite being ricotta-filled agnolotti with sage. The grilled sea bass with herb flavoring is always a delight, as are the tender and well-flavored lamb dishes. Enticing new additions are always cropping up on the chef's repertoire depending on what's good and fresh in any season.

26–29 Dean St., W1. ℂ **020/7437-9585.** Reservations required. Main courses £14–£19 ($26–$35). AE, DC, MC, V. Mon–Fri noon–2:30pm; Mon–Sat 5:30–10:30pm. Tube: Leicester Sq. or Tottenham Court Rd.

The Sugar Club ℛ PACIFIC RIM   This restaurant, with its adventurous menu, comes from the land Down Under. The chef attracts homesick Aussies with a kangaroo salad. The elegant and spacious setting is inviting, with soft textures, pale cream colors, and wooden floors. The restaurant offers a bar waiting area for diners and an open kitchen. Every area is nonsmoking except for the bar.

The flavors are often stunning—a good example is the amazingly fresh sashimi of Iki Jimi yellowtail with a black-bean-and-ginger salsa. Throughout the menu, flavors surprise the palate in the most exciting ways. You might dig into the duck leg braised in tamarind and star anise, with coconut rice, or try the pan-fried turbot with spinach, sweet potato, and red curry sauce. Many of the starters are vegetarian and can be upgraded to a main course. For dessert, the blood orange–curd sorbet is devastatingly delicious.

21 Warwick St., W1. ℂ **020/7437-7776.** Reservations recommended. Main courses £14–£23 ($26–$43). AE, DC, MC, V. Daily noon–3pm; Mon–Sat 5:30–11pm; Sun 6–10:30pm. Tube: Piccadilly Circus or Oxford Circus.

MODERATE

Bam-Bou ℛ FRENCH/VIETNAMESE   London's best Vietnamese-inspired eatery is spread over a series of dining rooms, alcoves, and bars in a town house with tattered French colonial decor. A favorite of young London, the restaurant is so popular that you may have to wait for 30 minutes to an hour for a table. The smell of lime and lemon grass lures you to the table—this combination is married perfectly in the chicken in lemon grass dish. Equally worthy is the caramelized ginger chicken. Also try such delights as tempura of soft-shell crab, or crispy beef with papaya and crabmeat flavored with a lime dressing. Rock lobster and spring chicken hot pot is an eternal favorite, as are the flavorful prawns with green herbs and coconut. Our favorite starter is spicy raw beef with aromatic basil, lime, and chile, or fried marinated squid. A winner for dessert is the dish of sweet banana rolls with chocolate sauce.

1 Percy St., W1. ✆ 020/7323-9130. Reservations required. Main courses £9–£14 ($17–$25). AE, DC, MC, V. Mon–Fri noon–3pm; Mon–Sat 6–11:30pm. Tube: Tottenham Court Rd.

The Criterion Brasserie ✿ FRENCH/MODERN BRITISH
Designed by Thomas Verity in the 1870s, this palatial neo-Byzantine mirrored marble hall is a glamorous backdrop for a superb cuisine, served under a golden ceiling, with theatrical peacock-blue draperies. The menu is wide ranging, offering everything from Paris brasserie food to "nouvelle-classical," a combination of classic French cooking techniques with some of the lighter, more experimental leanings of modern French cuisine. The food is excellent but falls short of sublime. Still, roast skate wing with deep-fried snails is delectable, as is roast saddle of lamb stuffed with mushrooms and spinach.

224 Piccadilly, W1. ✆ 020/7930-0488. Main courses £14–£23 ($26–$42); fixed-price 2-course lunch £15 ($28), 3-course lunch £18 ($33). AE, MC, V. Daily noon–2:30pm and 5:30–11pm. Tube: Piccadilly Circus.

Deca ✿✿ Finds FRENCH   At this brasserie-style restaurant, chef Jeremy Brown works his culinary magic, adding several innovative twists as well. His cooking is based upon sound French techniques and the lavish use of market-fresh ingredients. Tastes and textures come together in pleasing combinations, as characterized by the tender breast of chicken with wild mushrooms, and the breast of duck with honey and peppercorns. Freshness is the key to many dishes. The oysters are brought down from Loch Fyne in Scotland. The veal sweetbreads Pojarski have found many admirers.

23 Conduit St., W1. ✆ 020/7493-7070. Reservations required. Main courses £12–£20 ($22–$37); fixed-price lunch £13 ($23). AE, DC, MC, V. Mon–Sat noon–3pm and 5:30–11pm. Tube: Oxford Circus.

The Gay Hussar ✿ HUNGARIAN   Is it still the best Hungarian restaurant in the world? That's what some say. We can't agree until we've sampled every Hungarian restaurant in the world, but we're certain Gay Hussar would be near the top. Since 1953, it's been an intimate place with authentic cuisine, a loyal clientele of politicians, and a large international following, especially among visiting Hungarians. You can begin with a chilled wild-cherry soup or mixed Hungarian salami. Gutsy main courses might include cabbage stuffed with minced veal and rice, half a perfectly done chicken in mild paprika sauce with cucumber salad and noodles, roast duck with red cabbage and Hungarian-style caraway potatoes, and, of course, veal goulash with egg dumplings. Expect gigantic portions. For dessert, go with either the poppy-seed strudel or the walnut pancakes.

2 Greek St., W1. ⓒ 020/7437-0973. Reservations recommended. Main courses £10–£17 ($19–$31); fixed-price 2-course lunch £16 ($29), 3-course lunch £19 ($34). AE, DC, MC, V. Mon–Sat 12:15–2:30pm and 5:30–10:45pm. Tube: Tottenham Court Rd.

Hakkasan ⓡ *Finds* CHINESE   Asian mystique and pastiche are found in this offbeat restaurant, lying in a seedy alley off Tottenham Court Road. This is another London venture created by Alan Yau, who became a city-wide dining legend because of his Wagamama noodle bars. Designer Christian Liaigre created a dining room encapsulated in a lattice wood "cage" evocative of antique Chinese doors. The leather sofas are emblazoned with dragons, and a bar runs the length of the restaurant. Come here for great dim sum and tantalizing cocktails. Feast on such dishes as *har gau* (steamed prawn dumplings) and strips of tender barbecued pork. The spring roll is refreshing with the addition of fried mango and a delicate prawn-and-scallop filling. Steamed scallop shumai (dumplings) with tobiko caviar are fresh and meltingly soft. You may want to sample such delights as steamed asparagus with bamboo pith and dried shiitake, or fried taro croquettes. Desserts in most of London's Chinese restaurants are hardly memorable, but the offerings here are an exception to that rule, especially the layered banana sponge with chocolate cream.

8 Hanway Place. ⓒ 020/7907-1888. Reservations recommended. Main courses £8.50–£28 ($16–$52). AE, MC, V. Daily noon–3pm and 6–11pm. Tube: Tottenham Court Rd.

Mela ⓡ *Value* INDIAN   Serious foodies know that you'll likely be served some of London's finest Indian cuisine at this address. Both Carlton Television and the *London Evening Standard* named this the best Indian restaurant in Britain in 2001. Expect robust aromas and earthy flavors. Our spiced duck flavored with spring onions, ginger, and coriander evoked some of the best country dining in India. Eggplant came stuffed with a spicy lamb mince, and was superb, as was the whole fresh fish of the day in a spicy marinade flavored with saffron and cooked whole in a charcoal oven. Some of the best curries in the city are served here. Tawa cookery (which in India is street cookery on a hot plate) is a specialty. At Mela, the fresh meats and other ingredients are cooked straight on a hot plate. Look for the chef's special Tawa dish of the day, perhaps queen prawns cooked with onions and fresh tomatoes. Save room for one of their special desserts.

152–156 Shaftesbury Ave., WC2. ℭ **020/7836-8635**. Reservations required. Main courses £4.95–£7.95 ($9–$15); prix-fixe lunch £11 ($20), dinner (5:30–7pm) £15 ($28). AE, MC, V. Daily noon–2:30pm and 5:30pm–midnight. Tube: Tottenham Court Rd. or Leicester Sq.

Mezzo ASIAN/EUROPEAN   This 750-seat, blockbuster Soho spot—the creation of Sir Terence Conran—is the biggest restaurant in London. The mammoth space is the former site of rock's legendary Marquee club. Mezzo is actually composed of several restaurants: **Mezzonine** upstairs, serving Thai/Asian cuisine with a European flair (deep-fried salt-and-pepper squid flavored with garlic and coriander; and roast duck with Thai red curry and fragrant rice are some examples); swankier **Mezzo** downstairs, offering modern European cuisine in a 1930s Hollywood atmosphere; and **Mezzo Cafe,** where you can stop in for a simple sandwich and a drink.

The food is at its most ambitious downstairs at Mezzo, where 100 chefs work behind glass to feed up to 400 diners at a time. This is dinner-as-theater. Not surprisingly for a restaurant of this size, the cuisine tends to be uneven. We suggest the rotisserie rib of beef with red wine and creamed horseradish, or the roast cod, which is crisp-skinned and cooked to perfection. For dessert, you can't beat the butterscotch ice cream with a pitcher of hot fudge. A live jazz band entertains after 10pm from Wednesday to Saturday, and the world of Marlene Dietrich and Noel Coward comes alive again.

100 Wardour St., W1. ℭ **020/7314-4000**. Reservations recommended. Mezzo 3-course fixed-price dinner £17 ($31); Mezzonine 3-course dinner £15 ($27); Mezzo Cafe main courses £5–£10 ($9.25–$19). AE, DC, MC, V. Mezzo: Wed–Fri noon–3pm; Mon–Wed 5:30pm–1am; Thurs–Sat 5:30pm–3am. Mezzonine: Mon–Fri noon–3pm; Sat noon–4pm; Mon–Thurs 5:30pm–1am; Fri–Sat 5:30pm–3am. Mezzo Cafe: Mon–Sat 8am–11pm, Sun 4–10:30pm. Tube: Piccadilly Circus.

Satsuma JAPANESE   This funky Japanese canteen is all the rage in London. The clean lines, stark white walls, and long wooden tables might suggest an upmarket youth hostel. But patrons come for good food at reasonable prices. The restaurant is ideal for a pre-theater visit. Your meal comes in a lacquered bento box on a matching tray. Try the chicken teriyaki or fresh chunks of tuna and salmon. The dumplings are excellent, as is the miso soup. A specialty is the large bowl of seafood ramen, with noodles swimming in a well-seasoned broth studded with mussels, scallops, and prawns. Tofu steaks are a delight, as are udon noodles with wok-fried chicken and fresh vegetables. You can finish with deep-fried tempura ice cream.

56 Wardour St., W1. ⓒ 020/7437-8338. Reservations not accepted. Main courses £6–£16 ($11–$30). AE, MC, V. Mon–Tues noon–11pm; Wed–Thurs noon–11:30pm; Fri–Sat noon–midnight; Sun noon–10:30pm. Tube: Piccadilly Circus.

Soho Spice INDIAN   This is one of central London's most stylish Indian restaurants, combining a hip atmosphere with the flavors and scents of southern India. You might opt for a drink at the cellar bar before heading to the street-level dining room, decorated in saffron, cardamom, bay, and pepper hues. A staff member dressed in similarly vivid apparel will propose a wide array of choices, including slow-cooked Indian tandoori specials that feature lamb, chicken, fish, or vegetables with combinations of spices. The a la carte menu offers a variety of courses, including *Jhinga Hara Pyaz,* spicy queen prawns with fresh spring onions, and *Paneer Pasanda,* cottage cheese slices stuffed with spinach and served with almond sauce. The cuisine will satisfy traditionalists but also has a modern flair.

124–126 Wardour St., W1. ⓒ 020/7434-0808. Reservations recommended. Main courses £9.95–£15 ($18–$28); set dinner £20 ($37). AE, V. Mon–Thurs 11:30am–12:30am; Fri–Sat 11:30am–3am; Sun 12:30–10:30pm. Tube: Tottenham Court Rd.

INEXPENSIVE

Balans MODERN BRITISH   Located on one of the gayest streets in London, Old Compton Street, Balans is the best-known gay restaurant in London, and has been since its inauguration in 1993. Some of its diehard fans take all their meals here. Its extensive hours of service are almost without equal in London. Although the food is deemed "British," it is an eclectic cuisine, borrowing freely from whatever kitchen the chef chooses, from the Far East to America. You can fill up on one of the succulent pastas, such as linguine with crab, parsley, garlic and chili; tagliolini with wild mushrooms, fire-roasted sweet peppers, roast garlic, and truffle oil; or ricotta and spinach ravioli with Gorgonzola cream sauce. Grilled dishes delight the mostly male patrons, especially the tuna teriyaki or the charred roast chicken. Balans has a party pub atmosphere and is a good place to meet people.

60 Old Compton St., W1. ⓒ 020/7437-5212. Reservations recommended. Main courses £8–£17 ($15–$31). AE, MC, V. Mon–Sat 8am–5am; Sun 8am–2am. Tube: Piccadilly Circus or Leicester Sq.

Mildreds ☆ *Finds* VEGETARIAN   Mildreds may sound like a 1940s Joan Crawford movie, but it's one of London's most enduring vegetarian and vegan dining spots. It was vegetarian long before such restaurants became trendy. Jane Muir and Diane Thomas worked in various restaurants together before opening their own place. Today they run a busy, bustling diner with casual, friendly service. Sometimes it's a bit crowded and tables are shared. They do a mean series of delectable stir-fries. The ingredients in their dishes are naturally grown, and they strongly emphasize the best seasonal produce. The menu changes daily, but always features an array of homemade soups, casseroles, and salads. Organic wines are served, and portions are very large. Save room for the desserts, especially the nutmeg-and-mascarpone ice cream or the chocolate, rum, and amaretto pudding.

45 Lexington St., W1. ℂ 020/7494-1634. Reservations not accepted. Main courses £6.50–£8 ($12–$15). No credit cards. Mon–Sat noon–11pm. Tube: Tottenham Court Rd.

Veeraswamy *Value* INDIAN   The oldest Indian restaurant in England, originally established in the 1920s, Veeraswamy has been restyled and rejuvenated and is looking better than ever. Its menu has been redone, and today it serves some of the most affordable fixed-price menus in Central London, the heart of the city. Shunning the standard fare offered in most London-based Indian restaurants, Veeraswamy features authentic, freshly prepared dishes—the kind that would be served in a private Indian home. Try almost anything: spicy oysters, brochette of monkfish, chicken curry with almonds, succulent tandoori chicken, or tender and flavorful lamb curry. One of our favorite dishes is lamb with turnips from Kashmir, flavored with large black cardamoms, powdered fennel, and a red chile powder, giving the dish a savory flavor and a vivid red color.

Victory House, 99 Regent St., W1. ℂ 020/7734-1401. Reservations recommended. Lunch and pre-/post-theater menu £13–£15 ($23–$28). Sun 3-course menu £15 ($28). Lunch and dinner main courses £13–£22 ($24–$41). AE, DC, MC, V. Mon–Fri noon–2:30pm; Sat–Sun 12:30–3pm; daily 5:30–11pm. Tube: Piccadilly Circus.

TRAFALGAR SQUARE
MODERATE

Crivelli's Garden ☆ ITALIAN   In the National Gallery, this hot new dining choice lies over the foyer of the Sainsbury Wing, providing a panoramic view of fabled Trafalgar Square. The view's a bonus—it's the cuisine that attracts visitors. The restaurant is named for a striking mural by Paulo Rego that is painted on one side of a wall. The chefs are at home with Italian dishes, offering choices such as grilled skewered squid with eggplant and sun-dried tomato salad. The steamed salmon with leeks, cilantro, and ginger is an excellent dish, as is the red pepper ravioli in a chive sauce. There is a cafe offshoot of Crivelli's Garden in the basement of the main building, which is a good choice for sandwiches, pastas, soups, and pastries.

In the National Gallery, Trafalgar Sq., WC2. ℂ **020/7747-2869.** Reservations required. Fixed-price lunch and Wed dinner £16–£20 ($30–$37). AE, DC, MC, V. Daily 10am–5:30pm; Wed 6–8:30pm. Tube: Charing Cross.

The Portrait Restaurant ℛ MODERN BRITISH This rooftop restaurant is a sought-after dining ticket on the fifth floor of the National Portrait Gallery's Ondaatje Wing. Along with the view (Nelson's Column, the London Eye, Big Ben, and the like), you get superb meals. Patrons usually go for lunch, not knowing that the chefs also cook on Thursday and Friday nights. In spring, there's nothing finer than the green English asparagus. All the main courses are filled with flavor. The high quality of the produce really shines through in such dishes as the whole plaice cooked in shrimp butter, and the roasted organic chicken. For your "pudding," nothing is finer than the chocolate and pecan tart with espresso ice cream. Chefs aren't afraid of simple preparations mainly because they are assured of the excellence of their products. The wine list features some organic choices.

In the National Portrait Gallery, Trafalgar Sq., WC2. ℂ **020/7313-2490.** Reservations recommended. Main courses £11–£19 ($20–$35). AE, MC, V. Sat–Wed 10am–5pm; Thurs–Fri 5:30–8:30pm. Tube: Leicester Sq. or Charing Cross.

MAYFAIR
VERY EXPENSIVE

Le Gavroche ℛℛℛ FRENCH Although challengers come and go, this luxurious dining room remains the number-one choice in London for classical French cuisine. It may have fallen off briefly in the early 1990s, but it's fighting its way back to stellar ranks. There's always something special coming out of the kitchen of Burgundy-born Michel Roux; the service is faultless, and the ambience formally chic without being stuffy. The menu changes constantly, depending on the fresh produce that's available and the current inspiration of the chef. But it always remains classically French, though not of the "essentially old-fashioned bourgeois repertoire" that some critics suggest. Signature dishes have been honed over years of unswerving practice, including the soufflé Suissesse, papillote of smoked salmon (salmon cooked in a greased paper wrapper), or whole Bresse chicken with truffles and a Madeira cream sauce. Game is often served, depending on availability. New menu options include cassoulet of snails with frog thighs, seasoned with herbs; mousseline of lobster in champagne sauce; and filet of red snapper with caviar and oyster-stuffed tortellini.

43 Upper Brook St., W1. ℂ **020/7408-0881**. Fax 020/7491-4387. Reservations required as far in advance as possible. Main courses £24–£45 ($44–$83); fixed-price lunch £42 ($78); menu exceptional £82 ($152) per person. AE, MC, V. Mon–Fri noon–2pm and 7–11pm; Sat 7–11pm. Tube: Marble Arch.

Nobu 𝄢𝄢 JAPANESE   London's innovative Japanese restaurant owes much to its founders, actor Robert de Niro and chef Nobu Matsuhisa. The kitchen staff is brilliant and as finely tuned as their New York counterparts. The sushi chefs create gastronomic pyrotechnics. Those on the see-and-be-seen circuit don't seem to mind the high prices that go with these incredibly fresh dishes. Elaborate preparations lead to perfectly balanced flavors. Where else can you find an excellent sea urchin tempura? Salmon tartare with caviar is a brilliant appetizer. Follow with a perfectly done filet of sea bass in a sour bean paste or soft-shell crab rolls. The squid pasta is sublime, as is sukiyaki; the latter dish is incredibly popular and with good reason. Cold sake arrives in a green bamboo pitcher.

In the Metropolitan Hotel, 19 Old Park Lane, W1. ℂ **020/7447-4747**. Reservations required. Main courses £16–£35 ($30–$65); sushi and sashimi £4–£6 ($7–$11) per piece; fixed-price menu £70 ($130). AE, DC, MC, V. Mon–Fri noon–2:15pm; Mon–Thurs 6–10:15pm; Fri–Sat 6–11pm; Sun 6–9:30pm. Tube: Hyde Park Corner.

Sketch 𝄢𝄢 CONTINENTAL/MODERN BRITISH   Inaugurated in 2003, this restaurant, tearoom, art gallery, bar, and patisserie became an overnight sensation. Food, art, and music are artfully harmonized. In a converted 18th-century building in Mayfair, Mourad ("Momo") Mazouz, along with a team of chefs and designers, masterminded this fashionable creation. The British press hailed Sketch as a "camp wonderland."

You can come here to dine elegantly but also to bar hop, as there are a number of venues which, to confuse matters, change their venues as the day progresses. The laser-lit West Bar is a cafe by day, an exclusive bar at night. Whimsical and informal, the Parlour is for light lunches and delectable teas. In the Lecture Room and Library, each dish represents different sensations. The Art Gallery becomes a restaurant and bar at night.

The menu showcases a cuisine that is both bold and imaginative—and also delicious. For starters, you get not only fresh

Gillardeau oysters, which are lightly poached, but they come with avocado purée, aquavit, and cucumber jelly. The fresh corn and lemon grass soup is always invigorating. Well-flavored, tender lamb is served with a beetroot cake, prunes, and hazelnuts, and the roasted and caramelized baby tuna comes with steamed zucchini, red pepper, and celery leaves, and toasted sesame seeds.

9 Conduit St., W1. © 0870/777-4488. Reservations essential for dining. Main courses £14–£22 ($26–$40). West Bar: 2-course fixed-price lunch £19 ($35), 3-course fixed-price lunch £24 ($44). Lecture Room and Library: 3-course fixed-price dinner £65 ($120), 5-course fixed-price dinner £80 ($148). Art Gallery: Daily 7pm–midnight; Lecture Room and Library Tues–Sat 7–10:30pm; Parlour Mon–Fri 8am–7pm, Sat 10am–7pm; West Bar daily noon–2am. AE, MC, V. Tube: Oxford Circus.

The Square 🏵🏵🏵 FRENCH   Hip, chic, casual, sleek, and modern, The Square still doesn't scare Le Gavroche as a competitor for first place on London's dining circuit, but it is certainly a restaurant to visit on a serious London gastronomic tour. Chef Philip Howard delivers the goods at this excellent restaurant. You get immaculate food in a cosseting atmosphere with abstract modern art on the walls. The chef has a magic touch, with such concoctions as apple soup with grouse sausage. We urge you to savor the crusted saddle of lamb flavored with a shallot purée and fresh rosemary. Surprise dishes await in every corner of the menu—for example, loin of monkfish with pearl barley. Roast foie gras is a dazzling appetizer. Fish is stunningly fresh, and the Bresse pigeon is as good as it is in its hometown in France. If you're a vegetarian, stay clear of this place, as many dishes are aimed at the true carnivore. For dessert, try the lemon and lime soufflé with coconut ice cream.

6–10 Bruton St., W1. © 020/7495-7100. Reservations required. Fixed-price lunch £25–£30 ($46–$56), dinner £55–£75 ($102–$139). AE, DC, MC, V. Mon–Fri noon–3pm; Mon–Sat 6:30–11pm; Sun 6:30–10pm. Tube: Bond St. or Green Park.

MODERATE

Greenhouse EUROPEAN   Head chef Paul Merrett is quite inspired by modern European food. Dishes from the heart of England include a roast breast of pheasant that Henry VIII would have loved. The produce is first-class and dishes are beautifully prepared, without ever destroying the natural flavor of the ingredients. Fine examples included pan-fried sea bass and breast of guinea fowl. The chef deftly handles essential flavors without interfering with them, as is the case with his filet of Scottish beef. To make this dish more interesting, though, he adds such wake-up-the-taste-buds sides as sautéed foie gras and red-onion jam. The menu is backed up by a very large wine list with some 500 selections. Some of the delightfully sticky desserts, including a moist bread-and-butter pudding and a baked ginger loaf with orange marmalade, would please a Midlands granny. Most dishes are at the lower end of the price scale.

27A Hays Mews, W1. ✆ 020/7499-3331. Reservations required. Main courses £15–£30 ($28–$56). AE, DC, DISC, MC, V. Mon–Fri noon–2:30pm and 5:30–11pm; Sat 6:30–11pm. Closed Christmas and bank holidays. Tube: Green Park.

Langan's Brasserie FRENCH/TRADITIONAL BRITISH   In its heyday in the early 1980s, this was one of the hippest restaurants in London, and the upscale brasserie still welcomes an average of 700 diners a day. The 1976 brainchild of actor Michael Caine and chef Richard Shepherd, Langan's sprawls over two noisy floors filled with potted plants and ceiling fans that create a 1930s feel. The menu is "mostly English with a French influence," and includes spinach soufflé with anchovy sauce, quail eggs in a pastry case served with a sautéed hash of mushrooms and hollandaise sauce, and roast crispy duck with applesauce and sage-lemon stuffing. There's always a selection of English pub fare, including bangers and mash, and fish and chips. The dessert menu is a journey into nostalgia: bread-and-butter pudding, treacle tart with custard, apple pie with clotted cream . . . wait, how did mango sorbet slip in here?

Stratton St., W1. ✆ 020/7491-8822. Reservations recommended. Main courses £14–£19 ($26–$34). AE, DC, MC, V. Mon–Fri 12:15pm–11:45pm; Sat 7pm–midnight. Tube: Green Park.

Momo MOROCCAN/NORTH AFRICAN   You'll be greeted at this restaurant by a friendly, casual staff member clad in a colorful T-shirt and black pants. The setting is like Marrakech, with stucco walls, a wood-and-stone floor, patterned wood window shades, burning candles, and banquettes. You can fill up on the freshly baked bread along with appetizers such as garlicky marinated olives and pickled carrots spiced with pepper and cumin. These starters are a gift from the chef. Other appetizers are also tantalizing, especially the *briouat:* paper-thin and very crisp triangular packets of puffed pastry filled with saffron-flavored chicken and other treats. One of the chef's specialties is *pastilla au pigeon,* a traditional poultry pie with almonds. Many diners visit for the *couscous maison,* among the best in London. Served in a decorative pot, this aromatic dish of raisins, meats (including merguez sausage), chicken, lamb, and chickpeas is given added flavor with *marissa,* a powerful hot sauce from the Middle East.

25 Heddon St., W1. ℭ **020/7434-4040.** Reservations required. Main courses £15–£32 ($27–$59); fixed-price 2-course lunch £20 ($37). AE, DC, MC, V. Mon–Sat noon–2:30pm and 7–11:30pm; Sun 7–11pm. Tube: Piccadilly Circus or Oxford Circus.

Noble Rot ℱ CONTINENTAL Danish-born Soren Jessen strikes again with this modern European venue. Ladies-who-lunch and shoppers drop in during the day, but at night the lighting is lowered and the atmosphere turns romantic. Some of the best regional specialties of the Continent are prepared in light variations here, with imaginative culinary twists. You might begin a meal with roast pumpkin soup and Pecorino cheese, or else foie gras with a hazelnut dressing. Main dishes are concise, focused, and delicious, especially the supreme of guinea fowl on a bed of spinach purée and truffle *jus,* and especially the poached truffled chicken breast with fresh morels in a Riesling sauce.

3–5 Mill St., W1. ℭ **020/7629-8877.** Reservations required. Main courses £17–£23 ($31–$42); fixed-price lunch £16–£20 ($30–$37). AE, MC, V. Mon–Fri noon–3pm; Mon–Sat 6–11pm. Tube: Oxford Circus.

Zen Central CANTONESE//INDIAN/SZECHUAN Movie stars always seem to have an advance scouting party informing them of the best places to dine in a foreign city. So when we heard that Eddie Murphy and Tom Cruise were heading here, we followed. We didn't spot any stars, but we found a designer-chic Mayfair restaurant with a cool, dignified decor in black and white. Mirrors cover much of the interior (maybe that's why movie stars like it?).

Served by a competent staff, the cuisine is first-rate. Start with the soft-shell crabs cooked in a crust of salt. The steamed sea bass is perfectly cooked and, for extra flavor, served with a black bean sauce. Pork chops with lemon grass have a Thai flavor, and the baked lobster with crushed roast garlic and slivers of tangerine peel is worth a trip from anywhere. Vegetarian meals are also available. The chef's braised fish cheeks, sharks' fins, and bird's nest soup serve up flavors enjoyed in China. There is little catering to conventional Western palates, so most dishes taste the same as they would in their homeland. Most dishes are at the lower end of the price scale.

20–22 Queen St., W1. ℭ **020/7629-8103.** Reservations recommended. Main courses £10–£35 ($19–$65). AE, DC, MC, V. Mon–Sat 12:15–2:45pm and 6:15–11:15pm; Sun 12:15–2:30pm and 6:15–11pm. Tube: Green Park.

INEXPENSIVE

The Granary *Value* TRADITIONAL BRITISH This family-operated country-style restaurant serves a simple flavor-filled array of home-cooked dishes listed daily on a blackboard. These might include lamb casserole with mint and lemon; pan-fried cod; or avocado stuffed with prawns, spinach, and cheese. Vegetarian meals include mushrooms stuffed with mixed vegetables, stuffed eggplant with curry sauce, and vegetarian lasagna. Tempting desserts are bread-and-butter pudding and apple brown betty (both served hot). The large portions guarantee you won't go hungry. The cooking is standard, but quite good for the price.

39 Albemarle St., W1. ℭ 020/7493-2978. Main courses £8.90–£9.90 ($16–$18). MC, V. Mon–Fri 11:30am–7pm; Sat 11:30am–3pm. Tube: Green Park.

ST. JAMES'S
EXPENSIVE

L'Oranger ℛ FRENCH   This bistro-cum-brasserie occupies a high-ceilinged space in an affluent neighborhood near the bottom of St. James's Street. Amid paneling, burnt-orange and forest-green paint, patterned carpeting, immaculate linens, flowers, and a uniformed waitstaff, you'll appreciate the choreographed set of fixed-price menus created by executive chef Michel Laurent. The clientele, whom pundits frequently refer to as "people who have made it," have praised the chef's arrangement of flavors. Depending on the chef's inspiration, the set menu may include filet of beef with "condiments" that include mashed potatoes and a croustillant of bone marrow in the Provençal style; leek and potato cappuccino garnished with flaked, garden-poached codfish; a salad of winter vegetables with black truffles and caviar; Dover sole with curried seasonal fruits and *fumet* dressing; and filet of wild sea bass with artichokes, pink radishes, and vanilla-flavored olive oil. Only fixed-price menus are served here.

5 St. James's St., SW1A. ℭ 020/7839-3774. Reservations recommended. Fixed-price lunches £24–£28 ($44–$52); dinner £12–£32 ($22–$60). AE, DC, MC, V. Mon–Fri noon–2pm; Mon–Sat 6:30–10:30pm. Tube: Green Park.

MODERATE

Circus *Value* INTERNATIONAL/MODERN BRITISH   This place buzzes during pre- and post-theater times with London foodies anxious to sample the wares of chef Richard Lee. A minimalist haven for power design and eating in the very heart of London, this restaurant took over the ground floor and basement of what used to be the Granada Television building at the corner of Golden Square and Beak Street. The place evokes a London version of a Left Bank Parisian brasserie. You may want to taste the divine skate wing with "crushed" new potatoes accompanied by a thick pestolike medley of rocket blended with black olives. Or else try the tasty sautéed chili-flavored squid with bok choy, made even more heavenly with a tamarind dressing. The sorbets are a nice finish to a meal, especially the delectable mango and pink grapefruit version. Of course, if you're ravenous, there's always the velvety smooth amaretto cheese-cake with a coffee sauce. Service is a delight.

1 Upper James St., W1. ✆ 020/7534-4000. Reservations required. Main courses £13–£19 ($24–$34); fixed-price menus £13–£15 ($23–$28) 5:45–7:15pm and 10:30pm–midnight. AE, DC, MC, V. Daily noon–2:30pm, Mon–Sat 6pm–midnight; bar menu daily noon–3am. Tube: Piccadilly Circus.

3 Westminster & Victoria

EXPENSIVE

Allium 🎝 *Finds* EUROPEAN/MODERN BRITISH   In this discreet residential district, chef Anton Elderman is winning the discerning palates of the area with his take on fine dining. In the dining room's sophisticated Art Deco setting, you can partake of the chef's excellent blend of flavors and his passion for new combinations. For starters, the ravioli here is not only stuffed with butternut squash but served with a pumpkin purée and a foie gras velouté (sauce). Rosemary-scented figs come baked with goat cheese. Well-prepared main dishes based on quality ingredients include a rump of lamb with black olives and rosemary *jus*, or roasted partridge with glazed chestnuts. The steamed filet of sea bass is our favorite, served with caviar, baby spinach, and a red wine *jus*. For dessert, you've arrived in heaven if you order the apricot and chocolate soufflé in its own sorbet.

Dolphin Sq., Chichester St., SW1. ✆ 020/7798-6767. Reservations required. Main courses £10–£24 ($19–$44). AE, DC, MC, V. Tues–Fri noon–2:30pm; Tues–Sat 6–10:30; Sun noon–2:30pm. Tube: Pimlico.

MODERATE

Tate Gallery Restaurant 🎝🎝 *Value* MODERN BRITISH   This restaurant is particularly attractive to wine fanciers. It offers what may be the best bargains for superior wines anywhere in Britain. Bordeaux and burgundies are in abundance, and the management keeps the markup between 40% and 65%, rather than the 100% to 200% added in most restaurants. In fact, the prices here are lower than they are in most wine shops. Wine begins at £15 ($28) per bottle, or £3.95 ($7.30) per glass. Oenophiles frequently come for lunch. The restaurant offers an English menu that changes about every month. Dishes might include pheasant casserole, pan-fried skate with black butter and capers, and a selection of vegetarian dishes. One critic found the staff and diners as traditional "as a Gainsborough landscape." Access to the restaurant is through the museum's main entrance on Millbank.

Millbank, SW1. ✆ 020/7887-8825. Reservations recommended. Main courses £11–£18 ($19–$33); fixed-price lunch 2 courses £18 ($32), 3 courses £21 ($38). AE, DC, MC, V. Mon–Sat noon–3pm; Sun noon–4pm. Tube: Pimlico. Bus: 77 or 88.

INEXPENSIVE

Jenny Lo's Teahouse CANTONESE/SZECHUAN   London's noodle dives don't get much better than this. Before its decline, Ken Lo's Memories of China offered the best Chinese dining in London. The late Ken Lo, whose grandfather was the Chinese ambassador to the Court of St. James, made his reputation as a cookbook author. Jenny Lo is Ken's daughter, and her father taught her many of his culinary secrets. Belgravia matrons and young professionals come here for perfectly prepared, reasonably priced fare. Ken Lo cookbooks contribute to the dining room decor of black refectory tables set with paper napkins and chopsticks. Opt for such fare as a vermicelli rice noodle dish (a large plate of noodles topped with grilled chicken breast and Chinese mushrooms) or white noodles with minced pork. Rounding out the menu are stuffed Peking dumplings, chili-garnished spicy prawns, and wonton soup with slithery dumplings. The black-bean-seafood noodle dish is a delight, as is the chili beef soup.

14 Eccleston St., SW1 9LT. ✆ 020/7259-0399. Reservations not accepted. Main courses £5.75–£8 ($11–$15). No credit cards. Mon–Fri 11:30am–3pm; Sat noon–3pm; Mon–Sat 6–10pm. Tube: Victoria Station.

4 Knightsbridge to South Kensington

KNIGHTSBRIDGE
EXPENSIVE

The Collection ✸ INTERNATIONAL/MODERN BRITISH
This is a temple to voyeurism and the vanities, catering to the aesthetics and preoccupations of the fashion industry. It occupies an echoing warehouse; the only access is by a 9m (30-ft.) catwalk that feels like it should have couture models striding along it. Don't worry about a snobbish chill: Manager Julian Shaw is one of the most adept and humorous in London, a celebrity in his own right because of his skill at dealing with big-ticket, big-ego fashion moguls. Yummy menu items include such appetizers as scallops

with a green-mango salad, and such main courses as seared yellowfin tuna with eggplant, cumin, and caperberries. For a change of pace, perhaps you'll opt for the grilled bison with mushrooms and a green peppercorn sauce. Don't overlook this place as a stop on your after-dark bar hop.

264 Brompton Rd., SW3. ℂ 020/7225-1212. Reservations recommended. Main courses £11–£25 ($20–$46); fixed-price menu £35–£40 ($65–$74). AE, DC, MC, V. Mon–Fri 6:30–midnight; Sat noon–4pm and 6:30–11:30pm; Sun noon–4:30pm and 6–11pm. Tube: South Kensington.

MODERATE

Drones 🅖 CONTINENTAL Britain's wonder chef, Marco Pierre White, took this once-famous but stale restaurant and has once again turned it into a chic dining venue, decorated with black-and-white photographs of the famous people lining the wall. Redesigned by David Collins, it is now referred to as "the Ivy of Belgravia." The food and Art Deco ambience is delightful, as is the staff. Food is fresh and delicately prepared, including such favorites as cauliflower cream soup with truffles and sea scallops, or smoked haddock and rice pudding. All the delectable meat and fish dishes are prepared with consummate care and served with a certain finesse. Always expect some unusual flavor combination, such as oxtail *en daube* with a rutabaga purée and a bourguignon garnish. For dessert, a summer specialty is *gelée* of red fruits with a raspberry syrup drizzle.

1 Pont St. SW1 ℂ 020/7235-9555. Reservations required. Main courses £9.50–£22 ($18–$41). Mon–Fri noon–2:30pm and 6–11pm; Sat 6–11pm; Sun noon–3:30pm. Tube: Knightsbridge.

INEXPENSIVE

Le Metro INTERNATIONAL Located just around the corner from Harrods, Le Metro draws a fashionable crowd to its basement precincts. The place serves good, solid, reliable food prepared with flair. The menu changes frequently, but try the chargrilled salmon with pesto, or the chicken and asparagus pie. You can order special wines by the glass.

28 Basil St., SW3. ℂ 020/7589-6286. Main courses £7–£11 ($13–$20). AE, DC, MC, V. Mon–Sat 7:30am–11pm. Tube: Knightsbridge.

CHELSEA
EXPENSIVE

Blue Bird 🅖 MEDITERRANEAN This enormous space resounds with clinking silverware and peals of laughter from a loyal clientele. Locals and staff alike refer to it as a *restaurant de gare*—a railway-station restaurant. Downstairs is a cafe, upscale deli, and housewares store under separate management. But most of the business occurs upstairs at this restaurant, which can hold 220 diners at a time. You'll find a color scheme of red-and-blue canvas cutouts in the shape of birds in flight. Tables are close together, but the scale of the place makes dining private and intimate. The massive menu emphasizes savory, precisely cooked cuisine, some emerging from a wood-burning stove used to roast everything from lobster to game. An immense shellfish bar stocks every crustacean you can think of, and the liquor bar does a thriving business with the Sloane Square subculture. Perennial favorites include the pan-fried halibut with mussels and baby leeks, as well as pasta and fresh fish. We're also fond of the chef's smoked haddock chowder. Most recently, we followed the chowder with deliciously seared scallops with an artichoke purée, and the filet of beef with pancetta and braised onions.

Oh, the name: Before it was a restaurant, the site was a garage that repaired the legendary Bluebird, an English sports car that is, alas, no longer produced.

350 King's Rd., SW3. ✆ 020/7559-1000. Reservations recommended. Main courses £8–£47 ($15–$87); fixed-price menu £15–£20 ($28–$37). AE, DC, MC, V. Mon–Fri 12:30–3pm and 6–11:30pm; Sat noon–3:30pm and 6–11:30pm; Sun noon–3:30pm and 6–10:30pm. Tube: Sloane Sq.

English Garden ⭐ TRADITIONAL BRITISH   This is a metropolitan restaurant par excellence. The decor in this historic town house is pretty and lighthearted: The Garden Room is whitewashed brick with a domed conservatory roof; vivid florals, rattan chairs, banks of plants, and candy-pink linens complete the scene. Every component of the meal is carried out perfectly. Some of the dishes sound as if they were copied directly from an English cookbook of the Middle Ages—and are they ever good. For a main course, opt for such delights as roast baron of rabbit with oven-dried tomato, prunes, and olive-oil mash; or saddle of venison with potted cabbage. Desserts, especially the rhubarb-and-cinnamon ice cream, and the candied-orange tart with orange syrup, would've pleased Miss Marple. Only fixed-price menus are served.

10 Lincoln St., SW3. ✆ 020/7584-7272. Reservations required. Fixed-price lunch £24 ($43), 3-course dinner £29 ($54). AE, DC, MC, V. Mon–Sat noon–3pm and 6:30–10:30pm. Tube: Sloane Sq.

INEXPENSIVE

Chelsea Kitchen INTERNATIONAL   This simple restaurant feeds large numbers of Chelsea residents in a setting that's changed little since 1961. The food and the clientele move fast, almost guaranteeing that the entire inventory of ingredients is sold out at the end of each day. Menu items usually include leek-and-potato soup, chicken Kiev, chicken parmigiana, steaks, sandwiches, and burgers. The clientele includes a broad cross-section of Londoners—all having a good and cost-conscious time.

98 King's Rd., SW3. ⓒ 020/7589-1330. Reservations recommended. Main courses £4–£6 ($7.40–$11); fixed-price menu £6.40 ($12). MC, V. Daily 7am–11:45pm. Tube: Sloane Sq.

KENSINGTON & SOUTH KENSINGTON
EXPENSIVE

Bibendum/The Oyster Bar ⓖ FRENCH/MEDITERRANEAN In trendy Brompton Cross, this still-fashionable restaurant occupies two floors of a garage that's now an Art Deco masterpiece. Though its heyday came in the early 1990s, the white-tiled room with stained-glass windows, lots of sunlight, and a chic clientele, is still an extremely pleasant place. The eclectic cuisine, known for its freshness and simplicity, is based on what's available seasonally. Dishes might include roast pigeon with celeriac purée and apple sauté, rabbit with artichoke and parsley sauce, or grilled lamb cutlets with a delicate sauce. Some of the best dishes are for splitting between two people, including Bresse chicken flavored with fresh tarragon, and grilled veal chops with truffle butter.

Simpler meals and cocktails are available in the **Oyster Bar** on the building's street level. The bar-style menu stresses fresh shellfish presented in the traditional French style, on ice-covered platters adorned with strands of seaweed. It's a crustacean-lover's dream.

81 Fulham Rd., SW3. ⓒ 020/7581-5817. Reservations required in Bibendum; not accepted in Oyster Bar. Main courses £16–£24 ($30–$44); fixed-price 3-course lunch £29 ($53); cold seafood platter in Oyster Bar £48 ($89) for 2. AE, DC, MC, V. Bibendum: Mon–Fri noon–2:30pm and 7–11pm, Sat–Sun 12:30–3pm and 7–11pm; Oyster Bar: Mon–Sat noon–10:30pm, Sun noon–3pm and 7–10:30pm. Tube: South Kensington.

Clarke's ⓖ MODERN BRITISH Sally Clarke is one of the finest chefs in London, and this is one of the hottest restaurants around. *Still.* She opened it in the Thatcher era, and it's still going strong. In this excellent restaurant, everything is bright and modern, with wood floors, discreet lighting, and additional space in the basement where tables are more spacious and private. Some people are put off by the fact that there is only a fixed-price menu, but the food is so well prepared that diners rarely object to what ends up in front of them. The menu, which changes daily, emphasizes chargrilled foods with herbs and seasonal veggies. You might begin with an appetizer salad of blood orange with red onions, watercress, and black olive–anchovy toast, then follow with roasted breast of chicken with black truffle, crisp polenta, and arugula. Desserts are likely to include a warm pear-and-raisin puff pastry with maple syrup ice cream. Just put yourself in Clarke's hands—you'll be glad you did.

124 Kensington Church St., W8. ✆ 020/7221-9225. Reservations recommended. Fixed-price lunch £15–£17 ($27–$31); 4-course dinner £50 ($92); Sat brunch £7.50–£11 ($14–$20). AE, DC, MC, V. Mon 12:30–2pm, Tues–Fri 12:30–2pm and 7–10pm; Saturday brunch 11am–2pm and dinner 7–10pm. Tube: High St. Kensington or Notting Hill Gate.

MODERATE

Blue Elephant 𝓡 THAI   This is the counterpart of the famous L'Éléphant Bleu restaurant in Brussels. In a converted factory building in West Brompton, the Blue Elephant has been all the rage since 1986. It remains the leading Thai restaurant in London, where the competition seems to grow daily. In an almost magical garden setting of tropical foliage, diners are treated to an array of MSG-free Thai dishes. You can begin with a "Floating Market" (shellfish in clear broth, flavored with chile paste and lemon grass), then go on to a splendid selection of main courses, for which many of the ingredients have been flown in from Thailand. We recommend the roasted-duck curry served in a clay cooking pot.

4–6 Fulham Broadway, SW6. ✆ 020/7385-6595. Reservations required. Main courses £10–£18 ($19–$33); Royal Thai banquet £35–£39 ($65–$72); Sun buffet £22 ($41). AE, DC, MC, V. Mon–Fri and Sun noon–2:30pm; daily 7pm–midnight. Tube: Fulham Broadway.

Kensington Place EUROPEAN   Rowley Leigh, the chef here, has attracted a devoted following of regulars. But word of his delicious cuisine is spreading, and now more and more visitors are rushing here to sample some of his signature dishes, such as griddled foie gras on a sweet-corn pancake, and scallops with pea purée and mint vinaigrette. His slow-braised lamb shank is one of the best dishes of its kind. Also look for Leigh's innovative seasonal dishes. The chef has a marvelous way with grouse, venison, roast partridge, and sea bass. He grills scallops to golden perfection, and goat-cheese mousse and olives enhance even the simplest chicken dish. Everybody from pop stars to Kensington dowagers flock to this animated, noisy bistro. The set lunch is one of the best values in the area. Save room for the steamed chocolate pudding with custard. Harking back to olde England, the chef still serves rhubarb fool or a summer trifle flavored with red fruits and liqueur.

201 Kensington Church St., W8. ℭ 020/7727-3184. Reservations required. Main courses £13–£27 ($23–$49); fixed-price lunch £17 ($31) Mon–Sat, £19 ($34) Sun. AE, DC, MC, V. Mon–Sat noon–3:30pm and 6:30–11:45pm; Sun noon–3:30pm and 6:30–10:15pm. Tube: Notting Hill Gate.

INEXPENSIVE

Admiral Codrington ℛ ⓕⁱⁿᵈˢ CONTINENTAL/MODERN BRITISH Once a lowly pub, this stylish bar and restaurant is now all the rage. The exterior has been maintained, but the old "Cod," as it is affectionately known, has emerged to offer plush dining with a revitalized decor by Nina Campbell and a glass roof that rolls back on sunny days. The bartenders still offer a traditional pint, but the sophisticated menu features such delectable fare as grilled calves' liver and crispy bacon, or pan-fried rib-eye with a truffled horseradish cream. Opt for the charbroiled tuna with eggplant caviar and a red-pepper vinaigrette.

17 Mossop St., SW3. ℭ 020/7581-0005. Reservations recommended. Main courses £10–£15 ($19–$28). AE, MC, V. Mon–Sat 11:30am–midnight; Sun noon–10:30pm. Tube: South Kensington.

5 Marylebone to Notting Hill Gate

MARYLEBONE

EXPENSIVE

Assaggi ℛℛ ⓕⁱⁿᵈˢ ITALIAN Some of London's finest Italian cuisine is served in this room above a pub. This place is a real discovery, and completely unpretentious. The relatively simple menu highlights the creative, outstanding cookery. All the ingredients are fresh and deftly handled by a skilled kitchen staff. Simplicity and flavor reign throughout. The appetizers, such as smoked swordfish salad or beef carpaccio, are so truly sublime that you'll want to make a meal entirely of them. At least three freshly made pastas are featured nightly. The tortellini (pocket-shaped noodles filled with cheese) with pork and a zesty tomato sauce is especially delicious. For a main course, opt for such delights as the thick, juicy, tender grilled veal, flavored with fresh rosemary; or the grilled sea bass with braised fennel. Another savory choice is a plate of lamb cutlets (without any fat) with eggplant and a raisin salad. The flourless chocolate cake is the finest you'll find this side of northern Italy.

39 Chepstow Place, W2. ℂ **020/7792-5501.** Reservations required (as far in advance as possible). Main courses £16–£20 ($30–$37). DC, MC, V. Mon–Fri 12:30–2:30pm and 7:30–11pm; Sat 1–2:30pm and 7:30–11pm. Closed 2 weeks at Christmas. Tube: Notting Hill Gate.

Odin's 𝒢 INTERNATIONAL   This elegant restaurant is one of at least four in London owned by chef Richard Shepherd and actor Michael Caine. Set adjacent to its slightly less expensive twin, Langan's Bistro, it features ample space between tables and an eclectic decor that includes evocative paintings and Art Deco accessories. As other restaurants nearby have come and gone, the cookery here remains solid and reliable. The standard of fresh ingredients and well-prepared dishes is always maintained. The menu changes with the seasons: Typical fare may include forest mushrooms in brioche, braised leeks glazed with mustard and tomato sauce, roast duck with applesauce and sage and onion stuffing, or roast filet of sea bass with a juniper cream sauce.

27 Devonshire St., W1. ℂ **020/7935-7296.** Reservations required. Fixed-price 2-course lunch or dinner £26 ($48), 3 courses £29 ($54). AE, DC, MC, V. Mon–Fri 12:30–2:30pm and 6:30–11pm. Tube: Regent's Park.

MODERATE

Caldesi ITALIAN   Good food, reasonable prices, fresh ingredients, and authentic Tuscan family recipes attract a never-ending stream of patrons to this eatery founded by owner and head chef Giancarlo Caldesi. The extensive menu includes a wide array of pasta, fish, and meat dishes. Start with the excellent *insalata Caldesi,* made with tomatoes slow-roasted in garlic and rosemary oil, and served with mozzarella flown in from Tuscany. Pasta dishes include an especially flavor-filled homemade tortellini stuffed with salmon. Monkfish and prawns are flavored with wild fennel and fresh basil, or you might sample the tender duck breast à l'orange, steeped in white wine, honey, thyme, and rosemary.

15–17 Marylebone Lane, W1. ℂ **020/7935-9226.** Reservations required. Main courses £9–£20 ($17–$37). AE, MC, V. Mon–Fri noon–2:30pm; Mon–Sat 6–11pm. Tube: Bond St.

Mash 𝒢 *finds* CONTINENTAL   What is it, you ask? A bar? A deli? A microbrewery? Actually, it's all of the above, plus a restaurant. Breakfast and weekend brunch are the highlights, but don't ignore dinner. The owners of the hot Atlantic Bar & Grill have opened this "sunken chill-out zone" created by leading designer John Currin. The atmosphere is trendy, hip, breezy, and arty. The novelty decor includes curvy sci-fi lines that might remind you of a *Star Trek* set, and lizard-eye lighting fixtures, but ultimately the food is the attraction.

Suckling pig with spring cannellini stew made us forget all about the trendy mirrored bathrooms. So did the terrific pizzas emerging from the wood-fired oven. On another occasion, we returned for sea bass freshly grilled over wood and presented enticingly with grilled artichoke. Also try the chargrilled tuna with sautéed new potatoes, wilted spinach, and puttanesca dressing.

19–21 Great Portland St., W1. ℂ 020/7637-5555. Reservations required. Main courses £9–£15 ($17–$28); fixed-price 2-course lunch £12 ($22), 3 courses £15 ($28). AE, DC, MC, V. Mon–Sat 7–11am, noon–3pm, and 6–11pm. Tube: Oxford Circus.

Villandry ✺ CONTINENTAL/INTERNATIONAL   Food lovers and gourmands flock to this food store, delicatessen, and restaurant, where racks of the finest meats, cheese, and produce in the world are displayed and changed virtually every hour. The best of the merchandise is whimsically transformed into the restaurant's menu choices. The setting is an oversize Edwardian-style storefront north of Oxford Circus. The inside is a kind of minimalist temple dedicated to the glories of fresh produce and esoteric foodstuffs. Ingredients here change so frequently that the menu is rewritten twice a day—during our latest visit, it proposed such perfectly crafted dishes as breast of duck with fresh spinach and a gratin of baby onions; and pan-fried turbot with deep-fried celery, artichoke hearts, and hollandaise sauce.

170 Great Portland St., W1. ℂ 020/7631-3131. Reservations recommended. Main courses £16–£21 ($30–$39). AE, DC, MC, V. Restaurant: Mon–Sat noon–3pm and 6–10:30pm; food store: Mon–Sat 8am–10pm, Sun 11am–4pm. Tube: Great Portland St.

PADDINGTON & BAYSWATER
MODERATE

Halepi ✺ *Finds* CYPRIOT/GREEK   Run by the Kazolides family since 1966, this establishment is hailed by the *Automobile Association of America Guide* as the best Greek restaurant in the world. Despite its reputation, the atmosphere is informal, with rows of brightly clothed tables, *bouzouki* background music, and a large native Greek clientele.

Portions are generous. Menu items rely heavily on lamb and include kabobs, *klefticon* (baby lamb prepared with aromatic spices), moussaka (minced lamb and eggplant with béchamel sauce), and *dolmades* (vine leaves stuffed with lamb and rice). Other main courses include scallops; sea bass; Scottish halibut; huge Indonesian shrimp with lemon juice, olive oil, garlic, and spring-onion sauce; and *afelia* (filet of pork cooked with wine and spices, served with potatoes and rice). The homemade baklava is recommended for dessert. The wine list features numerous selections from Greece and Cyprus. Most dishes are moderate in price.

18 Leinster Terrace, W2. ℂ 020/7262-1070. Reservations required. Main courses £10–£26 ($19–$48); set-price menu £18–£29 ($33–$53). AE, DC, MC, V. Daily noon–1am. Closed Dec 25–26. Tube: Queensway.

Veronica's ☆☆ *Finds* TRADITIONAL BRITISH   Called the "market leader in cafe salons," Veronica's offers traditional—and historical—fare at prices you won't mind paying. It's a celebration of British cuisine over a 2,000-year period, with dishes based on medieval, Tudor, and even Roman-age recipes. The chef gives these traditional dishes imaginative, modern twists. One month she'll focus on Scotland; another month she'll concentrate on Victorian foods; during yet another she'll feature dishes from Wales; the next she'll offer an all-Irish menu; and so on. Your appetizer might be a salad called *salmagundy,* made with crunchy pickled vegetables, that Elizabeth I enjoyed in her day. Another concoction might be "Tweed Kettle," a 19th-century salmon stew recipe. Many dishes are vegetarian, and everything tastes even better when followed with a British farmhouse cheese or a pudding. The restaurant offers a moderated menu to help keep cholesterol down. The interior is brightly and attractively decorated, and the service is warm and ingratiating.

3 Hereford Rd., W2. ℂ 020/7229-5079. Reservations required. Main courses £12–£18 ($22–$32); fixed-price meals £15–£19 ($28–$35). AE, MC, V. Mon–Sat 6pm–midnight; Sun 6–10pm. Tube: Bayswater.

NOTTING HILL GATE
MODERATE

The Cow ☆ *Finds* MODERN BRITISH   You don't have to be a young fashion victim to enjoy the superb cuisine served here (although many of the diners are). Tom Conran (son of entrepreneur Sir Terence Conran) holds forth in this increasingly hip Notting Hill watering hole. It looks like an Irish pub, but the accents you'll hear are trustafarian rather than street-smart Dublin. With a pint of Fuller's or London Pride, you can linger over the modern European menu, which changes daily but is likely to include ox tongue poached in milk; mussels in curry and cream; or a mixed grill of lamb chops, calves' liver, and sweetbreads. The seafood selections are delectable. "The Cow Special"—a half-dozen Irish rock oysters with a pint of Guinness or a glass of wine for £7 ($13)—is the star of the show. A raw bar downstairs serves other fresh seafood choices. To finish, skip the filtered coffee served upstairs (it's wretched), and opt for an espresso downstairs.

89 Westbourne Park Rd., W2. ℭ 020/7221-0021. Reservations required. Main courses £14–£20 ($26–$37). MC, V. Mon–Sat 6–11pm, Sun 12:30–4pm (brunch) and 6:30–10pm; bar daily noon–4pm and 6pm–midnight. Tube: Westbourne Grove.

INEXPENSIVE

Prince Bonaparte INTERNATIONAL   This offbeat restaurant serves great pub grub in what used to be a grungy boozer before Notting Hill Gate became fashionable. Now pretty young things show up, spilling onto the sidewalk when the evenings are warm. The pub is filled with mismatched furniture from schools and churches; and CDs of jazz and lazy blues fill the air, competing with the babble. It may seem at first that the staff doesn't have its act together, but once the food arrives, you won't care—the dishes served here are very good. The menu roams the world for inspiration: Moroccan chicken with couscous is as good or better than any you'll find in Marrakech, and the seafood risotto is delicious. Roast lamb, tender and juicy, appears on the traditional Sunday menu. We recommend the London Pride or Grolsch to wash it all down.

80 Chepstow Rd., W2. ℭ 020/7313-9491. Reservations required. Main courses £9.50–£15 ($18–$28). AE, MC, V. Mon–Sat noon–11pm; Sun noon–10:30pm. Tube: Notting Hill Gate or Westbourne Park.

5

Exploring London

Dr. Samuel Johnson said, "When a man is tired of London, he is tired of life, for there is in London all that life can afford." It would take a lifetime to explore every alley, court, street, and square in this city, and volumes to discuss them. Since you don't have a lifetime to spend, we've chosen the best that London has to offer.

For the first-time visitor, the question is never what to do, but what to do first. The "Suggested Itineraries" and "The Top Attractions" should help.

A note about admission and open hours: In the listings below, children's prices generally apply to those 16 and under. To qualify for a senior discount, you must be 60 or older. Students must present a student ID to get discounts, where available. In addition to closing on bank holidays, many attractions close around Christmas and New Year's (and, in some cases, early in May), so always call ahead if you're visiting in those seasons. All museums are closed Good Friday, December 24 through 26, and New Year's Day.

1 The Top Attractions

British Museum ✸✸✸ Set in scholarly Bloomsbury, this immense museum grew out of a private collection of manuscripts purchased in 1753 with the proceeds of a lottery. It grew and grew, fed by legacies, discoveries, and purchases, until it became one of the most comprehensive collections of art and artifacts in the world. It's impossible to take in this museum in a day.

The overall storehouse splits basically into the national collections of antiquities; prints and drawings; coins, medals, and banknotes; and ethnography. Even on a cursory first visit, be sure to see the Asian collections (the finest assembly of Islamic pottery outside the Islamic world), the Chinese porcelain, the Indian sculpture, and the Prehistoric and Romano-British collections. Special treasures you might want to seek out on your first visit include the **Rosetta Stone,** in the Egyptian Room, whose discovery led to the deciphering of hieroglyphics; the **Elgin Marbles,** a series of pediments, metopes, and

London's Attractions

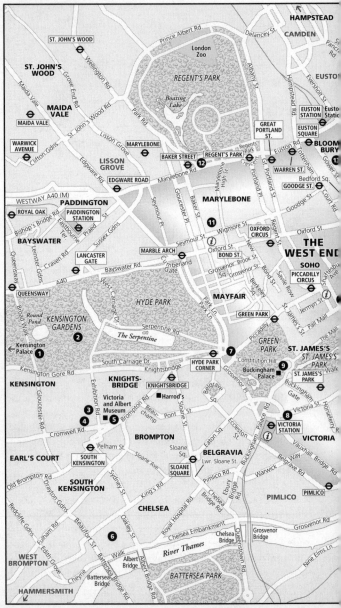

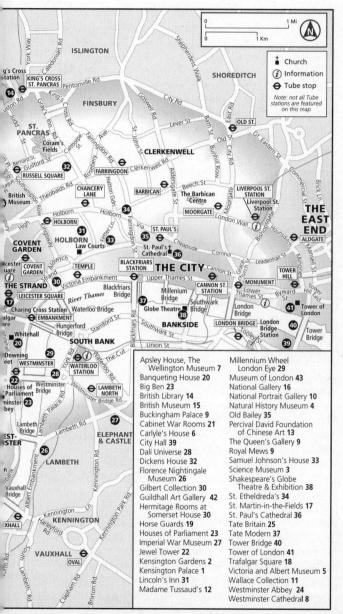

Legend

- ✝ Church
- ⓘ Information
- ⊖ Tube stop

Note: not all Tube stations are featured on this map

Apsley House, The Wellington Museum **7**	Millennium Wheel London Eye **29**
Banqueting House **20**	Museum of London **43**
Big Ben **23**	National Gallery **16**
British Library **14**	National Portrait Gallery **10**
British Museum **15**	Natural History Museum **4**
Buckingham Palace **9**	Old Bailey **35**
Cabinet War Rooms **21**	Percival David Foundation of Chinese Art **13**
Carlyle's House **6**	The Queen's Gallery **9**
City Hall **39**	Royal Mews **9**
Dalí Universe **28**	Samuel Johnson's House **33**
Dickens House **32**	Science Museum **3**
Florence Nightingale Museum **26**	Shakespeare's Globe Theatre & Exhibition **38**
Gilbert Collection **30**	St. Etheldreda's **34**
Guildhall Art Gallery **42**	St. Martin-in-the-Fields **17**
Hermitage Rooms at Somerset House **30**	St. Paul's Cathedral **36**
Horse Guards **19**	Tate Britain **25**
Houses of Parliament **23**	Tate Modern **37**
Imperial War Museum **27**	Tower Bridge **40**
Jewel Tower **22**	Tower of London **41**
Kensington Gardens **2**	Trafalgar Square **18**
Kensington Palace **1**	Victoria and Albert Museum **5**
Lincoln's Inn **31**	Wallace Collection **11**
Madame Tussaud's **12**	Westminster Abbey **24**
	Westminster Cathedral **8**

Tips **Timesaver**

With 4km (2½ miles) of galleries, the British Museum is over-whelming. To get a handle on it, we recommend taking a 1½-hour overview tour for £8 ($15), £5 ($9.25) for seniors, students and children under 16. Daily at 10:30am, 1pm, or 3pm. Afterwards, you can return to the galleries that most interest you. If you have limited time to spend on the museum, concentrate on the Greek and Roman rooms (nos. 1–15), which hold the golden hoard of booty both bought and stolen from the Empire's once far-flung colonies. For information on the British Library, see p. 141.

---

friezes from the Parthenon in Athens, in the Duveen Gallery; and the legendary **Black Obelisk,** dating from around 860 B.C., in the Nim-rud Gallery. Other treasures include the contents of Egyptian royal tombs (including mummies); fabulous arrays of 2,000-year-old jewelry, cosmetics, weapons, furniture, and tools; Babylonian astronomical instruments; and winged lion statues (in the Assyrian Transept) that guarded Ashurnasirpal's palace at Nimrud. The exhibits change throughout the year, so if your heart is set on seeing a specific treasure, call to make sure it's on display.

Insider's Tip: If you're a first-time visitor, you will, of course, want to concentrate on some of the fabled treasures previewed above. But what we do is duck into the British Museum several times on our visits to London, even if we have only an hour or two, to see the less heralded but equally fascinating exhibits. We recommend wandering rooms 33 and 34, and 91 to 94, to take in the glory of the Orient, covering Taoism, Confucianism, and Buddhism. The Chinese collection is particularly strong. Sculpture from India is as fine as anything at the Victoria and Albert. The ethnography collection is increasingly beefed up, especially the Mexican Gallery in room 33C, which traces that country's art from the 2nd millennium B.C. to the 16th century A.D. A gallery for the North American collection is also open nearby. Another section of the museum is devoted to the **Sainsbury African Galleries** ⚔, one of the finest collections of African art and artifacts in the world, featuring changing displays selected from more than 200,000 objects. Finally, the museum has opened a new Money Gallery in room 68, tracing the story of money. You'll learn that around 2000 B.C. in

Mesopotamia, money was grain, and that printed money came into being in the 10th century in China.

The museum's inner courtyard is now canopied by a lightweight, transparent roof, transforming the area into a covered square that houses a Centre for Education, exhibition space, bookshops, and restaurants. The center of the Great Court features the Round Reading Room, which is famous as the place where Karl Marx hung out while writing *Das Kapital.*

For information on the British Library, see p. 141.

Great Russell St., WC1. © **020/7323-8299** or 020/7636-1555 for recorded information. www.thebritishmuseum.ac.uk. Free admission. Sat–Wed 10am–5:30pm; Thurs–Fri 10am–8:30pm. Tube: Holborn, Tottenham Court Rd., Goodge St., or Russell Sq.

Buckingham Palace 👫👫 *(Kids)*   This massive, graceful building is the official residence of the queen. The redbrick palace was built as a country house for the notoriously rakish duke of Buckingham. In 1762, King George III, who needed room for his 15 children, bought it. It didn't become the official royal residence, though, until Queen Victoria took the throne; she preferred it to St. James's Palace. From George III's time, the building was continuously expanded and remodeled, faced with Portland stone, and twice bombed (during the Blitz). Located in a 40-acre garden, it's 108m (354 ft.) long and contains 600 rooms. You can tell whether the queen is at home by checking to see if the Royal Standard is flying from the mast outside. For most of the year, you can't visit the palace without an official invitation. Since 1993, though, much of it has been open for tours during an 8-week period in August and September, when the royal family is usually vacationing outside London. Elizabeth II agreed to allow visitors to tour the State Room, the Grand Staircase, the Throne Room, and other areas designed by John Nash for George IV, as well as the Picture Gallery, which displays masterpieces by Van Dyck, Rembrandt, Rubens, and others. The admission charges help pay for repairs to Windsor Castle, damaged by fire in 1992. You have to buy a timed-entrance ticket the same day you tour the palace. Tickets go on sale at 9am, but rather than lining up at sunrise with all the other tourists—this is one of London's most popular attractions—book by phone with a credit card and give yourself a few more hours of sleep.

During the 8 weeks of summer, visitors are also allowed to stroll through the royal family's garden, along a 4,455m (14,612-ft.) walk on the south side of the grounds, with views of a lake and the usually

---

> ⌒Tips **The Guard Doesn't Change Every Day**
>
> The schedule for the Changing of the Guard ceremony is vari-
> able at best. In theory, at least, the guard is changed daily
> from some time in April to mid-July, at which time it goes on
> its "winter" schedule—that is, alternating days. Always check
> locally with the tourist office to see if it's likely to be staged
> at the time of your visit. The ceremony has been cut at the
> last minute, leaving thousands of tourists feeling that they
> have missed out on a London must-see.

---

off-limits west side of the palace. The garden is home to 30 types of
birds, including the great crested grebe, plus 350 types of wildflowers.

Buckingham Palace's most famous spectacle is the vastly overrated
Changing of the Guard (daily Apr–July and on alternating days for
the rest of the year). The new guard, marching behind a band,
comes from either the Wellington or Chelsea barracks and takes
over from the old guard in the forecourt of the palace. The ceremony begins at 11:30am, although it's frequently canceled due to
bad weather, state events, and other harder-to-fathom reasons. We
like the changing of the guard at Horse Guards better (p. 137)
because you can actually see the men marching and you don't have
to battle such tourist hordes. However, few first-time visitors can
resist the Buckingham Place Changing of the Guard. If that's you,
arrive as early as 10:30am and claim territorial rights to a space in
front of the palace. If you're not firmly anchored here, you'll miss
much of the ceremony.

Insider's Tip: You can avoid the long queues for Buckingham
Palace tours by purchasing tickets before you go through **Global
Tickets,** 234 W. 44th St., Suite 1000, New York, NY 10034 (② **800/
223-6108**). You'll have to pick the exact date on which you'd like to
go. Visitors with disabilities can reserve tickets directly through the
palace by calling ② **020/7930-5526.**

At end of The Mall (on the road running from Trafalgar Sq.). ② **020/7839-1377** or
020/7321-2233. www.royal.gov.uk. Palace tours £13 ($23) adults, £11 ($19) seniors, £6.50 ($12) children under 17. Changing of the Guard free. Palace open for
tours Aug 6–Sept 28 daily 9:30am–4:30pm. Changing of the guard daily from
Apr–July at 11:30am, and alternating days for the rest of the year at 11am. Tube:
St. James's Park, Green Park, or Victoria.

Clarence House ⋒⋒   From 1953 until her death in 2002, the
Queen Mother lived at Clarence House in a wing of St. James's

Palace. It was constructed between 1825 and 1927 to the designs of John Nash. Today it is the official residence of the Prince of Wales, and is open to the public only during a specified period of the year (see below). The present Queen Elizabeth and the duke of Edinburgh lived here following their marriage in 1947.

After the death of the Queen Mother, the house was refurbished and redecorated, with antiques and art added from the royal collection. Visitors are taken on a guided tour of five of the staterooms, where much of the Queen's collection of works of art and furniture is on display, along with pieces added by Prince Charles. The Queen Mother had an impressive collection of 20th-century British art, including works by John Piper, Augustus John, and Graham Sutherland. She also was known for her superb collection of Fabergé and English porcelain and silver, especially pieces from her family collection (the Bowes-Lyon family).

Stable Yard Gate, SW1. ☎ **020/7766-7303**. www.royal.gov.uk. Admission £5.50 ($10) adults, £3 ($5.55) ages 5–17. Free for 4 and under. Aug 4–Oct 17 (dates subject to change—call first); daily 9:30am–6pm. Tube: Green Park or St. James's Park.

Houses of Parliament & Big Ben ☆☆   The Houses of Parliament, along with their trademark clock tower, Big Ben, are the ultimate symbols of London. They're the strongholds of Britain's democracy, the assemblies that effectively trimmed the sails of royal power. Both the House of Commons and the House of Lords are in the former royal Palace of Westminster, which was the king's residence until Henry VIII moved to Whitehall. The current Gothic Revival buildings date from 1840 and were designed by Charles Barry. (The earlier buildings were destroyed by fire in 1834.) Assisting Barry was Augustus Welby Pugin, who designed the paneled ceilings, tiled floors, stained glass, clocks, fireplaces, umbrella stands, and even the inkwells. There are more than 1,000 rooms and 3km (2 miles) of corridors. The clock tower at the eastern end houses the world's most famous timepiece. **"Big Ben"** refers not to the clock tower itself, but to the largest bell in the chime, which weighs close to 14 tons and is named for the first commissioner of works, Sir Benjamin Hall.

You may observe debates for free from the **Stranger's Galleries** in both houses. Sessions usually begin in mid-October and run to the end of July, with recesses at Christmas and Easter. The chances of getting into the House of Lords when it's in session are generally better than for the more popular House of Commons. Although we can't promise you the oratory of a Charles James Fox or a William

Pitt the Elder, the debates in the House of Commons are often lively and controversial (seats are at a premium during crises).

For years, London tabloids have portrayed members of the House of Lords as a bunch of "Monty Pythonesque upper-class twits," with one foreign secretary calling the House of Lords "medieval lumber." Today, under Tony Blair's Labour government, the House of Lords is being shaken up as lords lose their inherited posts. Panels are studying what to do with this largely useless house, its members often descendants of royal mistresses and ancient landowners.

Those who'd like to book a tour can do so, but it takes a bit of work. Both houses are open to the general public for guided tours only for a limited season in July and August. The palace is open Monday, Tuesday, Friday, and Saturday from 9:15am to 4:30pm during those times. All tour tickets cost £7 ($13) for adults, £5 ($9.25) for seniors, students, and children under 16. Under 4 years old may enter free. For advance tickets call ✆ **087/0906-3773.**

If you arrive just to attend a session, these are free. You line up at Stephen's Gate, heading to your left for the entrance into the Commons or to the right for the Lords. The London daily newspapers announce sessions of Parliament.

Insider's Tip: The hottest ticket and the most exciting time to visit is during "Prime Minister's Question Time" on Wednesdays, which is only from 3 to 3:30pm, but which must seem like hours to Tony Blair, who is on the hot seat. It's not quite as thrilling as it was back when Margaret Thatcher exchanged barbs with the MPs (members of Parliament), but Blair holds his own admirably against any and all who try to embarrass him and his government. He is given no mercy from these MPs, especially those who oppose his policies.

Across the street is the **Jewel Tower** ⍟, Abingdon Street (✆ **020/ 7222-2219**), one of only two surviving buildings from the medieval Palace of Westminster. It was constructed in 1365 as a place where Edward III could stash his treasure trove. The tower hosts an exhibition on the history of Parliament and makes for a great introduction to the inner workings of the British government. The video presentation on the top floor is especially informative. A touch-screen computer allows visitors to take a virtual tour of both houses of Parliament. The tower is open daily from 10am to 6pm April to September; 10am to 5pm in October; and 10am to 4pm November to March. Admission is £2.20 ($4.05) for adults, £1.70 ($3.15) for students and seniors, and £1.10 ($2.05) for children.

Westminster Palace, Old Palace Yard, SW1. House of Commons ✆ 020/7219-4272. House of Lords ✆ 020/7219-3107. www.parliament.uk. Free admission.

House of Lords open mid-Oct to Aug Mon–Wed from 2:30pm, Thurs from 11am, and sometimes Fri (check by phone). House of Commons mid-Oct to Aug Mon 2:30–10:30pm, Tues–Wed 11:30am–7:30pm, Thurs 11:30am–6pm, Fri not always open—call ahead. Both houses are open for tours (see above). Join line at St. Stephen's entrance. Tube: Westminster.

Kensington Palace 🐸 *Kids*   Once the residence of British monarchs, Kensington Palace hasn't been the official home of reigning kings since George II. William III and Mary II acquired it in 1689 as an escape from the damp royal rooms along the Thames. Since the end of the 18th century, the palace has housed various members of the royal family, and the State Apartments are open for tours.

It was here in 1837 that a young Victoria was awakened with the news that her uncle, William IV, had died and she was now the queen of England. You can view a collection of Victoriana, including some of her memorabilia. In the apartments of Queen Mary II is a striking 17th-century writing cabinet inlaid with tortoiseshell. Paintings from the Royal Collection line the walls. A rare 1750 lady's court dress and splendid examples of male court dress from the 18th century are on display in rooms adjacent to the State Apartments, as part of the Royal Ceremonial Dress Collection, which features royal costumes dating as far back as 200 years.

Kensington Palace was the London home of the late Princess Margaret, and is the current home of the duke and duchess of Kent. The palace was also the home of Diana, Princess of Wales, and her two sons. (Harry and William now live with their father at St. James's Palace.) The palace is probably best known for the millions of flowers placed in front of it during the days following Diana's death. The former apartment of the late Princess Margaret has opened to the public as an education center and an exhibition space for royal ceremonial dress.

Warning: You don't get to see the apartments where Princess Di lived or where both Di and Charles lived until they separated. Many visitors think they'll get to peek at these rooms and are disappointed. Charles and Di lived on the west side of the palace, still occupied today by minor royals.

The **Kensington Gardens** are open to the public for leisurely strolls through the manicured grounds and around the Round Pond. One of the most famous sights is the controversial Albert Memorial, a lasting tribute not only to Victoria's consort, but also to the questionable artistic taste of the Victorian era. There's a wonderful afternoon tea offered in The Orangery.

The Broad Walk, Kensington Gardens, W8. ⓒ 020/0751-5170. www.kensington-palace.org.uk. Admission £11 ($19) adults, £7 ($13) seniors/students, £6.50 ($12) children, £31 ($57) family. Mar–Oct daily 10am–7pm; Nov–Feb daily 10am–6pm. Tube: Queensway or Notting Hill Gate; High St. Kensington on south side.

National Gallery 𝔸𝔸𝔸   This stately neoclassical building contains an unrivaled collection of Western art spanning 7 centuries—from the late 13th to the early 20th—and covering every great European school. For sheer skill of display and arrangement, it surpasses its counterparts in Paris, New York, Madrid, and Amsterdam.

The largest part of the collection is devoted to the Italians, including the Sienese, Venetian, and Florentine masters. They're now housed in the Sainsbury Wing, which was designed by noted Philadelphia architects Robert Venturi and Denise Scott Brown and opened by Queen Elizabeth II in 1991. On display are such works as Leonardo's *Virgin of the Rocks;* Titian's *Bacchus and Ariadne;* Giorgione's *Adoration of the Magi;* and unforgettable canvases by Bellini, Veronese, Botticelli, and Tintoretto. Botticelli's *Venus and Mars* is eternally enchanting. The Sainsbury Wing is also used for large temporary exhibits.

Of the early Gothic works, the Wilton Diptych (French or English school, late 14th c.) is the rarest treasure; it depicts Richard II being introduced to the Madonna and Child by John the Baptist and the Saxon kings, Edmund and Edward the Confessor. Then there are the Spanish giants: El Greco's *Agony in the Garden* and portraits by Goya and Velázquez. The Flemish-Dutch school is represented by Brueghel, Jan van Eyck, Vermeer, Rubens, and de Hooch; the Rembrandts include two of his immortal self-portraits. None of van Eyck's art creates quite the stir that the **Arnolfini Portrait** does. You probably studied this painting from 1434 in your Art History 101 class. The stunning work depicts Giovanni di Nicolao Arnolfini and his wife (who is not pregnant as is often thought; she is merely holding up her full-skirted dress in the contemporary fashion). There's also an immense French Impressionist and post-Impressionist collection that includes works by Manet, Monet, Degas, Renoir, and Cézanne. Particularly charming is the peep-show cabinet by Hoogstraten in one of the Dutch rooms: It's like spying through a keyhole.

Guided tours of the National Gallery are offered daily at 11:30am and 2:30pm, with an extra tour at 6:30pm on Wednesday. A Gallery Guide Soundtrack is also available. A portable CD player provides audio information on paintings of your choice with the mere push of a button. Although this service is free, contributions are appreciated.

Insider's Tip: The National Gallery has a computer information center where you can design your own personal tour map for free. The computer room, located in the Micro Gallery, includes a dozen hands-on workstations. The online system lists 2,200 paintings and has background notes for each work. Using a touch-screen computer, you can design your own personalized tour by selecting a maximum of 10 paintings you would like to view. Once you have made your choices, you print a personal tour map with your selections.

North side of Trafalgar Sq., WC2. ✆ 020/7747-2885. www.nationalgallery.org.uk. Free admission. Thurs–Tues 10am–6pm; Wed 10am–9pm. Tube: Charing Cross or Leicester Sq.

National Portrait Gallery 🏛🏛   In a gallery of remarkable and unremarkable portraits (they're collected for their subjects rather than their artistic quality), a few paintings tower over the rest, including Sir Joshua Reynolds's first portrait of Samuel Johnson ("a man of most dreadful appearance"), Nicholas Hilliard's miniature of handsome Sir Walter Raleigh, a full-length of Elizabeth I, and a Holbein cartoon of Henry VIII. There's also a portrait of William Shakespeare (with a gold earring) by an unknown artist that bears the claim of being the "most authentic contemporary likeness" of its subject. One of the most famous pictures in the gallery is the group portrait of the Brontë sisters (Charlotte, Emily, and Anne) by their brother, Bramwell. An idealized portrait of Lord Byron by Thomas Phillips is also on display.

The galleries of Victorian and early-20th-century portraits were radically redesigned recently. The later 20th-century portraiture includes major works by such artists as Warhol and Hambling. Some of the more flamboyant personalities of the past 2 centuries are on show: T. S. Eliot; Disraeli; Macmillan; Sir Richard Burton (the explorer, not the actor); Elizabeth Taylor; and our two favorites, G. F. Watts's famous portrait of his great actress wife, Ellen Terry, and Vanessa Bell's portrait of her sister, Virginia Woolf. A portrait of the late Princess Diana is on the Royal Landing, and this painting seems to attract the most viewers.

In 2000, Queen Elizabeth opened the Ondaatje Wing of the gallery, increasing the gallery's exhibition space by over 50%. The most intriguing new space is the splendid Tudor Gallery, featuring portraits of Richard III and Henry II, Richard's conqueror in the Battle of Bosworth in 1485. There's also a portrait of Shakespeare that the gallery acquired in 1856. Rooms lead through centuries of English monarchs, with literary and artistic figures thrown in. A

Balcony Gallery taps into the cult of celebrity, displaying more recent figures whose fame has lasted longer than Warhol's 15 minutes. These include everybody from Mick Jagger to Joan Collins, and of course, the Baroness Thatcher.

The Gallery operates a cafe and art bookshop.

St. Martin's Place, WC2. ✆ **020/7306-0055**. www.npg.org.uk. Free admission; fee charged for certain temporary exhibitions. Mon–Wed 10am–6pm; Thurs–Fri 10am–9pm; Sat–Sun 10am–6pm. Tube: Charing Cross or Leicester Sq.

St. Paul's Cathedral ⭐⭐⭐ During World War II, newsreel footage reaching America showed St. Paul's Cathedral standing virtually alone among the rubble of the City, its dome lit by fires caused by bombings all around it. That the cathedral survived at all is a miracle, since it was badly hit twice during the early years of the bombardment of London during World War II. But St. Paul's is accustomed to calamity, having been burned down three times and destroyed by invading Norsemen. It was during the Great Fire of 1666 that the old St. Paul's was razed, making way for a new structure designed by Sir Christopher Wren and built between 1675 and 1710. The cathedral is architectural genius Wren's ultimate masterpiece.

The classical dome of St. Paul's dominates the City's square mile. The golden cross surmounting it is 110m (361 ft.) above the ground; the golden ball on which the cross rests measures 2m (6½ ft.) in diameter, though it looks like a marble from below. In the interior of the dome is the Whispering Gallery, an acoustic marvel in which the faintest whisper can be heard clearly on the opposite side. Sit on one side, have your traveling companions sit on the opposite side, and whisper away. You can climb to the top of the dome for a 360-degree view of London. From the Whispering Gallery a second steep climb leads to the **Stone Gallery,** opening onto a panoramic view of London. Another 153 steps take you to the **Inner Golden Gallery,** situated at the top of the inner dome. Here an even more panoramic view of London unfolds.

St. Paul's Churchyard, EC4. ✆ **020/7236-4128**. www.stpauls.co.uk. Cathedral and galleries £6 ($11) adults, £3 ($5.55) children 6–16. Guided tours £2.50 ($4.65) adults, £2 ($3.70) students and seniors, £1 ($1.85) children; recorded tours £3.50 ($6.50). Free for children 5 and under. Cathedral (excluding galleries) Mon–Sat 8:30am–4pm; galleries Mon–Sat 9:30am–4pm. No sightseeing Sun (services only). Tube: St. Paul's.

Tate Britain ⭐⭐⭐ Fronting the Thames near Vauxhall Bridge in Pimlico, the Tate looks like a smaller and more graceful relation of the British Museum. The most prestigious gallery in Britain, it houses the national collections, covering British art from the 16th century to the present day, as well as an array of international works. In the spring of 2000, the Tate moved its collection of 20th- and 21st-century art to the **Tate Modern** (see below). This split helped to open more display space at the Tate Britain, but the collection here is still much too large to be displayed all at once; so the works on view change from time to time.

The older works include some of the best of Gainsborough, Reynolds, Stubbs, Blake, and Constable. William Hogarth is well represented, particularly by his satirical *O the Roast Beef of Old England* (known as *The Gate of Calais*). You'll find the illustrations of William Blake, the incomparable mystical poet, including such works as *The Book of Job, The Divine Comedy,* and *Paradise Lost.* The collection of works by J. M. W. Turner is the Tate's largest collection of works by a single artist—Turner himself willed most of his paintings and watercolors to the nation.

Also on display are the works of many major 19th- and 20th-century painters, including Paul Nash, Matisse, Dalí, Modigliani, Munch, Bonnard, and Picasso. Truly remarkable are the several enormous abstract canvases by Mark Rothko, the group of paintings and sculptures by Giacometti, and the paintings by one of England's best-known modern artists, Francis Bacon. Sculptures by Henry Moore and Barbara Hepworth are also occasionally displayed.

Insider's Tip: After you've seen the grand art, don't hasten away. Drop in to the Tate Gallery Shop for some of the best art books and postcards in London. The gallery sells whimsical T-shirts with art masterpieces on them. Those ubiquitous Tate Gallery canvas bags seen all over London are sold here, as are the town's best art posters (all make great souvenirs). Invite your friends for tea at the Coffee Shop with its excellent cakes and pastries, or lunch at the Tate Gallery Restaurant (p. 104). You'll get to enjoy good food, Rex Whistler art, and the best and most reasonably priced wine list in London.

Millbank, SW1. ℂ 020/7887-8000. www.tate.org.uk. Free admission; special exhibitions sometimes incur a charge varying from £3–£8.50 ($5.55–$16). Daily 10:30am–5:40pm. Tube: Pimlico.

Tate Modern ☆☆☆ In a transformed Bankside Power Station in Southwark, this museum, which opened in 2000, draws some 2 million visitors a year to see the greatest collection of international 20th-century art in Britain. How would we rate the collection? At the same level of the Pompidou in Paris, with a slight edge over New York's Guggenheim. Of course, New York's Museum of Modern Art remains in a class of its own. Tate Modern is also viewer-friendly, with eye-level hangings. All the big painting stars are here, a whole galaxy ranging from Dalí to Duchamp, from Giacometti to Matisse and Mondrian, from Picasso and Pollock to Rothko and Warhol. The Modern is also a gallery of 21st-century art, displaying new and exciting art recently created.

You can cross the Millennium Bridge, a pedestrian-only walk from the steps of St. Paul's, over the Thames to the new gallery. Or else you can take the **Tate to Tate** boat (© 020/7887-8888), which takes art lovers on an 18-minute journey across the Thames from the Tate Britain to the Tate Modern, with a stop at the London Eye and the Saatchi Gallery. A day pass costs £4.50 ($8.35). Leaving from Millbank Pier, this catamaran is decorated by the trademark colorful dots of that *enfant terrible* artist, Damien Hirst.

The Tate Modern makes extensive use of glass for both its exterior and interior, offering panoramic views. Galleries are arranged over three levels and provide different kinds of space for display. Instead of exhibiting art chronologically and by school, the Tate Modern, in a radical break from tradition, takes a thematic approach. This allows displays to cut across movements.

Bankside, SE1. © 020/7887-8008. www.tate.org.uk. Free admission. Sun–Thurs 10am–6pm; Fri–Sat 10am–10pm. Tube: Southwark.

Tower Bridge 🏰🏰

This is one of the world's most celebrated landmarks, and possibly the most photographed and painted bridge on earth. (Presumably, this is the one the Arizona businessman thought he was getting, instead of the London Bridge.) Despite its medieval appearance, Tower Bridge was built in 1894.

In 1993, an exhibition opened inside the bridge to commemorate its century-old history; it takes you up the north tower to high-level walkways between the two towers with spectacular views of St. Paul's, the Tower of London, and the Houses of Parliament. You're then led down the south tower and into the bridge's original engine room, containing the Victorian boilers and steam engines that used to raise and lower the bridge for ships to pass. Exhibits in the bridge's towers use animatronic characters, video, and computers to illustrate the history of the bridge.

At Tower Bridge, SE1. © 020/7403-3761. www.towerbridge.org.uk. Tower Bridge Experience £5.50 ($10) adults; £3.30 ($6.10) children 5–15, students, and seniors; free for children 4 and under. Tower Bridge Experience open daily 9:30am–6pm (last entrance 5pm). Closed Christmas Eve and Christmas Day. Tube: Tower Hill or London Bridge.

Tower of London ★★★ *(Kids)*   This ancient fortress continues to pack in the crowds with its macabre associations with the legendary figures imprisoned and/or executed here. There are more spooks here per square foot than in any other building in the whole of haunted Britain. Headless bodies, bodiless heads, phantom soldiers, icy blasts, clanking chains—you name them, the Tower's got them. Centuries after the last head rolled on Tower Hill, a shivery atmosphere of impending doom still lingers over the Tower's mighty walls. Plan on spending a lot of time here.

The Tower is actually an intricately patterned compound of structures built throughout the ages for varying purposes, mostly as expressions of royal power. The oldest is the **White Tower,** begun by William the Conqueror in 1078 to keep London's native Saxon population in check. Later rulers added other towers, more walls, and fortified gates, until the buildings became like a small town within a city. Until the reign of James I (beginning in 1603), the Tower was also one of the royal residences. But above all, it was a prison for distinguished captives.

Every stone of the Tower tells a story—usually a gory one. In the **Bloody Tower,** according to Shakespeare, Richard III's henchmen murdered the two little princes (the sons of Edward IV). Richard knew that his position as king could not be secure as long as his nephews were alive. There seems no reasonable doubt that the little princes were murdered in the Tower on orders of their uncle. Attempts have been made by some historians to clear his name, but Richard remains the chief suspect, and his deed caused him to lose the "hearts of the people," according to the *Chronicles of London* at the time.

Sir Walter Raleigh spent 13 years in the Bloody Tower before his date with the executioner. On the walls of the **Beauchamp Tower,** you can still read the last messages scratched by despairing prisoners. Through **Traitors' Gate** passed such ill-fated, romantic figures as Robert Devereux, the second earl of Essex and a favorite of Elizabeth I. A plaque marks the eerie place at **Tower Green** where two wives of Henry VIII, Anne Boleyn and Catherine Howard, plus Sir Thomas More, and the 4-day queen, Lady Jane Grey, all lost their lives.

The Tower, besides being a royal palace, a fortress, and a prison, was also an armory, a treasury, a menagerie, and in 1675, an astronomical observatory. Reopened in 1999, the White Tower holds the **Armouries,** which date from the reign of Henry VIII, as well as a display of instruments of torture and execution that recall some of the most ghastly moments in the Tower's history. In the Jewel House, you'll find the tower's greatest attraction, the **Crown Jewels.** Here, some of the world's most precious stones are set into robes, swords, scepters, and crowns.

In the latest development here, the presumed prison cell of Sir Thomas More opened to the public in 2000. More left this cell in 1535 to face his executioner after he'd fallen out with King Henry VIII over the monarch's desire to divorce Catherine of Aragon, the first of his six wives. More is believed to have lived in the lower part of the Bell Tower, here in this whitewashed cell, during the last 14 months of his life, although some historians doubt this claim.

A **palace** inhabited by King Edward I in the late 1200s stands above Traitors' Gate. It's the only surviving medieval palace in Britain. Guides at the palace are dressed in period costumes, and reproductions of furniture and fittings, including Edward's throne, evoke the era, along with burning incense and candles.

Oh, yes—don't forget to look for the **ravens**. Six of them (plus two spares) are all registered as official Tower residents. According to a legend, the Tower of London will stand as long as those black, ominous birds remain, so to be on the safe side, one of the wings of each raven is clipped.

A 21st-century addition to the Tower complex is the New Armories restaurant, offering a range of snacks and meals, including the traditional cuppa for people about to lose their heads from too many attractions and not enough to eat.

One-hour guided tours of the entire compound are given by the Yeoman Warders (also known as "Beefeaters") every half-hour, starting at 9:30am, from the Middle Tower near the main entrance. The last guided walk starts about 3:30pm in summer, 2:30pm in winter—weather permitting, of course.

You can attend the nightly **Ceremony of the Keys,** the ceremonial locking-up of the Tower by the Yeoman Warders. For free tickets, write to the Ceremony of the Keys, Waterloo Block, Tower of London, London EC3N 4AB, and request a specific date, but also list alternate dates. At least 6 weeks' notice is required. Accompany all requests with a stamped, self-addressed envelope (British stamps only) or two International Reply Coupons. With ticket in hand, a Yeoman Warder will admit you at 9:35pm. Frankly, we think it's not worth the trouble you go through to see this rather cheesy ceremony, but we know some who disagree with us.

Tower Hill, EC3. ℂ **020/7709-0765.** www.hrp.org.uk/webcode/tower_home.asp. Admission £14 ($25) adults, £11 ($19) students and seniors, £9 ($17) children, free

---

Tips **Tower Tips**

You can spend the shortest time possible in the Tower's long lines if you buy your ticket in a kiosk at any Tube station before emerging above ground. Even so, choose a day other than Sunday—crowds are at their worst then—and arrive as early as you can in the morning.

---

for children under 5, £38 ($69) family ticket for 5 (but no more than 2 adults). Mar–Oct Mon–Sat 9am–6pm, Sun 10am–6pm; Nov–Feb Tues–Sat 9am–5pm, Sun–Mon 10am–5pm. Tube: Tower Hill.

Victoria and Albert Museum ⭐⭐⭐   The Victoria and Albert is the greatest decorative-arts museum in the world. It's also one of the liveliest and most imaginative museums in London—where else would you find the quintessential "little black dress" in the permanent collection?

The medieval holdings include such treasures as the early-English Gloucester Candlestick; the Byzantine Veroli Casket, with its ivory panels based on Greek plays; and the Syon Cope, a unique embroidery made in England in the early 14th century. An area devoted to Islamic art houses the Ardabil Carpet from 16th-century Persia.

The V&A boasts the largest collection of Renaissance sculpture outside Italy. A highlight of the 16th-century collection is the marble group *Neptune with Triton* by Bernini. The cartoons by Raphael, which were conceived as designs for tapestries for the Sistine Chapel, are owned by the queen and are on display here. A most unusual, huge, and impressive exhibit is the Cast Courts, life-size plaster models of ancient and medieval statuary and architecture.

The museum has the greatest collection of Indian art outside India, plus Chinese and Japanese galleries. In complete contrast are suites of English furniture, metalwork, and ceramics, and a superb collection of portrait miniatures, including the one Hans Holbein the Younger made of Anne of Cleves for the benefit of Henry VIII, who was again casting around for a suitable wife. The Dress Collection includes a collection of corsets through the ages that's sure to make you wince. There's also a remarkable collection of musical instruments.

V&A has recently opened 15 new galleries—the **British Galleries** ⭐⭐⭐—telling the story of British design from 1500 to 1900. No other museum in the world houses such a diverse collection of British design and decorative art. From Chippendale to Morris, all of the top British designers are featured in some 3,000 exhibits, ranging from the 5m (16-ft.) high Melville Bed (1697) with its luxurious wild-silk damask and red-velvet hangings, to 19th-century classics such as furniture by Charles Rennie Mackintosh. One of the most prized possessions is the "Great Bed of Ware," mentioned in Shakespeare's *Twelfth Night*. Also on exhibit is the wedding suite of James II. And don't miss the V&A's most bizarre gallery, Fakes and Forgeries.

Insider's Tip: In the winter of 2004, V&A opened a suite of five renovated painting galleries that were originally built in 1850. A trio of these galleries focus on British landscapes as seen through the eyes of Turner, Constable, and others. Constable's oil sketches were donated by his daughter, Isabel, in 1888. Another gallery showcases the bequest of Constantine Ionides, a Victorian collector, with masters such as Botticelli, Delacroix, Degas, Tintoretto, and Ingres. There's even a piano here designed by the famous Edward Burne-Jones, which once belonged to Ionides's brother.

Cromwell Rd., SW7. ℂ **020/7942-2000.** www.vam.ac.uk. Free admission. Daily 10am–5:45pm (Wed until 10pm). Tube: S. Kensington.

Westminster Abbey ⭐⭐⭐   With its identical square towers and superb archways, this early-English Gothic abbey is one of the greatest examples of ecclesiastical architecture on earth. But it's far more than that: It's the shrine of a nation, the symbol of everything Britain has stood for and stands for, and the place in which most of its rulers were crowned and where many lie buried.

Nearly every figure in English history has left his or her mark on Westminster Abbey. Edward the Confessor founded the Benedictine abbey in 1065 on this spot overlooking Parliament Square. The first English king crowned in the Abbey may have been Harold, in January 1066. The man who defeated him at the Battle of Hastings later that year, William the Conqueror, had the first recorded coronation in the Abbey on Christmas Day in that year. The coronation tradition has continued to the present day. The essentially early-English Gothic structure existing today owes more to Henry III's plans than to those of any other sovereign, although many architects, including Wren, have contributed to the Abbey.

Built on the site of the ancient Lady Chapel in the early 16th century, the **Henry VII Chapel** is one of the loveliest in Europe, with its fan vaulting, Knights of Bath banners, and Torrigiani-designed tomb for the king himself, near which hangs a 15th-century Vivarini painting, *Madonna and Child*. Also here, ironically buried in the same tomb, are Catholic Mary I and Protestant Elizabeth I (whose archrival, Mary Queen of Scots, is entombed on the other side of the Henry VII Chapel). In one end of the chapel, you can stand on Cromwell's memorial stone and view the **Royal Air Force Chapel** and its Battle of Britain memorial window, unveiled in 1947 to honor the Royal Air Force.

You can also visit the most hallowed spot in the abbey, the **shrine of Edward the Confessor** (canonized in the 12th c.). Near the tomb of Henry V is the Coronation Chair, made at the command of Edward I in 1300 to display the mystical Stone of Scone (which some think is the sacred stone mentioned in Genesis and known as Jacob's Pillar). Scottish kings were once crowned on the stone (it has since been returned to Scotland).

When you see a statue of the Bard, with one arm resting on a stack of books, you've arrived at **Poets' Corner.** Shakespeare himself is buried at Stratford-upon-Avon, but resting here are Chaucer, Samuel Johnson, Tennyson, Browning, Dickens, and many others have memorials; There's even an American, Henry Wadsworth Longfellow, as well as monuments to just about everybody: Milton, Keats, Shelley, Henry James, T. S. Eliot, George Eliot, and others. The most stylized monument is Sir Jacob Epstein's sculptured bust of William Blake. More recent tablets commemorate poet Dylan Thomas and Lord Laurence Olivier.

Statesmen and men of science—Disraeli, Newton, Charles Darwin—are also interred in the abbey or honored by monuments. Near the west door is the 1965 memorial to Sir Winston Churchill. In the vicinity of this memorial is the tomb of the **Unknown Warrior,** commemorating the British dead of World War I.

Although most of the Abbey's statuary commemorates notable figures of the past, 10 new statues were unveiled in July 1998. Placed in the Gothic niches above the West Front door, these statues honor 10 modern-day martyrs drawn from every continent and religious denomination. Designed by Tim Crawley and carved under his general direction from French Richemont limestone, the sculptures include Elizabeth of Russia, Janani Luwum, and Martin Luther King Jr., representatives of those who have sacrificed their lives for their beliefs.

Off the Cloisters, the **College Garden** is the oldest garden in England, under cultivation for more than 900 years. Established in the 11th century as the abbey's first infirmary garden, this was once a magnificent source of fruits, vegetables, and medicinal herbs. Five of the trees in the garden were planted in 1850 and they continue to thrive today. Surrounded by high walls, flowering trees dot the lawns, and park benches provide comfort where you can hardly hear the roar of passing traffic. The garden is only open Tuesday through Thursday, April through September from 10am to 6pm, and October through March from 10am to 4pm.

Insider's Tip: Far removed from the pomp and glory is the **Abbey Treasure Museum,** which displays a real bag of oddities in the undercroft—or crypt—part of the monastic buildings erected between 1066 and 1100. You'll find royal effigies that were used instead of the real corpses for lying-in-state ceremonies because they smelled better. You'll see the almost lifelike effigy of Admiral Nelson (his mistress arranged his hair) and even that of Edward III, his lip warped by the cerebral hemorrhage that felled him. Other oddities include Henry V's funeral armour, an unique corset from Elizabeth I's effigy and the Essex Ring that Elizabeth I gave to her favorite (Robert Devereux, the earl of Essex) when she was feeling good about him.

On Sundays, the Abbey is not open to visitors; the rest of the church is open unless a service is being conducted. For times of services, phone the **Chapter Office** (© **020/7222-5152**).

Broad Sanctuary, SW1. © **020/7654-4900.** www.westminster-abbey.org. Admission £7.50 ($14) adults; £5 ($9.25) for students, seniors, and children 11–18; free for children under 11; family ticket £15 ($28). Mon–Tues and Thurs–Fri 9:30am–3:45pm; Wed 9:30am–7pm, Sat 9am–1:45pm. Tube: Westminster or St. James's Park.

2 More Central London Attractions

CHURCHES & CATHEDRALS

Many of London's churches offer free lunchtime concerts; a full list is available from the London Tourist Board. It's customary to leave a small donation.

St. Etheldreda's The oldest Roman Catholic church in London, St. Etheldreda's stands on Ely Place, off Charterhouse Street, at Holborn Circus. Built in 1251, it was mentioned by the Bard in both Richard II and Richard III. A survivor of the Great Fire of 1666, the church and the area surrounding it were the property of the diocese of the city of Ely, in the days when many bishops had episcopal houses in London, as well as in the cathedral cities in which they held their sees. The property still has a private road, with impressive iron gates and a lodge for the gatekeeper. Six elected commissioners manage the church and area.

St. Etheldreda, whose name is sometimes shortened to St. Audrey, was a 7th-century king's daughter who left her husband and established an abbey on the Isle of Ely. St. Etheldreda's has a distinguished musical tradition, with the 11am mass on Sunday sung in Latin. Other masses are on Sunday at 9am, Monday through Friday at 8am and 1pm, and Saturday at 9:30am. Lunch, with a varied choice of hot and cold dishes, is served Monday through Friday from 11:30am to 2pm in the Pantry.

Ely Place, Holborn Circus, EC1. ℂ **020/7405-1061.** Free admission. Daily 7:30am–6:30pm; Sat mass 9:30am, Sun masses 9 and 11am, weekday masses Mon–Fri 8am and 1pm. Tube: Farringdon or Chancery Lane.

St. Martin-in-the-Fields 🉀   Designed by James Gibbs, a disciple of Christopher Wren, and completed in 1726, this classical church stands at the northeast corner of Trafalgar Square, opposite the National Gallery. Its spire, added in 1824, towers 56m (184 ft.) higher than Nelson's Column, which also rises on the square. The steeple became the model for many churches in colonial America. Since the first year of World War I (1914), the homeless have sought "soup and shelter" at St. Martin, a tradition that continues.

At one time, the crypt held the remains of Charles II (he's in Westminster Abbey now), who was christened here, giving St. Martin a claim as a royal parish church. His mistress, Nell Gwynne, and the highwayman Jack Sheppard are both interred here. The floors of the crypt are actually gravestones, and the walls date from the 1500s. The little restaurant, **Café in the Crypt,** is still called "Field's" by its devotees. Also in the crypt is **The London Brass Rubbing Centre** (ℂ **020/7930-9306**) with 88 exact copies of bronze portraits ready for use. Paper, rubbing materials, and instructions on how

---

Fun Fact **The Case of the Wobbling Bridge**

The first major new crossing over the Thames in a century, and the first ever dedicated to pedestrians, the £26 million ($48 million) **Millennium Bridge** had to be closed 3 days after it opened in the summer of 2000. Under certain conditions, the bridge designed by Sir Norman Foster wobbled. Nearly 100 dampers and shock absorbers were installed beneath the 315m (1,033-ft.) span, and independent consultants have pronounced the bridge stable for pedestrians. The bridge links Tate Modern on the South Bank of the river to St. Paul's Cathedral on the northern side.

to begin are furnished, and there's classical music for you to enjoy as you proceed. Fees to make the rubbings range from £3 to £16 ($5.55–$30), the latter price for the largest—a life-size Crusader knight. There's also a gift shop with brass-rubbing kits for children, budget-priced ready-made rubbings, Celtic jewelry, miniature brasses, and model knights. The center is open Monday through Saturday from 10am to 6pm and Sunday from noon to 6pm.

Insider's Tip: In back of the church is a crafts market. Also, lunchtime and evening concerts are staged Monday, Tuesday, and Friday at 1:05pm, and Thursday through Saturday at 7:30pm. Tickets cost £6.50 to £16 ($12–$29).

Trafalgar Sq., WC2. (*Ⓒ*) 020/7766-1100. Mon–Fri 7:45am–6pm; Sat–Sun 8:45am–7:30pm as long as no service is taking place. Concerts Mon, Tues, Fri 1pm and Thurs–Sat 7:30pm. Tube: Charing Cross.

Westminster Cathedral ☆ This spectacular brick-and-stone church (1903) is the headquarters of the Roman Catholic Church in Britain. Adorned in early-Byzantine style, it's massive: 108m (354 ft.) long and 47m (154 ft.) wide. One hundred different marbles compose the richly decorated interior, and eight marble columns support the nave. Eight yellow-marble columns hold up the huge canopy over the high altar. Mosaics emblazon the chapels and the vaulting of the sanctuary. If you take the elevator to the top of the 82m (269-ft.) campanile, you'll be rewarded with sweeping views that take in Buckingham Palace, Westminster Abbey, and St. Paul's Cathedral. There is a cafe serving light snacks and soft drinks from 9am to 5pm and a gift shop open from 9:30am to 5:15pm.

Ashley Place, SW1. (*Ⓒ*) 020/7798-9055. www.westminstercathedral.org.uk. Cathedral free. Audio tours £2.50 ($4.65). Tower £3 ($5.55). Cathedral services Mon–Fri 7am–7pm; Sat 8am–6pm; Sun 8am–7pm. Tower May–Nov daily 9am–12:30pm and 1–5pm; Dec–Apr Thurs–Sun 9am–5pm. Tube: Victoria.

HISTORIC BUILDINGS

Banqueting House ☆☆ The feasting chamber in Whitehall Palace is probably the most sumptuous dining hall on earth. (Unfortunately, you can't dine here unless you're a visiting head of state.) Designed by Inigo Jones and decorated with, among other things, original ceiling paintings by Rubens, the hall is dazzling enough to make you forget food altogether. Among the historic events that took place here were the beheading of King Charles I, who stepped through a window onto the scaffold outside, and the restoration ceremony of Charles II, marking the return of monarchy after Cromwell's brief Puritan Commonwealth.

Whitehall Palace, Horse Guards Ave., SW1. © 0870/7515-178. www.hrp.org.uk. Admission £4 ($7.40) adults, £3 ($5.55) seniors and students, £2.60 ($4.85) children. Mon–Sat 10am–5pm (last admission 4:30pm). Tube: Westminster or Embankment.

Cabinet War Rooms 🐾 Visitors today can see the **Cabinet War Rooms,** the bombproof bunker suite of rooms, just as they were when abandoned by Winston Churchill and the British government at the end of World War II. You can see the Map Room with its huge wall maps, the Atlantic map a mass of pinholes (each hole represents at least one convoy). Next door is Churchill's bedroom-cum-office, which has a bed and a desk with two BBC microphones on it for his famous speech broadcasts that stirred the nation. In 2003, nine more underground Cabinet War Rooms were restored and opened to the public, including the Chiefs of Staff map room, Churchill's kitchen and dining room, Sir Winston's private detectives' room, and Mrs. Churchill's bedroom. There's everything here from a pencil cartoon of Hitler to a mousetrap in the kitchen to the original chamber pots under the beds (they had no flush toilets).

The **Transatlantic Telephone Room,** its full title, is little more than a broom closet, but it housed the Bell Telephone Company's special scrambler phone, called *Sigsaly,* and it was where Churchill conferred with Roosevelt. Visitors are provided with a step-by-step personal sound guide, providing a detailed account of each room's function and history.

Clive Steps, at end of King Charles St. (off Whitehall near Big Ben), SW1. © 020/7930-6961. www.iwm.org.uk. Admission £7.50 ($14) adults, £6 ($11) seniors and students, free for children 16 and under. Apr–Sept daily 9:30am–6pm (last admission at 5:15pm); Oct–Mar daily 10am–6pm. Tube: Westminster or St. James's.

City Hall On the South Bank of the Thames, adjacent to Tower Bridge, this is the new home of the mayor of London and the London Assembly. Her Majesty dedicated the gleaming, egg-shaped building—a 10-story steel-and-glass structure—in July 2002. Foster and Partners, one of Britain's leading architectural firms, designed the building. The new home of the city government has become London's latest—and some say, most controversial—landmark. Half of City Hall is open to the public. The views from the rooftop gallery are worth the trek over to the South Bank. An exhibition space displays changing cultural exhibits, and there is a cafe on-site.

The Queen's Walk, SE1. © 020/7983-4100. www.london.gov.uk. Free admission. Visitors Center daily 9:30am–5pm; cafe daily 8am–8pm. Tube: London Bridge.

Horse Guards 🐾 North of Downing Street, on the west side of Whitehall, is the building of the Horse Guards, which is the headquarters of the British Army. The building was designed by William Kent, chief architect to George II. The real draw here is the Horse Guards themselves: the Household Cavalry Mounted Regiment, a combination of the oldest and most senior regiments in the British Army—the Life Guards and the Blues and Royals. In theory, their duty is to protect the sovereign. Life Guards wear red tunics and white plumes, and Blues and Royals are attired in blue tunics with red plumes. Two much-photographed mounted members of the Household Cavalry keep watch daily from 10am to 4pm. The mounted sentries change duty every hour as a benefit to the horses. Foot sentries change every 2 hours. The chief guard rather grandly inspects the troops here daily at 4pm. The guard, with flair and fanfare, dismounts at 5pm.

We prefer the **changing of the guards** here to the more famous ceremony at Buckingham Palace. Beginning around 11am Monday through Saturday and 10am on Sunday, a new guard leaves the Hyde Park Barracks on horseback, rides down Pall Mall, and arrives at the Horse Guards building, all in about 30 minutes. The old guard then returns to the barracks.

If you pass through the arch at Horse Guards, you'll find yourself at the **Horse Guards Parade,** which opens onto St. James's Park. This spacious court provides the best view of the various architectural styles that make up Whitehall. Regrettably, the parade ground itself is now a parking lot.

The military pageant—the most famous in Britain—known as **Trooping the Colour,** celebrating the queen's birthday, takes place in June at the Horse Guards Parade (see "London Calendar of Events," p. 6). The "Colour" refers to the flag of the regiment. For devotees of pomp and circumstance, "Beating the Retreat" is staged here 3 or 4 evenings a week during the first 2 weeks of June. It's only a dress rehearsal, though, for Trooping the Colour.

Whitehall, SW1. © 020/7414-2479. www.army.mod.uk. Free admission. Tube: Charing Cross, Westminster, or Embankment.

Lincoln's Inn 🏛🏛 Lincoln's Inn is the oldest of the four Inns of Court. Between the City and the West End, Lincoln's Inn comprises 4.4 hectares (11 acres), including lawns, squares, gardens, a 17th-century chapel (open Mon–Fri noon–2pm), a library, and two halls. One of these, Old Hall, dates from 1490 and has remained almost unaltered, with its linenfold paneling, stained glass, and wooden screen by Inigo Jones. It was once the home of Sir Thomas More, and it was where barristers met, ate, and debated 150 years before the *Mayflower* sailed on its epic voyage. Old Hall is the scene for the opening chapter of Charles Dickens's *Bleak House*. The other hall, Great Hall, remains one of the finest Tudor Revival buildings in London and was opened by Queen Victoria in 1843. It's now the center of the inn and is used for the formal ceremony of calling students to the bar.

Lincoln's Inn Fields, WC2. ✆ 020/7405-1393. www.lincolnsinn.org.uk. Free admission to grounds. Mon–Fri 10am–4pm. Tube: Holborn or Chancery Lane.

Old Bailey   This courthouse replaced the infamous Newgate Prison, once the scene of hangings and other forms of "public entertainment." It's affectionately known as the "Old Bailey" after a street that runs nearby. It's fascinating to watch the bewigged barristers presenting their cases to the high-court judges. Entry is strictly on a first-arrival basis, and guests line up outside; security will then direct you to one of the rooms where cases are being tried. It's impossible to predict how long a line you might face. If there's a London equivalent of the O. J. Simpson trial, forget about it—you'll never get in. On a day with trials attracting little attention, you can often enter after only 15 minutes or so. You never know until you show up. The best time to line up is 10am. You enter courts 1 to 4, 17, and 18 from Newgate Street, and the others from Old Bailey Street.

Newgate St., EC4. To get here from the Temple, travel east on Fleet St., which becomes Ludgate Hill; cross Ludgate Circus and turn left at the Old Bailey, a domed structure with the figure of *Justice* atop it. ✆ 020/7248-3277. Free admission. Court in session Mon–Fri 10:30am–1pm and 2–4pm. Children under 14 not admitted; children 14–16 must be accompanied by a responsible adult. No cameras, tape recorders, or cellphones (and there are no coat-checking facilities). Tube: St. Paul's.

LITERARY & MUSICAL LANDMARKS

Besides the homes of the authors and composers listed below, you can also visit Apsley House, the former mansion of the Duke of Wellington (p. 141).

Carlyle's House   From 1834 to 1881, Thomas Carlyle, author of *The French Revolution,* and Jane Baillie Welsh Carlyle, his noted letter-writing wife, resided in this modest 1708 terraced house. Furnished essentially as it was in Carlyle's day, the house is located about half a block from the Thames, near the Chelsea Embankment, along

King's Road. It was described by his wife as being "of most antique physiognomy, quite to our humour; all wainscoted, carved, and queer-looking, roomy, substantial, commodious, with closets to satisfy any Bluebeard." The second floor contains Mrs. Carlyle's drawing room, but the most interesting chamber is the not-so-soundproof "soundproof" study in the skylit attic. Filled with Carlyle memorabilia—his books, a letter from Disraeli, personal effects, a writing chair, even his death mask—this is where the author did his work.

24 Cheyne Row, SW3. ✆ 020/7352-7087. Admission £3.80 ($7) adults, £1.80 ($3.33) children 5–16, free for children 4 and under. Apr–Oct Wed–Sun 11am–5pm. Closed Nov–Mar. Tube: Sloane Sq.

Dickens House   Here in Bloomsbury stands the simple abode in which Charles Dickens wrote *Oliver Twist* and finished *The Pickwick Papers* (his American readers actually waited at the dock for the ship that brought in each new installment). The place is almost a shrine: It contains his study, manuscripts, and personal relics, as well as reconstructed interiors. During Christmas week (including Christmas Day), the museum is decorated in the style of Dickens's first Christmas there. During Christmas, the raised admission prices of £10 ($19) for adults and £5 ($9.25) for children include hot mince pies and a few glasses of "Smoking Bishop," Dickens's favorite hot punch, as well as a copy of the museum's guidebooks.

48 Doughty St., WC1. ✆ 020/7405-2127. www.dickensmuseum.com. Admission £5 ($9.25) adults, £4 ($7.40) students, £1 ($1.85) children, £14 ($26) families. Mon–Sat 10am–5pm; Sun 11am–5pm. Tube: Russell Sq.

Samuel Johnson's House 𝕲𝕲   Dr. Johnson and his copyists compiled his famous dictionary in this Queen Anne house, where the lexicographer, poet, essayist, and fiction writer lived from 1748 to 1759. Although Johnson also lived at Staple Inn in Holborn and at a number of other places, the Gough Square house is the only one of his residences remaining in modern London. The 17th-century building has been painstakingly restored, and it's well worth a visit.

After you're done touring the house, you might want to stop in at **Ye Olde Cheshire Cheese,** Wine Office Court, 145 Fleet St. (✆ 020/ 7353-6170), Johnson's favorite locale. He must have had some lean nights at the pub because by the time he had compiled his dictionary, he'd already spent his advance of 1,500 guineas. G. K. Chesterton, author of *What's Wrong with the World* (1910) and *The Superstition of Divorce* (1920), was also a familiar patron at the pub.

17 Gough Sq., EC4. Walk up New Bridge St. and turn left onto Fleet; Gough Sq. is tiny and hidden, north of Fleet St. ✆ 020/7353-3745. www.drjh.dircon.co.uk.

Admission £4 ($7.40) adults, £3 ($5.55) students and seniors, £1 ($1.85) children, free for children 10 and under. Oct–Apr Mon–Sat 11am–4:45pm; May–Sept Mon–Sat 11am–5:30pm. Tube: Blackfriars or Chancery Lane.

MUSEUMS & GALLERIES

Apsley House, The Wellington Museum ✿   This was the mansion of the Duke of Wellington, the "Iron Duke," one of Britain's greatest generals, who defeated Napoleon at Waterloo. Later, for a short period while he was prime minister, the duke had to have iron shutters fitted to his windows to protect him from a mob outraged by his autocratic opposition to reform. (His unpopularity soon passed, however.)

The house is crammed with art treasures, including three original Velázquez paintings, and military mementos that include the duke's medals and battlefield orders. Apsley House also holds some of the finest silver and porcelain pieces in Europe, displayed in the Plate and China Room. Grateful to Wellington for saving their thrones, European monarchs showered him with treasures. The collection includes a Sèvres Egyptian service that was intended as a divorce present from Napoleon to Josephine (but she refused it); Louis XVIII eventually presented it to Wellington. Another treasure, the Portuguese Silver Service, created between 1812 and 1816, has been hailed as the single greatest artifact of Portuguese neoclassical silver.

149 Piccadilly, Hyde Park Corner, SW1. ✆ 020/7499-5676. www.apsleyhouse.org. uk. Admission £4.50 ($8.35) adults, £3 ($5.55) seniors, free for children under 18. Tues–Sun 11am–5pm. Tube: Hyde Park Corner.

British Library ✿✿   In December 1996, one of the world's great libraries began moving its collection of some 12 million books, manuscripts, and other items from the British Museum to its very own home in St. Pancras. In the new building, you get modernistic beauty rather than the fading glamour and the ghosts of Karl Marx, Thackeray, and Virginia Woolf of the old library at the British Museum. You are also likely to get the book you want within an hour instead of 3 days. Academics, students, writers, and bookworms from the world over come here. On a recent visit, we sat next to a student researching the history of pubs.

The bright, roomy interior is far more inviting than the rather dull redbrick exterior suggests (the writer Alain de Botton likened the exterior to a supermarket). Still, Colin St. John Wilson, the architect, says he has been delighted by the positive response to his building. The most spectacular room is the Humanities Reading Room, constructed on three levels with daylight filtered through the ceiling.

Value   A Money-Saving Pass

The **London Pass** provides admission to 60 attractions in and around London, £5 ($9.25) worth of phone calls, "timed" admission at some attractions (bypassing the queues), plus free travel on public transport (buses, Tubes, and trains) and a pocket guidebook. It costs £23 ($43) for 1 day, £44 ($81) for 3 days, or £72 ($133) for 6 days (children pay £15/$28, £29/$54, or £41/$76), and includes admission to St. Paul's Cathedral, HMS *Belfast,* the Jewish Museum, and the Thames Barrier Visitor Centre—and many other attractions. Visit the website at **www.london pass.com**. Purchase the pass before you go because passes purchased in London do not include free transportation.

The fascinating collection includes such items of historic and literary interest as two of the four surviving copies of the *Magna Carta* (1215), a Gutenberg Bible, Nelson's last letter to Lady Hamilton, and the journals of Captain Cook. Almost every major author—Dickens, Jane Austen, Charlotte Brontë, Keats, and hundreds of others—is represented in the section devoted to English literature. Beneath Roubiliac's 1758 statue of Shakespeare stands a case of documents relating to the Bard, including a mortgage bearing his signature and a copy of the First Folio of 1623. There's also an unrivaled collection of stamps and stamp-related items.

Visitors can view the *Diamond Sutra,* dating from 868 and said to be the oldest surviving printed book. Using headphones set around the room, you can hear thrilling audio snippets such as James Joyce reading a passage from *Finnegans Wake.* Curiosities include the earliest known tape of a birdcall, dating from 1889. Particularly intriguing is an exhibition called "Turning the Pages," where you can, for example, electronically read a complete Leonardo da Vinci notebook by putting your hands on a special computer screen that flips from one page to another. An entire day spent here will only scratch the surface.

Walking tours of the library cost £6 ($11) for adults and £4.50 ($8.35) for seniors, students, and children. They are conducted Monday, Wednesday, and Friday at 3pm, and Saturday at 10:30am and 3pm. Library tours that include a visit to one of the reading rooms take place on Sundays and bank holidays at 11:30am and

3pm; £7 ($13) adults, £5.50 ($10) for seniors and students. Reservations can be made up to 2 weeks in advance.

96 Euston Rd., NW1. ✆ 020/7412-7000. www.bl.uk. Free admission. Mon, Wed, Thurs, Fri 9:30am–6pm; Tues 9:30am–8pm; Sat 9:30am–5pm; Sun and bank holidays 11am–5pm. Tube: King's Cross/St. Pancras, or Euston.

Dalí Universe ⋒ *Finds* Next to the "London Eye," this exhibition is devoted to the remarkable Spanish artist Salvador Dalí (1904–89), and is one of London's newest attractions. Featuring more than 500 works of art, including the Mae West Lips sofa, the exhibitions are divided into a trio of themed areas: Sensuality and Femininity, Religion and Mythology, and Dreams and Fantasy. Showcased are important Dalí sculptures, rare graphics, watercolors, and even furnishings and jewelry. You can feast on such surreal works as Dalí's monumental oil painting for the Hitchcock movie *Spellbound*, or view a series of original watercolors and collages including the mystical *Tarot Cards*. You can also see the world's largest collection of rare Dalí graphics, illustrating themes from literature. See the "London's Attractions" map.

County Hall, Riverside Bldg., South Bank, SE1. ✆ 020/7620-2720. www.dali universe.com. Admission £8.50 ($16) adults, £7 ($13) students and seniors, £5.50 ($10) ages 5–16, and £23 ($43) family ticket. Daily 10am–5:30pm. Tube: Waterloo.

Gilbert Collection ⋒⋒⋒ *Finds* In 2000, Somerset House became the permanent home for the Gilbert Collection of decorative arts, one of the most important bequests ever made to England. Sir Arthur Gilbert made his gift of gold, silver, mosaics, and gold snuffboxes to the nation in 1996, at which time the value was estimated at £75 million ($139 million). The collection of some 800 objects in three fields (gold and silver, mosaics, and gold snuffboxes) is among the most distinguished in the world. The silver collection here is arguably better than the one at the V&A. The array of mosaics is among the most comprehensive ever gathered, with Roman and Florentine examples dating from the 16th to the 19th centuries. The gold and silver collection has exceptional breadth, ranging from the 15th to the 19th centuries, spanning India to South America. It is strong in masterpieces of great 18th-century silversmiths, such as Paul de Lamerie. Such exhibits as the Maharajah pieces, the "Gold Crown," and Catherine the Great's Royal Gates are fabulous. The gallery also displays one of the most representative collections of gold snuffboxes in the world, with some 200 examples. Some of the snuffboxes were owned by Louis XV, Frederick the Great, and Napoleon. The Gilbert Collection is only one of three major museums and galleries at Somerset House. See the Hermitage Rooms below.

Somerset House, the Strand WC2. ✆ **020/7240-9400**. www.gilbert-collection.org. uk. Admission £5 ($9.25) adults, free for full-time students under 18. Daily 10am–6pm. Tube: Temple, Covent Garden, Charing Cross, or Embankment.

Guildhall Art Gallery ☆ In 1999, Queen Elizabeth opened a new £70 million ($130 million) gallery in the City, a continuation of an original gallery that was launched in 1886 but burned down in a severe air raid in May 1941. Many famous and much-loved pictures, which for years were known only through temporary exhibitions and reproductions, are again available for the public to see in a permanent setting. The new gallery can display only 250 of the 4,000 treasures it owns. The art ranges from classical to modern. A curiosity is the huge double-height wall built to accommodate Britain's largest independent oil painting, John Singleton Copley's *The Defeat of the Floating Batteries at Gibraltar, September 1782.* The Corporation of London in the City owns these works and has been collecting them since the 17th century. The most popular art is in the Victorian collection, including such well-known favorites as Millais's *My First Sermon* and *My Second Sermon,* and Landseer's *The First Leap.* There is also a landscape of Salisbury Cathedral by John Constable. Since World War II, all paintings acquired by the gallery concentrate on London subjects.

Guildhall Yard, EC2 2P2EJ. ✆ **020/7332-3700**. www.guildhall-art-gallery.org.uk. Admission £2.50 ($4.65) adults, £1 ($1.85) seniors and students. Free for children under 16. Free Fri and after 3:30pm on every other day. Mon–Sat 10am–5pm; Sun noon–4pm. Tube: Bank, St. Paul's, Mansion House, or Moorgate.

Hermitage Rooms at Somerset House ☆☆☆ This is a virtual branch of St. Petersburg's State Hermitage Museum, which owns a great deal of the treasure trove left over from the Czars, including possessions of art-collecting Catherine the Great. Now you don't have to go to Russia to see some of Europe's great treasures.

The rotating exhibitions will change, but you'll get to see such Czarist treasures as medals, jewelry, portraits, porcelain, clocks, and furniture. A rotating "visiting masterpiece" overshadows all the other collections. Some items that amused us on our first visit (and you are likely to see similar novelties) were a wig made entirely out of silver thread for Catherine the Great; a Wedgwood "Green Frog" table service; and two very rare Chinese silver filigree toilet sets. The rooms themselves have been designed in the style of the Winter

Palace at St. Petersburg. *Note:* Because this exhibit attracts so much interest, tickets should be purchased in advance. Tickets are available from Ticketmaster at ✆ **020/7413-3398** (24 hr.). You can book online at **www.ticketmaster.co.uk**. The other museum at Somerset House, the Gilbert Collection, was previewed above.

Somerset House, the Strand, WC2. ✆ **020/7845-4600**. www.hermitagerooms.com. Admission £5 ($9.25) adults, £4 ($7.40), free for students under 16 and seniors. Daily 10am–6pm. Tube: Temple, Covent Garden, Charing Cross, or Holborn.

Imperial War Museum ✪   One of the few major sights south of the Thames, this museum occupies 1 city block the size of an army barracks, greeting you with 38cm (15 in.) guns from the battleships *Resolution* and *Ramillies.* The large domed building, constructed in 1815, was the former Bethlehem Royal Hospital for the insane, known as "Bedlam."

A wide range of weapons and equipment is on display, along with models, decorations, uniforms, posters, photographs, and paintings. You can see a Mark V tank, a Battle of Britain Spitfire, and a German one-man submarine, as well as a rifle carried by Lawrence of Arabia. In the Documents Room, you can view the self-styled "political testament" that Hitler dictated in the chancellery bunker in the closing days of World War II, witnessed by henchmen Joseph Goebbels and Martin Bormann, as well as the famous "peace in our time" agreement that Neville Chamberlain brought back from Munich in 1938. (Of his signing the agreement, Hitler later said, "[Chamberlain] was a nice old man, so I decided to give him my autograph.") It's a world of espionage and clandestine warfare in the major permanent exhibit known as the "Secret War Exhibition," where you can discover the truth behind the image of James Bond— and find out why the real secret war is even stranger and more fascinating than fiction. Displays include many items never before seen in public: coded messages, forged documents, secret wirelesses, and equipment used by spies from World War I to the present day.

Public film shows take place on weekends at 4pm and on certain weekdays during school holidays and on public holidays.

Supported by a £12.6 million ($23.3 million) grant from the Heritage Lottery Fund, a permanent Holocaust exhibition now occupies two floors. Through original artifacts, documents, film, and photographs, some lent to the museum by former concentration camps in Germany and Poland, the display poignantly relates the story of Nazi Germany and the persecution of the Jews. In addition, the exhibition brings attention to the persecution of other groups under Hitler's regime, including Poles, Soviet prisoners of war, people with disabilities, and homosexuals.

Another new exhibition, called "Crimes Against Humanity," explores the theme of genocide.

Lambeth Rd., SE1. ✆ **020/7416-5000** or 020/7416-5320 (info line). www.iwm. org.uk. Free admission. Daily 10am–6pm. Closed Dec 24–26. Tube: Baker Line to Lambeth North or Elephant and Castle.

Jewish Museum This museum tells the story of Jewish life in Britain. Arriving at the time of the Norman Conquest, Jews survived in England until King Edward I forced them out in 1290. From that time, no Jews (or at least no known Jews) lived in Britain until a small community returned in 1656 during the reign of Elizabeth I. The museum has recently been awarded designated status by the Museums and Galleries Commission for its outstanding collection of Jewish ceremonial art. On display are silver Torah bells made in London, and two loving cups presented by the Spanish and Portuguese Synagogue to the lord mayor in the 18th century. The museum's Ceremonial Art Gallery contains a beautiful 16th-century Venetian ark, one of the oldest preserved in the world. An old English lord bought it from a furniture dealer without knowing what it was, and for years his maid used it as a wardrobe until someone discovered its true identity. The museum also sponsors **walking tours of Jewish London.**

The Jewish Museum has another location in Finchley, which focuses attention on Jewish immigration and settlement in London. On display there are reconstructions of East End tailoring and furniture workshops. Holocaust education is also a fundamental feature of this museum. The Finchley branch is open Monday through Thursday 10:30am to 5pm, and Sunday from 10:30am to 4:30pm; admission is £2 ($3.70) adults, £1 ($1.85) seniors and students. Children are admitted free. For further information, call ✆ **020/8349-1143.**

129–131 Albert St., Camden Town, NW1. ✆ **020/7284-1997.** www.jewish museum.org.uk. Main branch admission £3.50 ($6.50) adults, £2.50 ($4.65) seniors, £1.50 ($2.80) children. Main branch: Sun 10am–5pm; Mon–Thurs 10am–4pm. Closed Fri, Sat, bank holidays, and Jewish festivals. Tube: Camden Town.

Madame Tussaud's *Overrated* *Kids* Madame Tussaud's is not so much a wax museum as an enclosed amusement park. A weird, moving, sometimes terrifying (to children) collage of exhibitions, panoramas, and stage settings, it manages to be most things to most people, most of the time.

Madame Tussaud attended the court of Versailles and learned her craft in France. She personally took the death masks from the guillotined heads of Louis XVI and Marie Antoinette (which you'll find among the exhibits). She moved her original museum from Paris to England in 1802. Her exhibition has been imitated in every part of the world, but never with the realism and imagination on hand here. Madame herself molded the features of Benjamin Franklin, whom she met in Paris. All the rest—from George Washington to John F. Kennedy, Mary Queen of Scots to Sylvester Stallone—have been subjects for the same painstaking (and often breathtaking) replication.

In the well-known Chamber of Horrors—a kind of underground dungeon—are all kinds of instruments of death, along with figures of their victims. The shadowy presence of Jack the Ripper lurks in the gloom as you walk through a Victorian London street. Present-day criminals are portrayed within the confines of prison. The latest attraction to open here is "The Spirit of London," a musical ride that depicts 400 years of London's history, using special effects that include audio-animatronic figures that move and speak. Visitors take "time-taxis" that allow them to see and hear "Shakespeare" as he writes and speaks lines, be received by "Queen Elizabeth I," and feel and smell the Great Fire of 1666 that destroyed London.

We've seen these changing exhibitions so many times over the years that we feel they're a bit cheesy, but we still remember the first time we were taken here as a kid. We thought it fascinating back then.

Insider's Tip: To avoid the long lines, sometimes more than an hour in summer, call the waxworks in advance and reserve a ticket for fast pickup at the entrance. If you don't want to bother with that, be aggressive and form a group of nine people waiting in the queue. A group of nine or more can go in almost at once through the "group door." Otherwise, go when the gallery first opens or late in the afternoon when crowds have thinned.

Marylebone Rd., NW1. ℂ **0870/400-3000.** www.madame-tussauds.com. Admission £18 ($33) adults, £15 ($28) seniors, £14 ($26) children under 16. *Note:* Admission prices can go higher at certain peak periods Sat–Sun. Mon–Fri 9:30am–5:30pm; Sat–Sun 9am–6pm. Tube: Baker St.

Museum of London 𝄃𝄃   In London's Barbican district, near St. Paul's Cathedral and overlooking the city's Roman and medieval walls, this museum traces the history of London from prehistoric times to the 20th century through archaeological finds; paintings and prints; social, industrial, and historic artifacts; and costumes, maps, and models. Exhibits are arranged so that you can begin and end your chronological stroll through 250,000 years at the main entrance to the museum. The museum's pièce de résistance is the Lord Mayor's Coach, a gilt-and-scarlet fairy-tale coach built in 1757 and weighing in at 3 tons. You can also see the Great Fire of London in living color and sound in an audiovisual presentation; the death mask of Oliver Cromwell; cell doors from Newgate Prison, made famous by Charles Dickens; and most amazing of all, a shop counter showing pre–World War II prices. Early in 2002, the museum unveiled its latest permanent gallery, occupying an entire floor. Called the World City Gallery, the exhibit examines life in London between 1789 and 1914, the beginning of World War I. Some 2,000 objects are on view. See the "London's Attractions" map on p. 116.

150 London Wall, EC2. ℂ 020/7600-3699. www.museumoflondon.org.uk. Free admission. Mon–Sat 10am–5:50pm; Sun noon–5:50pm. Tube: St. Paul's or Barbican.

National Army Museum 🏛 *Kids*   The National Army Museum occupies a building adjoining the Royal Hospital, a home for retired soldiers. Whereas the Imperial War Museum is concerned with wars of the 20th century, the National Army Museum tells the colorful story of British armies from 1485 on. Here you'll find uniforms worn by British soldiers in every corner of the world, plus weapons and other gear, flags, and medals. Even the skeleton of Napoleon's favorite charger is here. Also on display are Florence Nightingale's jewelry, the telephone switchboard from Hitler's headquarters (captured in 1945), and Orders and Medals of HRH the Duke of Windsor. A more recent gallery, "The Rise of the Redcoats," contains exhibitions detailing the life of the British soldier from 1485 to 1793. Included in the exhibit are displays on the English Civil War and the American War of Independence.

Royal Hospital Rd., SW3. ℂ 020/7730-0717. www.national-army-museum.ac.uk. Free admission. Daily 10am–5:30pm. Closed Good Friday, 1st Mon in May, and Dec 24–26. Tube: Sloane Sq.

Natural History Museum 🏛🏛 *Kids*   This is the home of the national collections of living and fossil plants, animals, and minerals, with many magnificent specimens on display. The zoological displays are quite wonderful—not up to the level of the Smithsonian in Washington, D.C., but still definitely worthwhile. The Mineral Gallery displays marvelous examples of crystals and gemstones. Visit the Meteorite Pavilion, which exhibits fragments of rocks that have crashed into the earth, some from the farthest reaches of the galaxy. What attracts the most attention is the dinosaur exhibit, displaying 14 complete skeletons. The center of the show depicts a trio of full-size robotic Deinonychus enjoying a freshly killed Tenontosaurus. "Earth Galleries" is an exhibition outlining humankind's relationship with planet Earth. Here, in the exhibition "Earth Today and Tomorrow," visitors are invited to explore the planet's dramatic history from the big bang to its inevitable death. The latest development here is the new Darwin Centre, dedicated to the great naturalist Charles Darwin, with final completion scheduled for 2007, although there is much on view now. You're given an insider look at the storage facilities—including 22 million preserved specimens—and the laboratories of the museum. Fourteen behind-the-scenes free tours (ages 10 and up only) are given daily; you should book immediately upon entering the museum if you're interested.

Cromwell Rd., SW7. ☏ 020/7942-5000. www.nhm.ac.uk. Free admission. Mon–Sat 10am–5:50pm; Sun 11am–5:50pm. Tube: S. Kensington.

Percival David Foundation of Chinese Art ☏ This foundation displays the greatest collection of Chinese ceramics outside China. Approximately 1,700 ceramic objects reflect Chinese court taste from the 10th to 18th centuries and include many pieces of exceptional beauty. An extraordinary collection of stoneware from the Song (960–1279) and Yuan (1279–1368) dynasties includes examples of rare Ru and Guan wares. Among the justifiably famous blue-and-white porcelains are two unique temple vases, dated by inscription to A.D. 1351. A wide variety of polychrome wares is also represented; they include examples of the delicate doucai wares from the Chenghua period (1465–87), as well as a remarkable group of 18th-century porcelains.

53 Gordon Sq., WC1. ☏ 020/7387-3909. www.pdfmuseum.org.uk. Free admission; donations encouraged. £4 ($7.40) per person for a guided tour of 10–20 people. Admission to the library must be arranged with the curator ahead of time. There is a charge for use of the library. Mon–Fri 10:30am–5pm. Tube: Russell Sq. or Euston Sq.

The Queen's Gallery ☏☏ The refurbished gallery at Buckingham Palace reopened to the public in 2002 in time for the Golden Jubilee celebration of Queen Elizabeth II. Visitors going through the Doric portico entrance will find three times as much space as before. A chapel for Queen Victoria in 1843, the 1831 building by John Nash was destroyed in an air raid in 1940. The gallery is dedicated to changing exhibitions of the wide-ranging treasure trove that forms the Royal Collection. Anticipate special exhibitions of paintings, prints, drawings, watercolors, furniture, porcelain, miniatures, enamels, jewelry, and other works of art. At any given time, expect to see such artistic peaks as Van Dyck's equestrian portrait of Charles I, the world-famous *Lady at the Virginal* by Vermeer, a dazzling array of gold snuffboxes, paintings by Monet from the collection of the late Queen Mother, personal jewelry, studies by Leonardo da Vinci, and even the recent and very controversial portrait of the present queen by Lucian Freud.

Buckingham Palace, SW1. ⓒ 020/7321-2233. www.royalgov.uk. Admission £4.50 ($8.35) adults, £3.50 ($6.50) students and seniors, £2 ($3.70) children 5–16, free for children 4 and under. Daily 10am–5:30pm. Tube: Hyde Park Corner, Green Park, or Victoria.

Royal Mews 🟠🟠 This is where you can get a close look at Her Majesty's State Coach, built in 1761 to the designs of Sir William Chambers and decorated with paintings by Cipriani. Traditionally drawn by eight gray horses, it was used by sovereigns when they traveled to open Parliament and on other state occasions; Queen Elizabeth traveled in it to her 1953 coronation and in 1977 for her Silver Jubilee Procession. There are other state coaches to see here. You can also pay a visit to the queen's carriage horses, which are housed here. See the "London's Attractions" map.

Buckingham Palace, Buckingham Palace Rd., SW1. ⓒ **020/7766-7302**. www.royal.gov.uk. Admission £5.50 ($10) adults, seniors and students £4.50 ($8.35), children 5–17, free for children under 5. Mon–Thurs and Sat–Sun 11am–3:15pm; summer hours daily 10am–5pm (last entrance at 4:15pm). Tube: Green Park or Victoria.

Saatchi Gallery 🟠🟠🟠 Art lovers either define the controversial collector, Charles Saatchi, as the vision of the 21st century—or else they demand he be jailed at once and the key thrown away. If you're not among the faint-of-heart, you can make your way to this river-bordering Edwardian pile on the South Bank, a one-time seat of city government until Margaret Thatcher did away with the local council. Saatchi's taste for cocksure spectacle and his outrageous showcases defined modern British art in the 1990s. This former ad man has been called everything from a "modern day Medici" to "a Machiavellian mogul." He could even outrage part of New York City with his Chris Ofili's glittery Madonna with elephant dung, which went on show in Brooklyn (it now rests peacefully in this gallery).

It's all here, ranging from Sarah Lucas's photographs of herself with cash stuffed between her legs or fried eggs on her breasts, to Damien Hirst's pickled shark. Hirst's sliced-up cow appears butchered in separate glass containers that evoke Donald Judd boxes. Take delight—or horror—at Richard Wilson's famous *"20:50"*, a surrealistic chest-high lake of smelly sump oil. And, of course, you can't leave the gallery without checking out Marc Quinn's frozen "head," cast from nine pints of blood plasma extracted from the artist over a period of several months, or Marcus Harvey's *Myra*, a portrait of the child murderer, Myra Hindley.

County Hall, Southbank, SE1. © 020/7823-2363. Admission £8.50 ($16) adults, £6.50 ($12) seniors and students, £25 ($46) family ticket. Sun–Thurs 10am–8pm; Fri–Sat 10am–10pm. Tube: Waterloo.

Science Museum 🐨🐨🐨 *Kids*   This museum traces the development of science and industry and their influence on everyday life. These scientific collections are among the largest, most comprehensive, and most significant anywhere. On display is Stephenson's original rocket and the tiny prototype railroad engine; you can also see Whittle's original jet engine and the *Apollo 10* space module. The King George III Collection of scientific instruments is the highlight of a gallery on science in the 18th century. Health Matters is a permanent gallery on modern medicine. The museum has two hands-on galleries, as well as working models and video displays.

The museum also presents a behind-the-scenes look at the science and technology that went into making the film trilogy, *The Lord of the Rings.*

Insider's Tip: A large addition to this museum explores such topics as genetics, digital technology, and artificial intelligence. Four floors of a new Welcome Wing shelter half a dozen exhibition areas and a 450-seat IMAX theater. One exhibition explores everything from drug use in sports to how engineers observe sea life with robotic submarines. On an upper floor, visitors can learn how DNA was used to identify living relatives of the Bleadon Man, a 2,000-year-old Iron Age Man. On the third floor is the computer that Tim Berners-Lee used to design the World Wide Web outside Geneva, writing the first software for it in 1990.

Exhibition Rd., SW7. © 0870/870-4868. www.sciencemuseum.org.uk. Free admission. Daily 10am–6pm. Closed Dec 24–26. Tube: S. Kensington.

Shakespeare's Globe Theatre & Exhibition 🐨   This is a recent re-creation of what was probably the most important public theater ever built, Shakespeare's Globe, on the exact site where many of Shakespeare's plays opened. The late American filmmaker Sam Wanamaker worked for some 20 years to raise funds to re-create the theater as it existed in Elizabethan times, thatched roof and all. A fascinating exhibit tells the story of the Globe's construction, using the material (including goat hair in the plaster), techniques, and craftsmanship of 400 years ago. The new Globe isn't an exact replica: It seats 1,500 patrons, not the 3,000 who regularly squeezed in during the early 1600s, and this thatched roof has been specially treated with a fire retardant. Guided tours of the facility are offered throughout the day.

21 New Globe Walk, Southwark, SE1. © 020/7902-1400. www.shakespeares-globe. org. Admission £8 ($15) adults, £5.50 ($10) children 15 and under, £6.50 ($12) seniors and students. Oct–Apr daily 10am–5pm; May–Sept daily 9am–noon and 12:30–5pm. Tube: Mansion House or London Bridge.

Wallace Collection 🕮🕮 *Finds*   Located in a palatial setting (the modestly described "town house" of the late Lady Wallace), this collection is a contrasting array of art and armaments. The collection is evocative of the Frick Museum in New York and the Musée d'Jacque André in Paris. The art collection (mostly French) includes works by Watteau, Boucher, Fragonard, and Greuze, as well as such classics as Frans Hals's *Laughing Cavalier* and Rembrandt's portrait of his son Titus. The paintings of the Dutch, English, Spanish, and Italian schools are outstanding. The collection also contains important 18th-century French decorative art, including furniture from a number of royal palaces, Sèvres porcelain, and gold boxes. The European and Asian armaments, on the ground floor, are works of art in their own right: superb inlaid suits of armor, some obviously for parade rather than battle, with more businesslike swords, halberds, and magnificent Persian scimitars.

Manchester Sq., W1. © 020/7563-9500. www.the-wallace-collection.org.uk. Free admission. Mon–Sat 10am–5pm; Sun noon–5pm. Tube: Bond St. or Baker St.

PARKS & GARDENS

London's parks are the most advanced system of "green lungs" in any large city on the globe. Although not as rigidly maintained as those of Paris (Britons traditionally prefer a more natural look), they're cared for with a loving and lavishly artistic hand that puts their American counterparts to shame.

The largest of the central London parks is **Hyde Park** 🕮🕮 (Tube: Marble Arch, Hyde Park Corner, or Lancaster Gate), once a favorite deer-hunting ground of Henry VIII. With the adjoining Kensington Gardens (see below), it covers 246 hectares (608 acres) of central London with velvety lawns interspersed with ponds, flowerbeds, and trees. Running through its width is a 16.5-hectare (41-acre) lake known as the **Serpentine,** where you can row, sail model boats, or swim (provided you don't mind sub-Florida water temperatures). **Rotten Row,** a 2.5km (1½-mile) sand riding track, attracts some skilled equestrians on Sunday. You can rent a paddleboat or a rowboat from the boathouse (open Mar–Oct) on the north side of **Hyde Park's Serpentine** (© 020/7262-1330).

At the northeastern tip, near Marble Arch, is **Speakers Corner** (www.speakerscorner.net). Since 1855 (before the legal right to assembly was guaranteed), people have been getting on their soapboxes about any and every subject under the sky. In the past you might have heard Karl Marx, Frederick Engels, or Lenin, certainly William Morris and George Orwell. The corpse of Oliver Cromwell was hung here in a cage for the public to gape at or throw rotten eggs at. The king wanted to warn others against what might happen to them if they wished to abolish the monarchy. Hecklers, often aggressive, are part of the fun. Anyone can speak; just don't blaspheme, use obscene language, or start a riot.

Blending with Hyde Park and bordering the grounds of Kensington Palace, well-manicured **Kensington Gardens** (Tube: High St. Kensington or Queensway) contains the famous statue of Peter Pan, with bronze rabbits that toddlers are always trying to kidnap. The park is also home to that Victorian extravaganza, the Albert Memorial. The Orangery is an ideal place to take afternoon tea.

East of Hyde Park, across Piccadilly, stretch **Green Park** ⚜ (Tube: Green Park) and **St. James's Park** ⚜ (Tube: St. James's Park), forming an almost unbroken chain of landscaped beauty. These parks are ideal for picnics; you'll find it hard to believe that this was once a swamp near a leper hospital. There's a romantic lake stocked with ducks and some surprising pelicans, descendants of the pair that the Russian ambassador presented to Charles II in 1662.

Regent's Park ⚜⚜⚜ (Tube: Regent's Park or Baker St.) covers most of the district of that name, north of Baker Street and Marylebone Road. Designed by the 18th-century genius John Nash to surround a palace for the prince regent (the palace never materialized), this is the most classically beautiful of London's parks. Its core is a rose garden planted around a small lake alive with waterfowl and spanned by Japanese bridges; in early summer, the rose perfume in the air is as heady as wine. As at all the local parks, hundreds of chairs are scattered around the lawns, waiting for sunbathers. The deck-chair attendants, who rent the chairs for a small fee, are mostly college students on break. Rowboats and sailing dinghies are available in **Regent's Park** (© 020/7486-7905). Sailing and canoeing cost around £6 ($11) for 1½ hours.

The hub of England's—and perhaps the world's—horticulture is in Surrey, at the **Royal Botanic Gardens at Kew** (also known as Kew Gardens).

3 Organized Tours

BUS TOURS

For the first-timer, the quickest and most economical way to bring the big city into focus is to take a bus tour. One of the most popular is **The Original London Sightseeing Tour,** which passes by all the major sights in just about 1½ hours. The tour, which uses a traditional double-decker bus with live commentary by a guide, costs £15 ($28) for adults, £10 ($19) for children under 16, free for those under 5. The tour allows you to hop on or off the bus at any point in the tour at no extra charge. The tour plus admission to Madame Tussaud's is £28 ($52) for adults, £20 ($37) for children.

Departures are from convenient points within the city; you can choose your departure point when you buy your ticket. Tickets can be purchased on the bus or at a discount from any London Transport or London Tourist Board Information Centre. Most hotel concierges also sell tickets. For information or phone purchases, call ℂ 020/8877-1722. It's also possible to book online at **www.the originaltour.com**.

Big Bus Company Ltd., Waterside Way, London SW17 (ℂ **020/ 8944-7810** or 0800/169-1365; www.bigbus.co.uk), operates a 2-hour tour in summer, departing frequently between 8:30am and 4:30pm daily from Marble Arch by Speakers Corner, Green Park by the Ritz Hotel, and Victoria Station (Buckingham Palace Rd. by the Royal Westminster Hotel). Tours cover the highlights—18 in all—ranging from the Houses of Parliament and Westminster Abbey to the Tower of London and Buckingham Palace (exterior looks only), accompanied by live commentary. The cost is £17 ($31) for adults, £8 ($15) for children. A 1-hour tour follows the same route but covers only 13 sights. Tickets are valid all day; you can hop on and off the bus as you wish.

WALKING TOURS

The Original London Walks, 87 Messina Ave., P.O. Box 1708, London NW6 4LW (ℂ **020/7624-3978**), the oldest established walking-tour company in London, is run by an Anglo-American journalist/actor couple, David and Mary Tucker. Their hallmarks are variety, reliability, reasonably sized groups, and—above all—superb guides. The renowned crime historian Donald Rumbelow, the leading authority on Jack the Ripper and author of the classic guidebook *London Walks,* is a regular guide, as are several prominent actors (including classical actor Edward Petherbridge). Walks are regularly scheduled daily and cost £5 ($9.25) for adults, £4 ($7.40) for students and seniors; children under 15 go free. Call for schedule; no reservations needed.

Discovery Walks, 67 Chancery Lane, London WC2 (© **020/8530-8443;** www.Jack-the-Ripper-Walk.co.uk), are themed walks, led by Richard Jones, author of *Frommer's Memorable Walks in London.*

6

Shopping

Although London is one of the world's best shopping cities, it often seems made for wealthy visitors. To find real values, do what most Londoners do: Search out discount stores or look for sales, traditionally held in January and July.

1 Central London Shopping

Thankfully for those pressed for time, several key streets offer some (or even all) of London's best retail stores, compactly located in a niche or neighborhood so you can just stroll and shop.

THE WEST END As a neighborhood, the West End includes Mayfair and is home to the core of London's big-name shopping. Most of the department stores, designer shops, and multiples (chain stores) have their flagships in this area.

The key streets are **Oxford Street** (in either direction) for affordable shopping (start at Marble Arch Tube station if you're ambitious, or Bond St. station if you only care to see some of it), and **Regent Street,** which intersects Oxford Street at Oxford Circus (Tube: Oxford Circus). The Oxford Street flagship (at Marble Arch) of the private-label department store Marks & Spencer ("Marks & Sparks" in the local parlance) is worth visiting for quality goods. Regent Street has more upscale department stores (including the famed Liberty of London), chains (Laura Ashley), and specialty dealers.

Parallel to Regent Street, **Bond Street** (Tube: Bond St.) connects Piccadilly with Oxford Street and is synonymous with the luxury trade. Divided into New and Old, it has experienced a recent revival and is the hot address for international designers—Donna Karan has two shops here. A slew of international hotshots, from Chanel to Ferragamo to Versace, have digs nearby.

Burlington Arcade (Tube: Piccadilly Circus), the famous glass-roofed, Regency-style passage leading off Piccadilly, looks like a period exhibition and is lined with intriguing shops and boutiques. Its small, smart stores specialize in fashion, jewelry, Irish linen, cashmere, and more. If you linger there until 5:30pm, you can watch the beadles (the last London representatives of Britain's oldest police force), in their black-and-yellow livery and top hats, ceremoniously place the iron grills that block off the arcade until 9am, at which time they just as ceremoniously remove them to start a new business day. Also at 5:30pm, a hand bell called the Burlington Bell is sounded, signaling the end of trading.

For a total contrast, check out **Jermyn Street** (Tube: Piccadilly Circus), on the far side of Piccadilly, a tiny 2-block-long street devoted to high-end men's haberdashers and toiletries shops; many have been doing business for centuries. Several hold royal warrants, including Turnbull & Asser, where HRH Prince Charles has his pj's made. A bit to the northwest, Savile Row (between Regent St. and New Bond St.) is synonymous with the finest in men's tailoring.

The West End theater district borders two more shopping areas: the still-not-ready-for-prime-time **Soho** (Tube: Tottenham Court Rd.), where the sex shops are slowly converting into cutting-edge designer shops, and **Covent Garden** (Tube: Covent Garden), a shopping masterpiece full of fashion, food, books, and everything else. The original Covent Garden marketplace has overflowed its boundaries and eaten up the surrounding neighborhood; it's fun to wander the narrow streets and shop. Covent Garden is mobbed on Sundays.

Just a stone's throw from Covent Garden, **Monmouth Street** is somewhat of a London shopping secret: Londoners know they can find a wide array of stores in a space of only 2 blocks. Many shops here are outlets for British designers, such as Alexander Campbell, who specializes in outfits made of wispy materials. Some shops along this street sell both used and new clothing. Besides clothing, stores specialize in everything from musical instruments from the Far East to palm and crystal-ball readings.

KNIGHTSBRIDGE & CHELSEA Knightsbridge (Tube: Knightsbridge), the home of Harrods, is the second-most-famous London retail district. (Oxford St. edges it out.) Nearby Sloane Street is chock-a-block with designer shops.

Walk southwest on **Brompton Road** (toward the Victoria and Albert Museum) and you'll find **Cheval Place,** lined with designer resale shops, and Beauchamp (*Bee*-cham) Place. It's only a block long, but it's very "Sloane Ranger" or "Sloanie" (as the Brits would say), featuring the kinds of shops where young British aristocrats buy their clothing for the "season."

If you walk farther along Brompton Road, you'll connect to **Brompton Cross,** another hip area for designer shops made popular when Michelin House was rehabbed by Sir Terence Conran,

Tips How to Get Your VAT Refund

You *must* get your VAT refund form from the retailer. Don't leave the store without a form—it must be completed by the retailer on the spot.

Global Refund (www.taxfree.se) is your best bet for getting VAT refunds at the airport. Shop where you see the Global Refund Tax-Free Shopping sign, and ask for a Global Refund Tax-Free check when you purchase your items.

Fill out your form and then present it—with the goods, receipts, and passports—at the Customs office in the airport. Allow a half-hour to stand in line. *Remember:* You're required to show the goods, so put them in your carry-on.

Once the paperwork has been stamped, you have two choices: You can mail the papers (remember to bring a stamp) and receive your refund as a British check (no!) or a credit card refund (yes!), or go to the Cash VAT Refund desk at the airport and get your refund in cash. Know that if you accept cash other than British pounds, you will lose money on the conversion.

Many stores charge a fee for processing your refund, so £3 to £5 ($5.55–$9.25) may be deducted from the total you receive. But since the VAT in Britain is 17.5%, it's worth the trouble to get the money back.

Note: If you're heading to other countries in the European Union, you should file all of your VAT refunds at once at your final E.U. destination.

becoming the Conran Shop. Seek out **Walton Street,** a tiny snake of a street running from Brompton Cross back toward the museums. Most of the shops along this street specialize in nonessential luxury products. This is where you'll find aromatherapy from Jo Malone, needlepoint, and costume jewelry. **King's Road** (Tube: Sloane Sq.), the main street of Chelsea, will forever remain a symbol of the Swinging '60s. It's still popular with the young crowd, but there are fewer mohawk haircuts and Bovver boots than before. More and more, King's Road is a lineup of markets and "multistores," conglomerations of indoor stands, stalls, and booths within one building or enclosure. About a third of King's Road is devoted to "multi-store" antiques markets; another third houses design-trade showrooms and stores of housewares; and the remaining third is faithful to the area's teenybopper roots.

Finally, don't forget all those museums in nearby **South Kensington**—they all have great gift shops.

KENSINGTON, NOTTING HILL & BAYSWATER **Kensington High Street** (Tube: High St. Kensington) is the hangout of the classier breed of teen, one who has graduated from Carnaby Street and is ready for street chic. While there are a few staples of basic British fashion here, most of the stores feature items that stretch; are very, very short; very, very tight; and very, very black.

From Kensington High Street, you can walk up **Kensington Church Street,** which, like Portobello Road, is one of the city's main shopping avenues for antiques, selling everything from antique furniture to Impressionist paintings.

Kensington Church Street dead-ends at the Notting Hill Gate Tube station, jumping-off point for Portobello Road, whose antiques dealers and weekend market are 2 blocks beyond.

Not far from Notting Hill Gate is **Whiteleys of Bayswater,** Queensway, W2 (© **020/7229-8844;** Tube: Bayswater or Queensway), an Edwardian mall whose chief tenant is Marks & Spencer. Whiteleys also contains 75 to 85 other shops, mostly specialty outlets, plus restaurants, cafes, bars, and an eight-screen movie theater.

2 The Department Stores

Contrary to popular belief, Harrods is not the only department store in London. The British invented the department store, and they have lots of them, mostly in Mayfair, and each has its own customer profile.

Fortnum & Mason ✹✹✹ Catering to well-heeled clients as a full-service department store since 1707, Fortnum & Mason recently spent £14 million ($26 million) on an overhaul of its premises and inventories. Offerings include one of the most comprehensive delicatessens and food markets in London, as well as stationery, gift items, porcelain and crystal, and lots and lots of clothing for men, women, and children. 181 Piccadilly, W1. © **020/7734-8040.** Tube: Piccadilly Circus.

Harrods Harrods remains an institution, but in the last decade or so it has grown increasingly dowdy and is not nearly as cutting edge as it used to be. For the latest trends, shop elsewhere. However, we always stop here during our visits to London. As entrenched in English life as Buckingham Palace and the Ascot Races, it's still an elaborate emporium. Goods are spread across 300 departments, and the range, variety, and quality will still dazzle the visiting out-of-towner.

The whole fifth floor is devoted to sports and leisure, with a wide range of equipment and attire. Toy Kingdom is on the fourth floor, along with children's wear. The Egyptian Hall, on the ground floor, sells crystal from Lalique and Baccarat, plus porcelain.

There's also a barber, a jewelry department, and a fashion department for younger customers. You'll have a choice of 18 restaurants and bars. Best of all are the **Food Halls,** with a huge variety of foods and several cafes. Harrods began as a grocer in 1849, and food and drinks are still at the heart of the business. The motto remains, "If you can eat or drink it, you'll find it at Harrods." 87–135 Brompton Rd., Knightsbridge, SW1. ℂ 020/7730-1234. Tube: Knightsbridge.

Harvey Nichols   Locals call it "Harvey Nicks." Once a favorite of the late Princess Di, this store is large, but it doesn't compete directly with Harrods because it has a more upmarket, fashionable image. Harvey Nicks has its own gourmet food hall and fancy restaurant, **The Fifth Floor,** and is crammed with the best in designer home furnishings, gifts, and fashions for all, although women's clothing is the largest segment of its business. The store carries many American designer brands; avoid them, as they're more expensive in London than they are in the U.S. 109–125 Knightsbridge, SW1. ℂ 020/7235-5000. Tube: Knightsbridge.

Liberty 𝒶𝒶   This department store is celebrated for its Liberty Prints: top-echelon fabrics, often in floral patterns, prized by decorators for the way they add a sense of English tradition to a room. The front part of the Regent Street store isn't particularly distinctive, but don't be fooled: Other parts of the place have been restored to Tudor-style splendor that includes half-timbering and interior paneling. There are six floors of fashion, china, and home furnishings, including the famous Liberty Print fashion fabrics, upholstery fabrics, scarves, ties, luggage, gifts, and more. 214–220 Regent St., W1. ℂ 020/7734-1234. Tube: Oxford Circus.

3 Goods A to Z
ANTIQUES
Also check out the description of **Portobello Market** on p. 173.

Alfie's Antique Market   This is the biggest (and one of the best-stocked) conglomerate of antiques dealers in London, crammed into the premises of a 19th-century store. It has more than 370 stalls, showrooms, and workshops in over 35,000 square feet of floor space. You'll find the biggest Susie Cooper (a well-known designer of tableware and ceramics for Wedgwood) collection in Europe here. A whole antiques district has grown up around Alfie's along Church Street. 13–25 Church St., NW8. © 020/7723-6066. Fax 020/7724-0999. Tube: Marylebone or Edgware Rd.

Bond Street Antiques Centre ★★ This place, in the heart of London's finest shopping district, enjoys a reputation for being London's preeminent center for antique jewelry, silver, watches, porcelain, glass, and Asian antiques and paintings. 124 New Bond St., W1. © 020/7351-5353 or 020/7493-1854. Tube: Bond St. or Green Park.

Grays Antiques and Grays Mews These markets have been converted into walk-in stands with independent dealers. The term "antiques" covers items from oil paintings to, say, the 1894 edition of the *Encyclopedia Britannica*. Also sold are antique jewelry; silver; gold; maps and prints; bronzes and ivories; arms and armor; Victorian and Edwardian toys; furniture; Art Nouveau and Art Deco items; antique lace; scientific instruments; craft tools; and Asian, Persian, and Islamic pottery, porcelain, miniatures, and antiquities. There's a cafe in each building. Check out the 1950s-style **Victory Cafe** on Davies Street for their homemade cakes. 58 Davies St. and 1–7 Davies Mews, W1. © 020/7629-7034. Tube: Bond St.

The Mall at Camden Passage The Mall contains one of Britain's greatest concentrations of antiques dealers. In individual shops, you'll find some 35 dealers offering fine furniture, porcelain, and silver. The area expands into a street market on Wednesday and Saturday. Islington, N1. © 020/7351-5353. Tube: Northern Line to Angel.

ART & CRAFTS

ACAVA *Finds* This London-based visual-arts organization provides studios and other services for professional artists, and represents about 250 artists working in spaces around London. Call for individual open-studio schedules, as well as dates for the annual Open Studios weekend. © 020/8960-5015.

Contemporary Applied Arts ★ This association encourages traditional and progressive contemporary artwork. Many of Britain's best-established craftspeople, as well as promising talents, are represented within this contemporary-looking space. The gallery houses a diverse display of glass, ceramics, textiles, wood, furniture, jewelry, and metalwork—all by contemporary artisans. A program of special exhibitions, including solo and small-group shows, focuses on innovations in craftwork. There are new exhibitions every 6 weeks. 2 Percy St., W1. © 020/7436-2344. Tube: Tottenham Court Rd.

Crafts Council Gallery ⊛⊛   This gallery is run by the Crafts Council, the national body promoting contemporary crafts. You'll discover some of today's most creative work here. There's a shop specializing in craft objects and publications, and a reference library. The gallery is closed on Mondays. 44A Pentonville Rd., Islington, N1. © 020/7278-7700. Tube: Northern Line to Angel.

England & Co.   Under the guidance of Jane England, this gallery specializes in Outsider Art and Art in Boxes (that is, art which incorporates a box structure into the composition or frame of a three-dimensional work). The gallery focuses attention on neglected postwar British artists such as Tony Stubbings and Ralph Romney. One-person and group shows are mounted frequently, and many young artists get early exposure here. 216 Westbourne Grove, W11. © 020/7221-0417. Tube: Notting Hill Gate.

Gabriel's Wharf   This is a South Bank complex of shops, restaurants, and bars open Tuesday to Sunday 11am to 6pm (dining and drinking establishments are open later). Lying 2 minutes by foot from Oxo Tower Wharf, it is filled with some of London's most skilled craftspeople, turning out original pieces of sculpture, jewelry, ceramics, art, and fashion. Food, fashion, art, and crafts await you here, making this place a lot of fun to poke around. 56 Upper Ground, SE1. © 020/7401-2255. Tube: Blackfriars, Southwark, Waterloo, or Embankment.

Grosvenor Prints   London's largest stock of antique prints, ranging from the 17th up to the 20th century, is on sale here. Obviously, views of London are the biggest-selling items. Some prints depict significant moments in the city's history, including the Great Fire. Of course, the British are great animal lovers, so expect plenty of prints of dogs and horses. 28 Shelton St., WC2. © 020/7836-1979. Tube: Covent Garden.

BATH & BODY
The Body Shop   There's a branch of The Body Shop in every shopping area and tourist zone in London. Some are bigger than others, but all are filled with politically and environmentally friendly beauty, bath, and aromatherapy products. Prices are much lower in the U.K. than they are in the U.S. There's an entire children's line, a men's line, and lots of travel sizes and travel products.

374 Oxford St., W1. ✆ **020/7409-7868**. Tube: Bond St. Other locations throughout London.

Boots the Chemist   This store has branches all over Britain. The house brands of beauty products are usually the best, including original Boots products (try the cucumber facial mask), Boots' versions of The Body Shop (two lines, Global and Naturalistic), and Boots' versions of Chanel makeup (called No. 7). They also sell film, pantyhose (called tights), sandwiches, and all of life's other little necessities. 490 Oxford St., W1G. ✆ **020/7491-8546**. Tube: Marble Arch. Other locations throughout London.

Culpeper the Herbalist ✿   This store has another branch in Mayfair, at 21 Bruton St., W1 (✆ **020/7629-4559**), but the hours are better at the Covent Garden location. You'll have to put up with a cramped space to check out all the food, bath, and aromatherapy products, but it's worth it. Stock up on essential oils, or go for the dream pillows, candles, sachets, and many a shopper's fave—the aromatherapy fan, for home and the car. 8 The Piazza, Covent Garden, WC2. ✆ **020/7379-6698**. Tube: Covent Garden.

Floris ✿✿   A variety of toilet articles and fragrances fill Floris's floor-to-ceiling mahogany cabinets, which are architectural curiosities in their own right. They were installed relatively late in the establishment's history—that is, 1851—long after the shop had received its royal warrants as suppliers of toilet articles to the king and queen. 89 Jermyn St., SW1. ✆ **020/7930-2885**. Tube: Piccadilly Circus.

Penhaligon's ✿✿✿   This Victorian perfumery, established in 1870, holds royal warrants to HRH Duke of Edinburgh and HRH Prince of Wales. All items sold are exclusive to Penhaligon's. The store offers a large selection of perfume, aftershave, soap, and bath oils for women and men. Gifts include antique-silver scent bottles, grooming accessories, and leather traveling goods. Penhaligon's is now in more than 20 Saks Fifth Avenue stores across the United States. 41 Wellington St., WC2. ✆ **020/7836-2150**. Tube: Covent Garden.

BOOKS, MAPS & ENGRAVINGS

In addition to the bookstores below, you'll find well-stocked branches of the **Dillon's** chain around town, including one at 82 Gower St. (Tube: Euston Sq.).

Children's Book Centre   With thousands of titles, this is the best place to go for children's books. Fiction is arranged according to age, up to 16. There are also videos and toys for kids. 237 Kensington High St., W8. ✆ **020/7937-7497**. Tube: Kensington.

Foyle's Bookshop Claiming to be the world's largest bookstore, Foyle's has an impressive array of hardcovers and paperbacks, as well as travel maps, new records, CDs, videotapes, and sheet music. 113–119 Charing Cross Rd., WC2. © 020/7437-5660. Tube: Tottenham Court Rd. or Leicester Sq.

Gay's the Word Britain's leading gay and lesbian bookstore offers a large selection of books, as well as magazines, cards, and guides. There's also a used-books section. 66 Marchmont St., WC1. © 020/7278-7654. Tube: Russell Sq.

Hatchards On the south side of Piccadilly, Hatchards offers a wide range of books on all subjects and is particularly renowned in the areas of fiction, biography, travel, cookery, gardening, art, history, and finance. In addition, Hatchards is second to none in its range of books on royalty. 187 Piccadilly, W1. © 020/7439-9921. Tube: Piccadilly Circus or Green Park.

Stanfords Established in 1852, Stanfords is the world's largest map shop. Many maps, including worldwide touring and survey maps, are unavailable elsewhere. It's also London's best travel bookstore (with a complete selection of Frommer's guides!). 12–14 Long Acre, WC2. © 020/7836-1321. Tube: Covent Garden.

CASHMERE & WOOLENS

Belinda Robertson Some of the most beautiful and most chic cashmeres, in lovely colors, are sold at this centrally located outlet at Knightsbridge. Bold colors are a hallmark of Ms. Robertson's designs, ranging from carnival red to canary yellow. She designs for women, men, and children. 4 West Halkin St., SW1. © 020/7235-0519. Tube: Knightsbridge.

Berk This store boasts one of the largest collections of cashmere sweaters in London—at least the top brands. The outlet also carries capes, stoles, scarves, and camelhair sweaters. 46 Burlington Arcade, Piccadilly, W1. © 020/7493-0028. Tube: Piccadilly Circus or Green Park.

CHINA, GLASS & SILVER

London Silver Vaults ⭐ *Finds* Don't let the out-of-the-way location or the facade's lack of charm slow you down. Downstairs, you'll enter vaults—40 in all—that are filled with tons of silver and silverplate, plus collections of jewelry. It's a staggering selection of old and new, with excellent prices and friendly dealers. Chancery House, 53–64 Chancery Lane, WC2. © 020/7242-3844. Tube: Chancery Lane.

Reject China Shop *Value*   Don't expect too many rejects or too many bargains, despite the name. This shop sells seconds (sometimes) along with first-quality pieces of china with such names as Royal Doulton, Spode, and Wedgwood. You can also find a variety of crystal, glassware, and flatware. If you'd like to have your purchases shipped home for you, the shop can do it for a fee. 183 Brompton Rd., SW3. © 020/7581-0739. Tube: Knightsbridge. Other locations throughout London.

Royal Doulton ✸✸✸   Founded in the 1930s, this store has one of the largest inventories of china in Britain. A wide range of English bone china, as well as crystal and giftware, is sold. The firm specializes, of course, in Royal Doulton (plus Minton and Royal Crown Derby) china, Lladró figures, Border Fine Arts, and other famous names. The January and June sales are excellent. 167 Piccadilly, W1. © 020/7493-9121. Tube: Piccadilly Circus or Green Park.

Thomas Goode ✸✸   This is one of the most famous emporiums in Britain; it's worth visiting for its architectural interest and nostalgic allure alone. Originally built in 1876, Goode's has 14 rooms loaded with porcelain, gifts, candles, silver, tableware, and even a private museum. There's also a tearoom-cum-restaurant tucked into the corner. 19 S. Audley St., W1. © 020/7499-2823. Tube: Bond St., Green Park, Marble Arch, or Hyde Park.

FASHION

We have divided this category into "Classic," "Cutting Edge," and "Vintage & Secondhand," below.

CLASSIC

While every internationally known designer worth his or her weight in Shantung silk has a boutique in London, the best buys are on the sturdy English styles that last forever. See also the separate sections on "Cashmere & Woolens," "Jewelry," and "Shoes."

Austin Reed   Austin Reed has long stood for superior-quality clothing and excellent tailoring. Chester Barrie's off-the-rack suits, for example, are said to fit like tailor-made. The polite employees are unusually honest about telling you what looks good. The store always has a wide variety of top-notch jackets and suits, and men can outfit themselves from dressing gowns to overcoats. For women, there are carefully selected suits, separates, coats, shirts, knitwear, and accessories. 103–113 Regent St., W1. © 020/7534-7779. Tube: Piccadilly Circus.

Beau Monde   This outlet earns its fame selling chic but affordable "nouvelle couture" for women—fitted and adjusted to your body. All designs are by the locally famous London designer Sylvia Young. Her design philosophy is that a busy woman should be conscious of fashion, but not a victim of its whims, and that clothes should work for her—not against her. Her women's wear is comfortable to wear and fashionable, but not stuffy. 43 Lexington St., W1. © 020/7734-6563. Tube: Piccadilly Circus.

Burberry 🅰🅰🅰   The name has been synonymous with raincoats ever since Edward VII ordered his valet to "bring my Burberry" when the skies threatened. An impeccably trained staff sells the famous raincoats, plus excellent men's shirts, sportswear, knitwear, and accessories. Raincoats are available in women's sizes and styles as well. Prices are high, but you get quality and prestige. 18–22 Haymarket, SW1. © 020/7930-3343. Tube: Piccadilly Circus.

Designer Sale UK *Value*   Amazingly, you can sometimes get 90% off designer clothing for both men and women at this outlet. Of course, you've got to sift through 140 rails of clothing and accessories, much of which had a good reason for not selling in the first place. The shop claims it caters to both the discerning label lover and the devoted bargain hunter. Yes, those rails carry Armani, Vivienne Westwood, Alexander McQueen, and a lot of the lesser lights in designer fashion. £2 ($3.70) is charged to attend the sale. Atlantis Gallery, Old Truman Brewery, 146 Brick Lane, E1. © 01273/470-880. Tube: Aldgate E. or Liverpool St.

Hilditch & Key 🅰🅰   The finest name in men's shirts, Hilditch & Key has been in business since 1899. The two shops on this street both offer men's clothing (including a custom-made shirt service) and women's ready-made shirts. There's also an outstanding tie collection. Shirts go for half price during the twice-yearly sales (in Jan and June); men fly in from all over the world for them. 37 and 73 Jermyn St., SW1. © 020/7734-4707. Tube: Piccadilly Circus or Green Park.

Jigsaw   Branches of this fashion chain are numerous, but the Long Acre branch features trendy, middle-market womenswear and children's clothing. Around the corner, the Floral Street shop carries menswear, including a wide range of colored moleskin items. 21 Long Acre, WC2. © 020/7240-3855. Tube: Covent Garden.

Laura Ashley   This is the flagship store of the company whose design ethos embodies the flowery English country look. The store carries a wide choice of women's clothing, plus home furnishings. Prices are lower than in the United States. 256–258 Regent St., W1. © 020/7437-9760. Tube: Oxford Circus. Other locations around London.

Next   This chain of "affordable fashion" stores saw its heyday in the 1980s, when it was celebrated for its success in marketing avantgarde fashion ideas to a wide spectrum of the British public. No longer at its peak, it still merits a stop. The look is still very contemporary, with a Continental flair, and there are clothes for men, women, and kids. 15–17 Long Acre, WC2. ℭ 020/7420-8280. Tube: Covent Garden. Other locations throughout London.

Reiss   In a city where men's clothing often sells at exorbitant prices, Reiss is a haven of reasonable sporty and casual wear. Take your pick from everything from pullovers to rugged cargo pants. 114 King's Rd., SW3. ℭ 020/7225-4910. Tube: Sloane Sq.

Thomas Pink ⭐⭐⭐   This Jermyn Street shirt-maker, named after an 18th-century Mayfair tailor, gave the world the phrase "in the pink." It has a prestigious reputation for well-made cotton shirts for both men and women. The shirts are created from the finest two-fold Egyptian and Sea Island pure-cotton poplin. Some patterns are classic, others new and unusual. All are generously cut with long tails and finished with a choice of double cuffs or single-button cuffs. A small pink square in the tail tells all. 85 Jermyn St., SW1. ℭ 020/7930-6364. Tube: Green Park or Piccadilly Circus.

CUTTING EDGE

Currently, the most cutting-edge shopping area in London is on **Conduit Street,** W1, in Mayfair (Tube: Oxford Circus). Once known for its dowdy airline offices, it is now London's smartest fashion street. Trendy shops are opening between Regent Street and the "blue-chip" boutiques of New Bond Street. Current stars include **Vivienne Westwood,** 44 Conduit St., W1 (ℭ 020/7439-1109), who has left her punk origins behind and is now the grande dame of English fashion. See below for her flagship store. **Krizia,** 24 Conduit St., W1 (ℭ 020/7491-4987), the fashion rage of Rome since the 1950s, displays not only Krizia's clothing lines but her luxury home goods as well.

For muted fashion elegance, **Yohji Yamamoto,** 14–15 Conduit St., W1 (ℭ 020/7491-4129), is hard to beat, and **Issey Miyake,** 52 Conduit St., W1 (ℭ 020/7349-3300), is the Japanese master of minimalism.

Accessorize *Value*   This aptly named store is often packed with women who have an eye for bargains but want top-notch style. The store stays abreast of the latest fads and trends, especially in evening bags, which range from antique to high fashion. All sorts of treasures are stocked here, everything from hologram-flecked nail polish to silk scarves. 123A Kensington High St., W8. ℂ 020/7937-1433. Tube: Kensington High St.

Anya Hindmarch   Although her fashionable bags are sold at Harvey Nichols, Liberty, Harrods, and throughout the U.S. and Europe, this is the only place to see the complete range of Anya Hindmarch's handbags, wallets, purses, and key holders. Smaller items start at £45 ($83), whereas handbag prices start at £200 ($370), with alligator being the most expensive. There's a limited custom-made service; bring in your fabric if you want a bag to match. 15–17 Pont St., SW3. ℂ 020/7838-9177. Tube: Sloane Sq. or Knightsbridge.

Browns 𝕲𝕲   This is the only place in London to find the designs of Alexander McQueen, head of the House of Givenchy in Paris and one of the fashion industry's stars. Producing his own cottons, silks, and plastics, McQueen creates revealing, feminine women's couture and ready-to-wear, and has started a menswear line. McQueen made his reputation creating shock-value apparel that was more photographed than worn. But recently, fashion critics have called his new outfits "consumer friendly." Browns has introduced "Browns Living," an eclectic array of lifestyle products. 23–27 S. Molton St., W1. ℂ 020/7491-7833. Tube: Bond St.

Egg   This shop is hot, hot, hot with fashionistas. It features imaginatively designed, contemporary clothing by Indian textile designer Asha Sarabhai and knitwear by Eskandar. Designs, created from handmade textiles at a workshop in India, range from everyday dresses to hand-embroidered silk coats. Crafts and ceramics are also available. Closed Sunday and Monday. 36 Kinnerton St., SW1. ℂ 020/7235-9315. Tube: Hyde Park Corner or Knightsbridge.

H&M Hennes   Here are copies of hot-off-the-catwalk fashions at affordable prices. While the quality isn't to brag about, the prices are. For disposable cutting-edge fashion, you can't beat it. 261 Regent St., W1. ℂ 020/7493-4004. Tube: Oxford Circus.

The Library   Despite its name, this is a showcase for some of the best young designers for men. It's very cutting edge without dipping into the extremes of male fashion. The Library is famous for having introduced Helmut Lang to London, and now features such designers as Fabrizio del Carlo, Kostas Murkudis, and even Alexander McQueen. 268 Brompton Rd., SW3. ℂ 020/7589-6569. Tube: S. Kensington.

Vivienne Westwood 𝕲𝕲   No one in British fashion is hotter than the unstoppable Vivienne Westwood. While it's possible to purchase some Westwood pieces around the world, her U.K. shops are the best places to find her full range of fashion designs. The flagship location (on Davies St.) concentrates on her couture line, known as the Gold Label. One of the U.K.'s most watched designers, Westwood creates jackets, skirts, trousers, blouses, dresses, and evening dresses that manage to be elegant, alluring, and stylish all at the same time. Many of the fabrics and accessories for her garments are made in Britain, and at least some of them are crafted and tailored there as well. Westwood came out with her own fragrance in 1997. Westwood's World's End line of clothing focuses on casual designs for youthful bodies, including T-shirts, jeans, and sportswear. 6 Davies St., W1. ✆ 020/7629-3757. Tube: Bond St.; World's End branch: 430 King's Rd., SW3 ✆ 020/7352-6551. Tube: Sloane Sq.

VINTAGE & SECONDHAND

Note that there's no VAT refund on used clothing.

Annie's Vintage Costume and Textiles *(Finds)* This shop concentrates on carefully preserved dresses from the 1920s and 1930s, but also has a range of clothing and textiles from the 1880s through the 1960s. A 1920s fully beaded dress will run you about £300 ($555), but there are scarves for £15 ($28), camisoles for £30 ($56), and a range of exceptional pieces priced between £50 and £60 ($93–$111). Clothing is located on the main floor; textiles, including old lace, bed linens, and tapestries, are upstairs. 12 Camden Passage, N1. ✆ 020/7359-0796. Tube: Northern Line to Angel.

Pandora *(Value)* A London institution since the 1940s, Pandora stands in fashionable Knightsbridge, a stone's throw from Harrods. Several times a week, chauffeurs drive up with bundles packed anonymously by England's gentry. One woman voted best-dressed at the Ascot Horse Races several years ago was wearing a secondhand dress acquired here. Prices are generally one-third to one-half the retail value. Chanel and Anne Klein are among the designers represented. Outfits are usually no more than two seasons old. 16–22 Cheval Place, SW7. ✆ 020/7589-5289. Tube: Knightsbridge.

HOME DESIGN, FURNISHINGS & HOUSEWARES

Also see "Jewelry," and "Art & Crafts."

The Conran Shop You'll find Sir Terence Conran's high style at reasonable prices at this outlet. The fashion press cites Conran as "the director" of British middle-class taste since the 1960s. This place is great for gifts, home furnishings, and tabletop ware—or just for gawking. Michelin House, 81 Fulham Rd., SW3. ✆ 020/7589-7401. Tube: S. Kensington.

Designers Guild After more than 3 decades in business, creative director Tricia Guild and her young designers still lead the pack in all that's bright and whimsical. They are often copied but never outdone. There's an exclusive line of handmade furniture and accessories at the no. 267–271 location, and wallpaper and more than 2,000 fabrics at the neighboring no. 275–277 shop. The colors remain vivid forever, and the designs are always irreverent. Also available are children's accessories, toys, crockery, and cutlery. 267–271 and 275–277 King's Rd., SW3. ✆ 020/7351-5775. Tube: Sloane Sq.

Purves & Purves This store has a varied collection of modern furniture from Britain and the Continent. Many designers make individual pieces that are sold here. The light and airy store displays this eye-catching array of furniture, lighting, fabrics, rugs, and beds. 220 Tottenham Court Rd., W1. ✆ 020/7580-8223. Tube: Goodge St. or Tottenham Court Rd.

Summerill & Bishop Some of London's most sophisticated kitchenware is sold here, items that may not be available in your hometown store. The range is from Edward S. Wohl's charming bird's-eye maple breadboards to John Julian Sainsbury's black granite mortar with a stainless steel handled pestle. Some of the top designers in Britain created the unusual ware at this outlet. 100 Portland Rd., Holland Park W11. ✆ 020/7221-4566. Tube: Holland Park.

JEWELRY

Asprey & Garrard Previously known as Garrard & Co., this recently merged jeweler specializes in both antique and modern jewelry, and silverware. The in-house designers also produce pieces to order and do repairs. You can have a pair of pearl earrings or silver cufflinks for a mere £60 ($111)—but the prices go nowhere but up from there. 167 New Bond St., W1. ✆ 020/7493-6767. Tube: Green Park.

Lesley Craze Gallery/Craze 2/C2 Plus This complex has developed a reputation as a showcase of the best contemporary British jewelry and textile design. The gallery shop focuses on precious metals and includes pieces by such renowned designers as Wendy Ramshaw. Prices start at £60 ($111). Craze 2 features costume jewelry in materials ranging from bronze to paper, with prices starting at £25 ($46). C2 Plus features contemporary textile designs, including wall hangings, scarves, and ties by artists such as Jo Barker, Dawn DuPree, and Victoria Richards. 34 Clerkenwell Green, EC1. ✆ 020/7608-0393 (Gallery), ✆ 020/7251-0381 (Craze 2), ✆ 020/7251-9200 (C2 Plus). Tube: Farringdon.

MUSEUM SHOPS

Victoria and Albert Museum Gift Shop ✿✿ This is the best museum shop in London—indeed, one of the best in the world. It sells cards, a fabulous selection of art books, and the usual items, along with reproductions from the design museum archives. Cromwell Rd., SW7. ℂ **020/7942-2696**. Tube: S. Kensington.

MUSIC

Collectors should browse **Notting Hill,** because there are a handful of good shops near the Notting Hill Gate Tube stop. Also browse **Soho** in the Wardour Street area, near the Tottenham Court Road Tube stop. Sometimes dealers show up at Covent Garden on the weekends.

In addition to the two below, the ubiquitous **Our Price** chain is worth checking out for current chart-toppers at great prices.

Tower Records Attracting throngs in a neighborhood whose pedestrian traffic is almost overwhelming, this is one of the largest record and CD stores in Europe. Sprawling over four floors, it's practically a tourist attraction in its own right. In addition to a huge selection of music, you'll find everything that's on the cutting edge of music technology. 1 Piccadilly Circus, W1. ℂ **020/7439-2500**. Tube: Piccadilly Circus. Other locations throughout London.

Virgin Megastore If a record has just been released—and if it's worth hearing in the first place—chances are this store carries it. It's like a giant musical grocery store. You get to hear many of the new releases on headphones at listening stations before making a purchase. Even rock stars come here to pick up new releases. A large selection of classical and jazz recordings is sold, as are computer software and video games. In between selecting your favorites, you can enjoy a coffee at the cafe or purchase an airline ticket from the Virgin Atlantic office. 14–16 Oxford St., W1. ℂ **020/7631-1234**. Tube: Tottenham Court Rd. Also at King's Walk Shopping Centre, King's Rd., Chelsea, SW3. ℂ **020/7591-0957**. Tube: Sloane Sq.

SHOES

Koko This is a sprawling, hip, trendy, style-conscious shop that sells footwear, and only footwear, from three different vendors, the most famous and visible being Dr. Marten's. Dr. Marten's shoes have unisex punk-rock associations and you can expect lots of British rocker types trying on shoes around you. This store has the largest inventory of Doc Marten's in London. 9 Carnaby St., W1. ℂ **020/7734-8890**. Tube: Oxford Circus.

Office In spite of its dull name, this is a most unusual store for style-setters on a budget. Its imitations of some of the world's leading shoe designers have earned it the reputation of being the "Madame Tussaud's of footwear." All the shoe designers, from Kenneth Cole to Patrick Cox, get ripped off here. 107 Queensway, W2. © 020/7792-4000. Tube: Queensway.

Shelly's Shelly's flagship on Oxford Circus is the largest shoe store in London, selling footwear to fashionable young things and style-conscious individuals at affordable prices. They're famous for their Dr. Marten's, but there's much more. 266–268 Regent St., W1. © 020/7287-0927. Tube: Oxford Circus. Other locations throughout London.

SPORTING GOODS

Lillywhites Ltd. 𝄐𝄐𝄐 Europe's biggest and most famous sports store has floor after floor of sports clothing, equipment, and footwear. It also offers collections of fashionable leisurewear for men and women. 24–36 Lower Regent St., Piccadilly Circus, SW1. © 0870/3339-600. Tube: Piccadilly Circus.

TOYS

Hamleys This flagship is the finest toy shop in the world—more than 35,000 toys and games on seven floors of fun and magic. The huge selection includes soft, cuddly stuffed animals as well as dolls, radio-controlled cars, train sets, model kits, board games, outdoor toys, computer games, and more. 188–196 Regent St., W1. © 0870/333-2455. Tube: Oxford Circus. Also at Covent Garden and Heathrow Airport.

4 Street & Flea Markets

If Mayfair stores are not your cup of tea, don't worry; you'll have more fun, and find a better bargain, at any of the city's street and flea markets.

THE WEST END   Covent Garden Market 𝄐 (© 020/7836-9136; Tube: Covent Garden), the most famous market in all of England, offers several markets daily from 9am to 6:30pm (we think it's most fun to come on Sun). It can be a little confusing until you dive in and explore. **Apple Market** is the bustling market in the courtyard, where traders sell—well, everything. Many of the items are what the English call collectible nostalgia: a wide array of glassware and ceramics, leather goods, toys, clothes, hats, and jewelry. Some of the merchandise is truly unusual. Many items are handmade, with some of the craftspeople selling their own wares—except on Mondays, when antiques dealers take over. Some goods are new, some are very old. Out back is **Jubilee Market** (© 020/7836-2139), also an antiques market on Mondays. Tuesday to Sunday, it's sort of a fancy hippie market with cheap clothes and books. Out front there are a few tents of cheap stuff, except on Monday.

The indoor market section of Covent Garden Market (in a superbly restored hall) is one of the best shopping venues in London. Specialty shops sell fashions and herbs, gifts and toys, books and dollhouses, cigars, and much more. There are bookshops and branches of famous stores (Hamleys, The Body Shop), and prices are kept moderate.

St. Martin–in-the-Fields Market (Tube: Charing Cross) is good for teens and hipsters who don't want to trek all the way to Camden Market and are interested in imports from India and South America, crafts, and local football souvenirs. It's located near Trafalgar Square and Covent Garden; hours are Monday through Saturday from 11am to 5pm, and Sunday from noon to 5pm.

Berwick Street Market (Tube: Oxford Circus or Tottenham Court Rd.) may be the only street market in the world that's flanked by two rows of strip clubs, porno stores, and adult-movie dens. Don't let that put you off. Humming 6 days a week in the scarlet heart of Soho, this array of stalls and booths sells the best and cheapest fruit and vegetables in town. It also hawks ancient records, tapes, books, and old magazines, any of which may turn out to be a collector's item one day. It's open Monday through Saturday from 9am to 5pm.

On Sunday mornings along **Bayswater Road,** artists hang their work on the railings along the edge of Hyde Park and Kensington Gardens for more than 1.5km (1 mile). If the weather's right, start at Marble Arch and walk. You'll see the same thing on the railings of Green Park along Piccadilly on Saturday afternoon.

NOTTING HILL   Portobello Market 🎡🎡 (Tube: Notting Hill Gate) is a magnet for collectors of virtually anything. It's mainly a Saturday event, from 6am to 5pm. You needn't be here at the crack of dawn; 9am is fine. Once known mainly for fruit and vegetables (still sold throughout the week), in the past decades Portobello has become synonymous with antiques. But don't take the stallholder's word for it that the fiddle he's holding is a genuine Stradivarius left to him in the will of his Italian great-uncle; it might have been "nicked" from an East End pawnshop.

The market is divided into three major sections. The most crowded is the antiques section, running between Colville Road and Chepstow Villas to the south. (*Warning:* Be careful of pickpockets in this area.) The second section (and the oldest part) is the fruit and veg market, lying between Westway and Colville Road. In the third and final section, there's a flea market where Londoners sell bric-a-brac and lots of secondhand goods they didn't really want in the first place, but poking around this section still makes for interesting fun.

The serious collector can pick up a copy of a helpful official guide, *Saturday Antique Market: Portobello Road & Westbourne Grove,* published by the Portobello Antique Dealers Association. It lists where to find what, be it music boxes, lace, or 19th-century photographs.

Note: Some 90 antiques and art shops along Portobello Road are open during the week when the street market is closed. This is actually a better time for the serious collector to shop because you'll get more attention from dealers and you won't be distracted by the organ grinder.

London After Dark

London's pulsating nightlife scene is the most vibrant in Europe. Although pubs still close at 11pm, the city is staying up later, and more and more clubs have extended partying into the wee hours.

London is on a real high right now, especially in terms of music and dance-much of the currently popular techno and electronica originated in London clubs. Youth culture prevails here, as downtown denizens flock to the clubs where pop-culture superstars are routinely spotted.

London nightlife is always in a state of flux. What's hot today probably just opened, and many clubs have the lifespan of fruit flies. At the time of this writing, **Groucho,** at 45 Dean St., W1 (© 020/ 7439-4685), is still the *in* club, although it is members only. A few perennials, like Ronnie Scott's, are still favorites.

But London nightlife is not just about music and dance clubs. The city abounds with the world's best theater (sorry, New York!), loads of classical music, pubs oozing historic charm, and tons of other options for a night out.

1 The Play's the Thing: London's Theater Scene

Even more than New York, London is the theater capital of the world. Few things in London are as entertaining and rewarding as the theater. The number and variety of productions, and the standards of acting and directing, are unrivaled. The London stage accommodates both the traditional and the avant-garde and is, for the most part, accessible and reasonably affordable. The new Globe Theatre is an exciting addition to the theater scene (p. 179).

To find out what's on stage before you leave home, check www. officiallondontheatre.co.uk.

TICKET AGENCIES If your heart is set on seeing a specific show, particularly a big hit, reserve way in advance through one of London's ticket agencies. You can check www.officiallondontheatre.co.uk to find out what will be on stage when you're in London. For tickets and information before you go, try **Global Tickets,** 234 W. 44th

> *Tips* **Curtain Going Up!**
>
> Prices for shows vary from £18 to £70 ($33–$130), depend-
> ing on the theater and the seat. Matinees, performed
> Tuesday through Saturday, are cheaper than evening per-
> formances. Evening performances begin between 7:30 and
> 8:30pm, midweek matinees at 2:30 or 3pm, and Saturday
> matinees at 5:45pm. West End theaters are closed Sundays.
>   Many theaters accept telephone bookings at regular
> prices with a credit card. They'll hold your tickets for you
> at the box office, where you pick them up at show time
> with a credit card.

St., Suite 1000, New York, NY 10036 (© **800/223-6108** or 212/
398-1468; www.keithprowse.com). Their London office (which
operates under the name of both Global Tickets and First Call Tickets) is at the British Visitors Center, 1 Regent St., W1 V1PJ (© **020/
7014-8550**), or at the Harrods ticket desk, 87–135 Brompton Rd.
(© **020/7589-9109**), opposite the British Airways desk. They'll
mail your tickets, fax a confirmation, or leave your tickets at the
appropriate production's box office. Instant confirmations are
immediately available for most shows. A booking and handling fee
of up to 20% is added to the price of all tickets.

Another option is **Theatre Direct International (TDI)** (© **800/
334-8457,** U.S. only). TDI specializes in providing London fringe
theater tickets, but also has tickets to major productions, including
those at the Royal National Theatre and the Barbican. The service
allows you to arrive in London with your tickets or have them held
for you at the box office.

GALLERY & DISCOUNT TICKETS   Sometimes gallery seats
(the cheapest) are sold on the day of the performance. Head to the
box office early in the day to purchase these tickets and, since these
are not reserved seats, return an hour before the performance to grab
good seats. Many theaters offer reduced-price tickets to students on
a standby basis. When available, these tickets are sold 30 minutes
before curtain. Line up early for popular shows, as standby tickets
get snapped up quickly. Call the theater directly to find out if
gallery, discount, or standby tickets are offered for a particular show.
Of course, you'll need a valid student ID for student discounts.

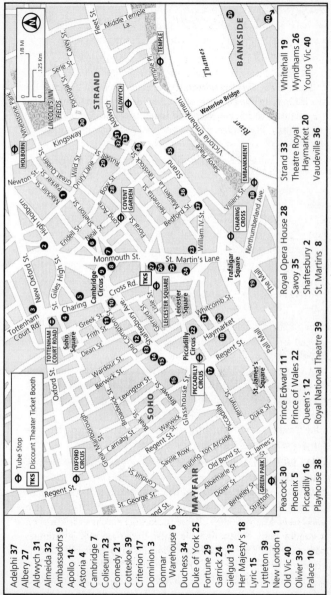

Adelphi **37**
Albery **27**
Aldwych **31**
Almeida **32**
Ambassadors **9**
Apollo **14**
Astoria **4**
Cambridge **7**
Coliseum **23**
Comedy **21**
Cottesloe **39**
Criterion **17**
Dominion **3**
Donmar
  Warehouse **6**
Duchess **34**
Duke of York **25**
Fortune **29**
Garrick **24**
Gielgud **13**
Her Majesty's **18**
Lyric **15**
Lyttelton **39**
New London **1**

Old Vic **40**
Olivier **39**
Palace **10**
Peacock **30**
Phoenix **5**
Piccadilly **16**
Playhouse **38**

Prince Edward **11**
Prince of Wales **22**
Queen's **12**
Royal National Theatre **39**

Royal Opera House **28**
Savoy **35**
Shaftesbury **2**
St. Martins **8**

Strand **33**
Theatre Royal
  Haymarket **20**
Vaudeville **36**

Whitehall **19**
Wyndhams **26**
Young Vic **40**

MAJOR THEATERS & COMPANIES

We have listed some of the most popular theaters and companies below. To find out what's on currently in all of the major and fringe theaters, pick up *Time Out London, Where,* a London daily newspaper, or "The Official London Theatre Guide" pamphlet (online at www.officiallondontheatre.co.uk), available at ticket brokers and all West End theaters.

Barbican Theatre—Royal Shakespeare Company   The Barbican is the London home of the Royal Shakespeare Company, one of the world's finest theater companies. The core of its repertoire remains, of course, the plays of William Shakespeare. It also presents a wide-ranging program in its two theaters. Three productions are in repertory each week in the Barbican Theatre—a 2,000-seat main auditorium with excellent sight lines throughout, thanks to a raked orchestra. The Pit, a small studio space, is where the company's new writing is presented. The Royal Shakespeare Company performs both here and at Stratford-upon-Avon. It is in residence in London during the winter months; in the summer, it tours in England and abroad. For more information on the company and its current productions, check **www.rsc.org.uk**. In the Barbican Centre, Silk St., Barbican, EC2Y. ✆ **0870/609-1110.** Barbican Theatre £5–£40 ($9.25–$74). The Pit £7–£24 ($13–$44) matinees and evening performances. Box office daily 9am–8pm. Tube: Barbican or Moorgate.

Royal National Theatre   Home to one of the world's greatest stage companies, the Royal National Theatre is not one but three theaters—the Olivier, reminiscent of a Greek amphitheater with its open stage; the more traditional Lyttelton; and the Cottesloe, with

---

(Value Ticket Bargains

The **Society of London Theatre** (✆ **020/7557-6700**) operates the tkts booth in Leicester Square (see the "Central London Theaters" map on p. 177 for the location), where same-day tickets for many shows are available at half price or 25% off, plus a £2.50 ($4.65) service charge. All major credit and debit cards are accepted. Tickets (limited to four per person) are sold only on the day of performance. You cannot return tickets. Hours are Monday through Friday from 10am to 6pm. We prefer this ticket agency to the others that populate Leicester Square.

its flexible stage and seating. The National presents the finest in world theater, from classic drama to award-winning new plays, including comedies, musicals, and shows for young people. A choice of at least six plays is offered at any one time. It's also a full-time theater center, with an amazing selection of bars, cafes, restaurants, free foyer music and exhibitions, short early-evening performances, bookshops, backstage tours, riverside walks, and terraces. You can have a three-course meal in Mezzanine, the National's restaurant; enjoy a light meal in the brasserie-style Terrace cafe; or have a snack in one of the coffee bars. South Bank, SE1. ✆ **020/7452-3000**. www.nt-online.org. Tickets £11–£40 ($20–$74); midweek matinees, Sat matinees, and previews cost less. Tube: Waterloo, Embankment, or Charing Cross.

Shakespeare's Globe Theatre   In May 1997, the new Globe Theatre—a replica of the Elizabethan original, thatched roof and all—staged its first slate of plays (*Henry V* and *A Winter's Tale*) yards away from the site of the 16th-century theater where the Bard originally staged his work.

Productions vary in style and setting; not all are performed in Elizabethan costume. In keeping with the historic setting, no lighting is focused just on the stage, but floodlighting is used during evening performances to replicate daylight in the theater—Elizabethan performances took place in the afternoon. Theatergoers sit on wooden benches of yore—in thatch-roofed galleries, no less—but these days you can rent a cushion to make yourself more comfortable. About 500 "groundlings" can stand in the uncovered yard around the stage, just as they did when the Bard was here. Mark Rylane, the artistic director of the Globe, wanted the theatergoing experience to be as authentic as possible—he told the press he'd be delighted if the audience threw fruit at the actors, as they did in Shakespeare's time.

From May to September, the company intends to hold performances Tuesday through Saturday at 2 and 7pm. There will be a limited winter schedule. In any season, the schedule may be affected by weather because this is an outdoor theater. Performances last 2½ to 4 hours, depending on the play.

For details on the exhibition that tells the story of the painstaking re-creation of the Globe, as well as guided tours of the theater, see p. 151. New Globe Walk, Bankside, SE1. ✆ **020/7902-1400**. Box office: ✆ 020/7902-1401. www.shakespeare-globe.org. Tickets £5 ($9.25) for groundlings, £11–£29 ($20–$54) for gallery seats. Exhibition tickets £8 ($15) adults, £6.50 ($12) seniors and students, £5 ($9.25) ages 5–15. Tube: Mansion House or Blackfriars.

FRINGE THEATER

Some of the best theater in London is performed on the "fringe"—at the dozens of theaters devoted to alternative plays, revivals, contemporary dramas, and musicals. These shows are usually more adventurous than established West End productions; they are also consistently lower in price. Expect to pay from £10 to £30 ($19–$56). Most offer discounted seats to students and seniors.

Fringe theaters are scattered around London. Check the weekly listings in *Time Out* for schedules and show times. Some of the more popular and centrally located theaters are listed below; call for details on current productions. Also check www.officiallondontheatre.co.uk and www.londontheatre.co.uk for current fringe show schedules and descriptions.

Almeida Theatre   The Almeida is known for its adventurous stagings of new and classic plays. The theater's legendary status is validated by consistently good productions at lower-than-average prices. Among the recent celebrated productions have been *Hamlet* with Ralph Fiennes and *Medea* with Dame Diana Rigg. Performances are usually held Monday through Saturday. The Almeida is also home to the Festival of Contemporary Music (also called the Almeida Opera) from mid-June to mid-July, featuring everything from atonal jazz to 12-tone chamber orchestra pieces. Almeida St., N1. ✆ **020/7359-4404.** Tickets £15–£27 ($28–$50). Box office Mon–Sat 10am–6pm. Tube: Northern Line to Angel or Victoria Line to Highbury & Islington.

Young Vic *(Kids*   In two showrooms, the Young Vic presents classical and modern plays in the round for theatergoers of all ages and backgrounds, but primarily caters to young adults. Recent productions have included Shakespeare, Ibsen, Arthur Miller, and specially commissioned plays for children. Performances are usually Monday through Saturday at 7:30pm, with a Saturday matinee at 2 or 2:30pm, but call for specific times as the schedule has been known to change. 66 The Cut, Waterloo, SE1. ✆ **020/7928-6363.** Tickets £20–£25 ($37–$46) adults, £15–£20 ($28–$37) seniors, £10 ($19) students and children. Box office Mon–Sat 10am–8pm. Tube: Waterloo or Southwark.

2 Classical Music, Dance & Opera

Currently, London supports five major orchestras—the London Symphony Orchestra (www.lso.co.uk), the Royal Philharmonic (www.rpo.co.uk), the London Philharmonic Orchestra (www.lpo.co.uk), the BBC Symphony (www.bbc.co.uk/orchestras/so), and the BBC

Philharmonic (www.bbc.co.uk/orchestras/philharmonic)—plus several choirs and operas, and many smaller chamber groups and historic-instrument ensembles. In addition to the big stars listed above, also look for the London Sinfonietta (www.londonsinfonietta.org.uk), a contemporary-music ensemble; the English Chamber Orchestra (www.englishchamberorchestra.co.uk); and the Academy of St. Martin-in-the-Fields (www.academysmif.co.uk). Concerts for many of the groups mentioned above are presented, with exceptions, in the South Bank Arts Centre or the Barbican. For smaller recitals, venues include Wigmore Hall and St. John's Smith Square. Check the websites to find out where and when the orchestras and ensembles listed here are performing.

Barbican Centre (home of the London Symphony Orchestra & more)   The largest art and exhibition center in Western Europe, the roomy and comfortable Barbican complex is the perfect setting for enjoying music and theater. Barbican Hall is the permanent home address of the London Symphony Orchestra, as well as host to visiting orchestras and performers of all styles, from classical to jazz, folk, and world music.

In addition to its hall and two theaters, Barbican Centre encompasses the Barbican Art Gallery, the Concourse Gallery, and foyer exhibition spaces; Cinemas One and Two, which show recently released mainstream films and film series; the Barbican Library, a general lending library that places a strong emphasis on the arts; the Conservatory, one of London's largest greenhouses; and restaurants, cafes, and bars. Silk St., the City, EC2. ✆ 020/7638-8891. www.barbican.org.uk. Tickets £8–£42 ($15–$78). Box office daily 9am–8pm. Tube: Barbican or Moorgate.

Kenwood Lakeside Concerts   These band and orchestral concerts on the north side of Hampstead Heath have been a British tradition for some 50 years. In recent years, laser shows and fireworks have been added to a repertoire that includes everything from rousing versions of the *1812 Overture* to jazz to operas such as *Carmen*. The final concert of the season always features some of the "Pomp and Circumstance" marches of Sir Edward Elgar. Music drifts across the lake to serenade wine-and-cheese parties on the grass. Concerts take place from July to early September, Saturday at 7:30pm. Kenwood, Hampstead Lane, Hampstead Heath, London NW3 7JR. ✆ 020/7413-1443. Tickets for adults £11 ($20) for seats on the grass lawn, £13–£18 ($24–$33) for reserved deck chairs. Reductions of 12.5% for students and persons over 60. Box office Mon–Sat 9:30am–6:30pm. Tube: Northern Line to Golders Green or Archway, then bus no. 210.

London Coliseum (home of the English National Opera)

Built in 1904 as a variety theater and converted into an opera house in 1968, the London Coliseum is the city's largest theater. One of two national opera companies, the English National Opera performs a range of works here, from classics to Gilbert and Sullivan to new experimental works. All performances are in English. The Opera presents a repertory of 18 to 20 productions 5 or 6 nights a week for 10 months of the year (the theater is dark mid-July to mid-Sept). The theater also hosts touring companies. Although balcony seats are cheaper, many visitors seem to prefer the upper circle or dress circle. London Coliseum, St. Martin's Lane, WC2. ℰ 020/7632-8300. Tickets £5–£12 ($9.25–$22) balcony, £20–£70 ($37–$130) upper or dress circle or stalls; about 100 discount balcony tickets sold on the day of performance from 10am. Box office Mon–Sat 10am–8pm. Tube: Charing Cross or Leicester Sq.

Royal Albert Hall

Opened in 1871 and dedicated to the memory of Victoria's consort, Prince Albert, this circular building holds one of the world's most famous auditoriums. With a seating capacity of 5,200, it's a popular place to hear music by stars. Occasional sporting events (especially boxing) figure strongly here, too.

Since 1941, the hall has hosted the BBC Henry Wood Promenade Concerts, known as "The Proms," an annual series that lasts for 8 weeks between mid-July and mid-September. The Proms, incorporating a medley of rousing, mostly British orchestral music, have been a British tradition since 1895. Although most of the audience occupies reserved seats, true aficionados usually opt for standing room in the orchestra pit, with close-up views of the musicians on stage. Newly commissioned works are often premiered here. The final evening is the most traditional; the rousing favorites "Jerusalem" or "Land of Hope and Glory" echo through the hall. Recently, the hall has seen performances by Liza Minnelli, an avant-garde production of Bizet's *Carmen,* orchestral and symphonic works from orchestras visiting from other cities, lots of British and European pop, and the London production of *Cirque du Soleil.* Kensington Gore, SW7 2AP. ℰ 020/7589-8212. Tickets £18–£52 ($33–$96), depending on the event. Box office daily 9am–9pm. Tube: S. Kensington.

Royal Festival Hall

Three of the most acoustically perfect concert halls in the world were erected here between 1951 and 1964: the Royal Festival Hall, the Queen Elizabeth Hall, and the Purcell Room, all located in this complex. Together, the halls present more than 1,200 performances a year, including classical music, ballet, jazz, popular music, and contemporary dance. Also here is the internationally renowned Hayward Gallery.

Royal Festival Hall, which opens daily at 10am, offers an extensive array of things to see and do, including free exhibitions in the foyers and free lunchtime music at 12:30pm. On Friday, Commuter Jazz in the foyer from 5:15 to 6:45pm is free. The Poetry Library is open Tuesday through Sunday from 11am to 8pm, and shops display a selection of books, records, and crafts. The Festival Buffet has food at reasonable prices, and bars dot the foyers. The People's Palace offers lunch and dinner with a panoramic view of the River Thames; making reservations by calling ✆ **020/7928-9999** is recommended. On the South Bank, SE1. ✆ 020/7960-4242. www.rfh.org.uk. Tickets £6–£55 ($11–$102). Box office daily 9am–8pm. Tube: Waterloo or Embankment.

The Royal Opera House (home of the Royal Ballet & the Royal Opera)   The Royal Ballet and the Royal Opera are at home again in this magnificently restored theater. Opera and ballet aficionados hardly recognize the renovated place, with its spectacular new public spaces, including the Vilar Floral Hall (a chamber-music venue), a rooftop restaurant, and bars and shops. The entire northeast corner of one of London's most famous public squares has been transformed, finally realizing Inigo Jones's original vision for this colonnaded plaza. Regular backstage tours are offered daily at 10:30am, and 12:30 and 2:30pm (not on Sun or matinee days).

Performances of the Royal Opera are usually sung in the original language, but supertitles are projected. The Royal Ballet, which ranks with top companies such as the Kirov and the Paris Opera Ballet, performs a repertory with a tilt toward the classics, including works by its earlier choreographer-directors Sir Frederick Ashton and Sir Kenneth MacMillan. Bow St., Covent Garden, WC2. ✆ 020/7304-4000. www.royalopera.org. Tickets £15–£170 ($28–$315). Box office Mon–Sat 10am–8pm. Tube: Covent Garden.

Sadler's Wells Theatre   This is a premier venue for dance and opera. It occupies the site of a series of theaters, the first built in 1683. In the early 1990s, the turn-of-the-century theater was mostly demolished, and construction began on an innovative new design completed at the end of 1998. The turn-of-the-century facade has been retained, but the interior has been completely revamped with a stylish cutting-edge theater design. The new theater offers classical ballet, modern dance of all degrees of "avant-garde-ness," and children's theatrical productions, including a Christmas ballet. Performances are usually at 8pm. Rosebery Ave., EC1. ✆ 0870/7333-9000.

www.sadlers-wells.com. Tickets £11–£50 ($19–$92). Box office Mon–Sat 9am–8:30pm. Tube: Northern Line to Angel.

3 Live Rock, Pop & Jazz

In addition to the venues listed below, see Bar Rumba, Cargo, Cuba, Electric Ballroom, The End, Equinox, and Fabric (all are dance clubs with live music) in section 4, "Dance Clubs."

ROCK & POP

The Bull & Gate   Outside central London, and smaller, cheaper, and often more animated and less touristy than many of its competitors, The Bull & Gate is the unofficial headquarters of London's pub rock scene. Indie and relatively unknown rock bands are served up in back-to-back handfuls at this somewhat battered Victorian pub. The place attracts a young crowd mainly in their 20s. If you like spilled beer, this is off-the-beaten-track London at its most authentic. Bands that have played here and later ascended to fame on Europe's club scene have included Madness, Blur, and Pulp. There's music nightly from 9pm to midnight. 389 Kentish Town Rd., NW5. ✆ 020/8806-8062. Cover £5 ($9.25). Tube: Northern Line to Kentish Town.

Sound   In the heart of London, this 700-seat venue books the big acts, everybody from Sinead O'Connor to Puff Daddy to the Spice Girls. Sound functions as a restaurant and bar every night, with limited live music and a DJ until 11pm; after 11pm, the mood changes, the menu is simplified to include only bar snacks, and the site focuses much more heavily on live music and dancing. The music program is forever changing; call to see what's on at the time of your visit and to reserve tickets. Crowds and age levels can vary here depending on what act is featured. Reservations are recommended for dinner, but reservations after 11pm are not accepted. Swiss Centre at 10 Wardour St., Leicester Sq., W1. ✆ 020/7287-1010. Tickets £8–£12 ($15–$22). Box office Mon–Sat 10am–8pm. Tube: Leicester Sq.

JAZZ

Bull's Head   This club has showcased live modern jazz every night of the week for more than 30 years. One of the oldest hostelries in the area, it was a 19th-century staging post where travelers on their way to Hampton Court could rest while coach horses were changed. Today, the bar features jazz by musicians from all over the world. Since it's way off the tourist trail, it attracts mainly locals in a wide age group, all of whom appreciate good music. Live jazz plays on

Sunday from 2 to 4pm and 8 to 10:30pm; Monday through Saturday, from 8:30 to 11pm. You can order lunch at the Carvery in the Saloon Bar or dinner in the 17th-century Stable Restaurant. The club is open Monday through Saturday from 11am to 11pm, and Sunday from noon to 10:30pm. 373 Lonsdale Rd., Barnes, SW13. © 020/8876-5241. Cover £5–£10 ($9.25–$19). Tube: Hammersmith, then bus 219 to Barnes Bridge, then retrace the path of the bus for some 90m (300 ft). on foot; or take Hounslow Look train from Waterloo Station and get off at Barnes Bridge Station, then walk 5 min. to the club.

100 Club Although less plush and expensive than some jazz clubs, 100 Club is a serious contender on the music front, with presentations of some remarkably good jazz. Its cavalcade of bands includes the best British jazz musicians and some of their Yankee brethren. Rock, R&B, and blues are also on tap. Serious devotees of jazz from 20 to 45 show up here. Open Monday through Thursday and Sunday from 7:30 to 11:30pm; Friday from noon to 3pm, and 8:30pm to 2am; and Saturday from 7:30pm to 1am. 100 Oxford St., W1. © 020/7636-0933. Cover nightly £7–£12 ($13–$22). Club members get a £1 ($1.85) discount. Tube: Tottenham Court Rd. or Oxford Circus.

Jazz Café Afro-Latin jazz fans know that this club hosts great combos from around the globe. Weekends, described by a patron as "bumpy jazzy-funk nights," are the best time to decide what that means. To fit in here, be young or dress the part. Call ahead for listings, cover, and table reservations (often necessary); opening times can vary. 5 Parkway, NW1. © 020/7916-6060. Reservations recommended. Cover £8–£20 ($15–$37). Tube: Camden Town.

Pizza Express Don't let the name fool you: This restaurant/bar serves up some of the best jazz in London by mainstream artists, along with thin-crust Italian pizza. You'll find local bands or visiting groups, often from the United States. The place draws an equal mix of Londoners and visitors in the 20s-to-40s age bracket. Although the club has been enlarged, it's still important to reserve ahead of time. The restaurant is open daily from noon to midnight; there is jazz from 9pm to midnight. 10 Dean St., W1. © 020/7437-9595. Cover £11–£20 ($20–$37). Tube: Tottenham Court Rd.

Ronnie Scott's Jazz Club Inquire about jazz in London and people immediately think of Ronnie Scott's, the European vanguard for modern jazz. Only the best English and American combos, often fronted by top-notch vocalists, are booked here. The programs make for an entire evening of cool jazz. In the heart of Soho, Ronnie Scott's is a 10-minute walk from Piccadilly Circus along Shaftesbury Avenue. In the Main Room, you can watch the show from the bar or sit at a table, at which you can order dinner. The Downstairs Bar is more intimate; among the regulars at your elbow may be some of the world's most talented musicians. This place is so well known that all visiting musicians show up here along with the diehard music fans. On weekends, the separate Upstairs Room has a disco called Club Latino. The club is open Monday through Saturday from 8:30pm to 3am. Reservations are recommended. 47 Frith St., W1. ℂ 020/7439-0747. Cover £15–£25 ($28–$46) for nonmembers, £5 ($9.25) for members, Fri and Sat £10 ($19). Tube: Leicester Sq. or Piccadilly Circus.

606 Club Located in a discreet basement in Chelsea, the 606, a jazz supper club in the boondocks of Fulham, presents live music nightly. Predominantly a venue for modern jazz, styles range from traditional to contemporary. Local musicians and some very big names play here, whether at planned gigs or informal jam sessions after they finish shows elsewhere in town. Because of license requirements, patrons can order alcohol only with food. Locals show up here along with a trendy crowd from more posh neighborhoods in London. Open Monday through Wednesday from 7:30pm to 1am; Thursday from 8pm to 1:30am; Friday and Saturday from 10pm to 2am; Sunday from 8:30 to 11:30pm. 90 Lots Rd., SW10. ℂ 020/7352-5953. Cover Mon–Thurs £7 ($13), Fri–Sat £9 ($17), Sun £6–£8 ($11–$15). Bus: 11, 19, 22, 31, 39, or C3. Tube: Earl's Court.

4 Dance Clubs

Bar Rumba Despite its location on Shaftesbury Avenue, this Latin bar and music club could be featured in a book of "Underground London." A hush-hush address, it leans toward radical jazz-fusion on some nights, and phat funk on other occasions. It boasts two full bars and a different musical theme every night. Tuesday and Wednesday are the only nights you probably won't have to queue at the door. Monday's "That's How It Is" showcase features jazz, hip-hop, and drum and bass; Friday provides R&B and swing; and Saturday's "Garage City" buzzes with house and garage. All the music here is live. On weeknights you have to be 18 or older; on Saturday and Sunday, nobody under 21 is allowed in. Open Monday through Thursday from 6pm to 3:30am, Friday from 6pm to 4am, Saturday from 7pm to 6am, and Sunday from 8pm to 1:30am. 36 Shaftesbury Ave., W1. ℂ 020/7287-6933. Cover £3–£12 ($5.55–$22). Tube: Piccadilly Circus.

Cargo   Another watering hole in ultra-trendy Hoxton draws a smart urban crowd from their expensive West End flats. Its habitués assure us it's the place to go for a "wicked time" and great live bands. If there are no bands on a particular night, then great DJs dominate the club. Music and dancing starts at 6pm and the joint is jumping by 9:30 nightly. It's fun and funky, with two big arched rooms, fantastic acoustics, and a parade of videos. As for the patrons, the bartender characterized it just right: "We get the freaks and the normal people." Drinks are reasonably priced, as is the self-styled "street food." Open Monday to Thursday 6pm to 1am, Friday and Saturday 6pm to 3am, and Sunday 6pm to midnight. Kingsland Viaduct, 83 Rivington St., Shoreditch, EC2. ℰ 020/7739-3440. Cover £5–£9 ($9.25–$17) after 10pm. Tube: Liverpool St.

Cuba   This Spanish/Cuban bar-restaurant, which has a music club downstairs, features live acts from Spain, Cuba, Brazil, and the rest of Latin America. The crowd is equal parts restaurant diners, after-work drinkers, and dancers. Salsa classes are offered daily from 7:30 to 9:30pm for £4 to £7 ($7.40–$13). Happy hour is Monday through Friday from 5 to 7:30pm. Open Monday through Thursday from 5pm to 2am; Sunday from 5 to 10:30pm; Friday to Saturday noon to 2am; Sunday all-day Happy Hour. 11 Kensington High St., W8. ℰ 020/7938-4137. Cover £3–£8 ($5.55–$15). Tube: High St. Kensington.

Electric Ballroom   Though this club's been around long enough to come down a few points on the trendiness scale, the joint is still packed and jumping with a mixture of Londoners and visitors having a hot time. Two floors are set aside for gyrating to live music throughout the night; another is set up for chilling out. Many nights are '70s and '80s retro. Call to see what's happening. Thursday night is often theme night, at which time the cover varies. Perhaps it'll be an alternative night called "Full Tilt," when you'll discover a parade of pierced flesh and leather. Open 10:30pm to 3am Friday and Saturday. 184 Camden High St., NW1. ℰ 020/7485-9006. Cover varies on weekdays; £7–£10 ($13–$19) Fri–Sat. Tube: Camden Town.

The End   This club is better than ever after its recent enlargement. Now you'll find a trio of large dance floors, along with four bars and a chill-out area. Speaker walls will blast you into orbit. The End is the best club in London for live house and garage music. It draws both straight and gay Londoners. "We can't tell the difference anymore," the club owner confessed, "and who cares anyway?" From its drinking fountain to its swanky toilets, the club is alluring. Dress for glam and to be seen on the circuit. Some big names in London appear on the weekends to entertain. Open Monday through Thursday from 10pm to 3am, Friday 10pm to 5am, and Saturday from 10pm to 7am. 16A W. Central St., WC1. ✆ **020/7419-9199.** Cover £4–£15 ($7.40–$28). Tube: Tottenham Court Rd.

Equinox   Built in 1992 on the site of the London Empire, a dance emporium that had witnessed the changing styles of social dancing since the 1700s, the Equinox has established itself as a perennial favorite. It contains nine bars, the largest dance floor in London, and a restaurant modeled after a 1950s American diner. With the exception of rave, virtually every kind of live dance music is featured, including dance hall, pop, rock, and Latin. The setting is illuminated with one of Europe's largest lighting rigs, and the crowd is as diverse as London itself. On Friday and Saturday nights, summer visitors can enjoy theme nights, which are geared toward entertaining a worldwide audience. Open Monday through Thursday from 9pm to 3am, and Friday and Saturday from 9pm to 4am. Leicester Sq., WC2. ✆ **020/7437-1446.** Cover £6–£12 ($11–$22) depending on the night of the week. Tube: Leicester Sq.

Fabric   While other competitors have come and gone, Fabric continues to draw crowds since opening in 1999. Its main allure is that it has a license for 24-hour music and dancing from Thursday to Sunday night. This is one of the most famous clubs in the increasingly trendy East London sector. It is said that when the owners power up the underfoot subwoofer, lights dim in London's East End. On some crazed nights, at least 2,500 members of young London, plus a medley of international visitors, crowd into this mammoth place. It has a trio of dance floors, bars wherever you look, unisex toilets, chill-out beds, and even a roof terrace. Live acts are presented every Friday, with DJs reigning on weekends. You'll hear house, garage, soca, reggae, and whatever else is on the cutting edge of London's underground music scene at the time. Open Thursday and Friday from 10pm to 7am, Saturday from 10:30pm to 7am, and Sunday from 10pm to 5am. 77A Charterhouse St., EC1. ✆ **020/7336-8898.** Cover £12–£15 ($22–$28). Tube: Farringdon.

Hippodrome   Near Leicester Square, the Hippodrome is London's granddaddy of discos, a cavernous place with DJed music, a great sound system, and lights to match. It was Lady Di's favorite in her bar-hopping days. Tacky and touristy, it's packed on weekends. Open Monday through Friday from 9pm to 3am, and Saturday from 9pm to 3:30am. Corner of Cranbourn St. and Charing Cross Rd., WC2. *©* **020/7437-4311.** Cover £8–£11 ($15–$20). Tube: Leicester Sq.

Ministry of Sound   Removed from the city center, this club-of-the-hour remains hot, hot, hot. With a large bar and huge sound system, it blasts garage and house music for the energetic crowds that pack the two dance floors. If music and lights in the rest of the club have gone to your head, you can chill in the lounge. *Note:* The cover charge is stiff, and bouncers decide who is cool enough to enter, so slip into your grooviest and most glamorous club gear. Open Friday from 10:30pm to 5am, and Saturday from 11pm to 8am. 103 Gaunt St., SE1. *©* **020/7740-8600.** Cover £12–£15 ($22–$28). Tube: Northern Line to Elephant & Castle.

The Office   This is an eclectic club with a bureaucratic name—nights feature more traditional recorded pop, rock, soul, and disco. Ambience wins out over decor. During the week, a social lounge atmosphere pervades; on the weekends, this place is pure dance club. Open Monday and Tuesday from noon to 11:30pm, Wednesday through Friday from noon to 3am, and Saturday from 9:30pm to 3am. 3–5 Rathbone Place, W1. *©* **020/7636-1598.** Cover £3–£9 ($5.55–$17). Tube: Tottenham Court Rd.

Trap   This is one of the leading clubs of the West End lying in the vicinity of Oxford and Regent streets. It's a stylish rendezvous, drawing a crowd in their 20s and 30s to its plush precincts. The young Mick Jagger or aspirant Madonna of today might be seen lounging on one of the large white-covered sofas across from the sleek bar. Drinks are expensive, so be duly warned. Recorded music plays for dancing; Thursday and Friday nights are especially busy. A supper club adjoins the joint and is open for most of the night. 201 Wardour St., W1. *©* **020/7434-3820.** Cover £5–£15 ($9.25–$28). Tues–Wed 5pm–midnight; Thurs–Fri 5pm–3am; Sat 5–10pm. Tube: Tottenham Court Rd. or Oxford Circus.

Zoo Bar   The owners spent millions of pounds outfitting this club in the slickest, flashiest, and most psychedelic decor in London. If you're looking for a true Euro nightlife experience replete with gorgeous *au pairs* and trendy Europeans, this is it. Zoo Bar upstairs is a menagerie of mosaic animals beneath a glassed-in ceiling dome. Downstairs, the music is intrusive enough to make conversation futile. Clients range from 18 to 35; androgyny is the look of choice. 13–18 Bear St., WC2. *©* **020/7839-4188.** Cover £3–£7 ($5.55–$13) after 10pm. Mon–Fri 4pm–3:30am; Sat 1pm–3:30am; Sun 4pm–12:30am. Tube: Leicester Sq.

5 The Best of London's Pubs: The World's Greatest Pub Crawl

Dropping into the local pub for a pint of real ale or bitter is the best way to soak up the character of the different villages that make up London. You'll hear local accents and slang and see firsthand how far removed upper-crust Kensington is from blue-collar Wapping. Catch the local gossip or football talk—and, of course, enjoy some of the finest ales, stouts, ciders, and malt whiskies in the world.

Anchor   You can follow in the footsteps of Shakespeare and Dickens by quenching your thirst at this pub. If literary heroes are not your bag, then perhaps you'll enjoy knowing that Tom Cruise had a pint or two here during the filming of *Mission Impossible*. Rebuilt in the mid–18th century to replace an earlier pub that managed to withstand the Great Fire of 1666, the rooms are worn and comfortable. You can choose from Scottish and Newcastle brews on tap. 34 Park St., Bankside, SE1. ℂ 020/7407-1577. Tube: Jubilee Line to London Bridge.

Black Friar   The Black Friar will transport you to the Edwardian era. The wedge-shaped pub is swimming in marble and bronze Art Nouveau, featuring bas-reliefs of monks, a low-vaulted mosaic ceiling, and seating recesses carved out of gold marble. It's popular with the City's after-work crowd, and it features Adams, Wadworths 6X, Tetleys, and Brakspears on tap. 174 Queen Victoria St., EC4. ℂ 020/7236-5474. Tube: Blackfriars.

Bow Wine Vaults   Bow Wine Vaults has existed since long before the wine-bar craze began in the 1970s. One of the most famous in London, the bar attracts cost-conscious diners and drinkers to its vaulted cellars for such traditional fare as deep-fried Camembert, lobster ravioli, and a mixed grill, along with fish. The cocktail bar is popular with City employees after work (open weekdays 11:30am–11pm). More elegant meals, served in the street-level dining room, include mussels in cider sauce, English wild mushrooms in puff pastry, beef Wellington, and steak with brown-butter sauce. Wines from around the world are available; the last time we were there the wine of the day was a Chilean chardonnay. 10 Bow Churchyard, EC4. ℂ 020/7248-1121. Tube: Mansion House, Bank, or St. Paul's.

Cittie of Yorke   This pub boasts the longest bar in Britain, rafters ascending to the heavens, and a row of immense wine vats, all of which give it the air of a great medieval hall—appropriate, since a pub has existed at this location since 1430. Samuel Smiths is on tap, and the bar offers novelties such as chocolate-orange-flavored vodka. 22 High Holborn, WC1. ℭ 020/7242-7670. Tube: Holborn or Chancery Lane.

Cutty Sark Tavern   Retreat here for great antiquarian ambience inside a 16th-century dwelling with flagstones, barrel tables, open fires, and rough-hewn brick walls. The pub has such an Old London feel that you may find yourself seeing Dickensian riffraff after a few pints of Bass or Worthington's Best. Ballast Quay, off Lassell St., SE10. ℭ 020/8858-3146. Train: Cutty Sark.

Dog & Duck   This snug little joint, a Soho landmark, is the most intimate pub in London. A former patron was the author George Orwell, who came here to celebrate his sales of *Animal Farm* in the United States. A wide mixture of ages and persuasions flock here, usually chatting amiably. Publicans here stock an interesting assortment of English beers, including Tetleys, Fuller London, and Timothy Taylor Landlord. In autumn, customers will ask for Addlestone's Cider. A lot of patrons head to Ronnie Scott's Jazz Club, which is close by, after having a few pints here. The cozy upstairs bar is also open. 18 Bateman St. (corner of Frith St.), W1. ℭ 020/7494-0697. Tube: Tottenham Court Rd. or Leicester Sq.

George   The existing structure was built in 1877 to replace the original pub, which was destroyed in the Great Fire of 1666. That pub's accolades date to 1598, when it was reviewed as a "faire inn for the receipt of travelers." The present pub was built in the typical "traditional Victorian" style, with stripped oak floors, paneled walls, a curved bar counter, brass ceiling lights, and windows with etched and cut glass. Three huge mirrors decorate the walls. It's still a great place to enjoy Flowers Original, Boddingtons, and London Pride Abbot on tap. Off 77 Borough High St., SE1. ℭ 020/7407-2056. Tube: Northern Line to London Bridge or Borough.

Grenadier   Tucked away in a mews, the Grenadier is one of London's reputedly haunted pubs, the ghost here being an 18th-century British soldier. Aside from the poltergeist, the basement houses the original bar and skittles alley used by the Duke of Wellington's officers. The scarlet front door of the one-time officers' mess is guarded by a scarlet sentry box and shaded by a vine. The bar is nearly always crowded. Lunch and dinner are offered daily—even on Sunday, when it's a tradition to drink Bloody Marys here. In the stalls along the side, you can order good-tasting fare based on seasonal ingredients. Well-prepared dishes include pork Grenadier, and a chicken-and-Stilton roulade. Snacks like fish and chips are available at the bar. 18 Wilton Row, SW1. ℭ 020/7235-3074. Tube: Hyde Park Corner.

World's Greatest Pub Crawl

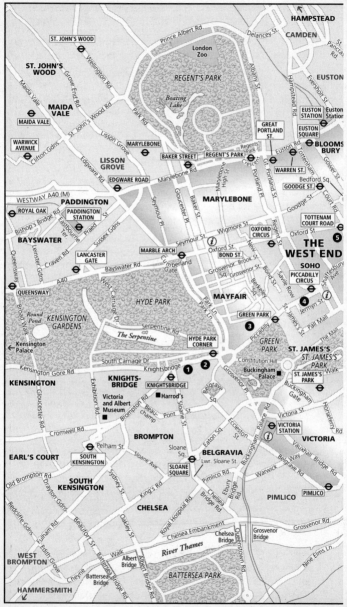

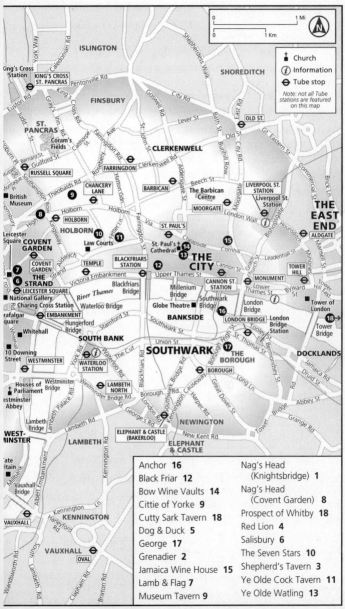

Anchor 16			**Nag's Head** (Knightsbridge) 1	
Black Friar 12			**Nag's Head** (Covent Garden) 8	
Bow Wine Vaults 14			**Prospect of Whitby** 18	
Cittie of Yorke 9			**Red Lion** 4	
Cutty Sark Tavern 18			**Salisbury** 6	
Dog & Duck 5			**The Seven Stars** 10	
George 17			**Shepherd's Tavern** 3	
Grenadier 2			**Ye Olde Cock Tavern** 11	
Jamaica Wine House 15			**Ye Olde Watling** 13	
Lamb & Flag 7				
Museum Tavern 9				

Jamaica Wine House This was one of the first coffeehouses in England and, reputedly, the Western world. For years, merchants and sea captains came here to transact deals over rum and coffee. Nowadays, the two-level house dispenses coffee, beer, ale, lager, and fine wines, among them a variety of ports. The oak-paneled bar is on the street level, and attracts crowds of investment bankers. You can order standard but filling dishes such as a ploughman's lunch and toasted sandwiches. St. Michael's Alley, off Cornhill, EC3. ☏ 020/7929-6972. Tube: Bank.

Lamb & Flag Dickens once frequented this pub, and the room has changed little from the days when he prowled the neighborhood. The pub has an amazing and scandalous history. Poet and author Dryden was almost killed by a band of thugs outside its doors in December 1679, and the pub gained the nickname the "Bucket of Blood" during the Regency era (1811–20) because of the bare-knuckled prizefights here. Tap beers include Courage Best and Directors, Old Speckled Hen, John Smiths, and Wadworths 6X. 33 Rose St., off Garrick St., WC2. ☏ 020/7497-9504. Tube: Leicester Sq.

Museum Tavern Across the street from the British Museum, this pub (ca. 1703) retains most of its antique trappings: velvet, oak paneling, and cut glass. It lies right in the center of the University of London area and is popular with writers, publishers, and researchers from the museum. Supposedly, Karl Marx wrote while dining here. Traditional English food is served: shepherd's pie, sausages cooked in English cider, turkey-and-ham pie, ploughman's lunch, and salads. Several English ales, cold lagers, cider, Guinness, wines, and spirits are available. Food and coffee are served all day. The pub gets crowded at lunchtime. 49 Great Russell St., WC1. ☏ 020/7242-8987. Tube: Holborn or Tottenham Court Rd.

Nag's Head This Nag's Head (not to be confused with the more renowned one at 10 James St.; see below) is on a back street a short walk from the Berkeley Hotel. Previously a jail dating from 1780, it's said to be the smallest pub in London. In 1921, it was sold for £12 ($22) and 6p(11¢). Have a drink up front or wander to the tiny bar in the rear. For food, you might enjoy "real ale sausage" (made with pork and ale), shepherd's pie, or the quiche of the day, all served by the welcoming staff. A cosmopolitan clientele—newspaper people, musicians, and travelers—patronizes this warm, cozy pub. This pub touts itself as an "independent," or able to serve any "real ale" they choose because of their lack of affiliation. 53 Kinnerton St., SW1. ☏ 020/7235-1135. Tube: Hyde Park.

Nag's Head This Nag's Head (as opposed to the one above) is one of London's most famous Edwardian pubs. In days of yore, patrons had to make their way through a fruit and flower market to drink here. Today, the pub is popular with young people. The draft Guinness is very good. Lunch (served noon–4pm) is typical pub grub: sandwiches, salads, pork cooked in cider, and garlic prawns. Snacks are available all afternoon. 10 James St., WC2. ✆ 020/7836-4678. Tube: Covent Garden.

Prospect of Whitby One of London's most historic pubs, Prospect was founded in the days of the Tudors, taking its name from a coal barge that made trips between Yorkshire and London. Come here for a tot, a noggin, or whatever it is you drink, and soak up the atmosphere. The pub has got quite a pedigree. Dickens and diarist Samuel Pepys used to drop in, and Turner came here for weeks at a time studying views of the Thames. In the 17th century, the notorious Hanging Judge Jeffreys used to get drunk here while overseeing hangings at the adjoining Execution Dock. Tables in the courtyard look out over river views. You can order a Morlands Old Speckled Hen from a hand-pump, or a malt whisky. 57 Wapping Wall, E1. ✆ 020/7481-1095. Tube: Wapping.

Red Lion This Victorian pub, with its early-1900s decorations and 150-year-old mirrors, has been compared to Manet's painting *A Bar at the Folies-Bergère* (on display at the Courtauld Gallery). You can order premade sandwiches, and on Saturday, homemade fish and chips are served. Wash down your meal with Ind Coope's fine ales or the house's special beer, Burton's, a brew made of spring water from the Midlands town of Burton-on-Trent. 2 Duke of York St. (off Jermyn St.), SW1. ✆ 020/7321-0782. Tube: Piccadilly Circus.

Salisbury Salisbury's cut-glass mirrors reflect the faces of English stage stars (and hopefuls) sitting around the curved buffet-style bar. A less prominent place to dine is the old-fashioned wall banquette with its copper-topped tables and Art Nouveau decor. The pub's specialties, home-cooked pies set out in a buffet cabinet with salads, are quite good and inexpensive. 90 St. Martin's Lane, WC2. ✆ 020/7836-5863. Tube: Leicester Sq.

The Seven Stars In 2001, its 399th year, this tranquil little pub facing the back of the Royal Courts of Justice was taken over by Roxy Beaujolais, author of the pub cookbook "Home From the Inn Contented," whose former pub was voted the Soho Society's Pub of the Year. Within the ancient charm of two narrow rooms that are listed landmarks, drinking in Queer Street (as Carey St. was called because of the bankruptcy courts) is pleasant. One can linger over pub food and real ales behind Irish-linen lace curtains, with litigants, barristers, reporters, and pit musicians from West End shows. Then, try to navigate to the lavatories up some comically narrow Elizabethan stairs. In mild weather, the law courts' stone balustrade under the trees provides customers with a long bar and beer garden. 53 Carey St., WC2. ✆ 020/7242-8521. Tube: Chancery Lane or Temple.

Shepherd's Tavern One of the focal points of the all-pedestrian shopping zone of Shepherd's Market, this pub occupies an 18th-century town house amid a warren of narrow, cobble-covered streets behind Park Lane. The street-level bar is cramped but congenial. Many of the regulars recall this tavern's popularity with the pilots of the Battle of Britain. Bar snacks include simple plates of shepherd's pie, and fish and chips. More formal dining is available upstairs in the cozy, cedar-lined Georgian-style restaurant. The classic British menu probably hasn't changed much since the 1950s, and you can always get Oxford ham or roast beef with Yorkshire pudding. 50 Hertford St., W1. ✆ 020/7499-3017. Tube: Green Park.

Ye Olde Cock Tavern Dating back to 1549, this tavern boasts a long line of literary patrons: Pepys mentioned it, Dickens frequented it, and Tennyson referred to it in a poem (a copy of which is proudly displayed near the front entrance). It's one of the few buildings in London that survived the Great Fire of 1666. At street level, you can order a pint as well as snacks, steak-and-kidney pie, or a cold chicken-and-beef plate with salad. At the Carvery upstairs, a meal includes a choice of appetizers, followed by lamb, pork, beef, or turkey. 22 Fleet St., EC4. ✆ 020/7353-8570. Tube: Temple or Chancery Lane.

Ye Olde Watling Ye Olde Watling was rebuilt after the Great Fire of 1666. On the ground level is a mellow pub. Upstairs is an intimate restaurant where, sitting at trestle tables under oak beams, you can dine on simple English main dishes for lunch. The menu varies daily, with such choices and reliable standbys as fish and chips, lasagna, fish cakes, and usually a vegetarian dish. All are served with two vegetables or salad, plus rice or potatoes. 29 Watling St., EC4. ✆ 020/7653-9971. Tube: Mansion House.

6 Bars & Cocktail Lounges

Beach Blanket Babylon Go here if you're looking for a hot singles bar that attracts a crowd in their 20s and 30s. This Portobello joint is very cruisy. The decor is a bit wacky, no doubt designed by an aspiring Salvador Dalí who decided to make it a fairy-tale grotto (or was he going for a medieval dungeon look?). It's close to the Portobello Market. Saturday and Sunday nights are the hot, crowded times for bacchanalian revelry. 45 Ledbury Rd., W11. ℂ 020/7229-2907. Tube: Notting Hill Gate.

Cantaloupe This bustling pub and restaurant is hailed as the bar that jump-started the increasingly fashionable Shoreditch scene. Businesspeople commuting from their jobs in the City mix with East End trendoids in the early evening at what has been called a "gastro pub/pre-club bar." Wooden tables and benches are found up front, although the Red Bar is more comfortable, as patrons lounge on Chesterfield chairs. The urban beat is courtesy of the house DJ. The restaurant and tapas menus are first rate. 35–42 Charlotte Rd., Shoreditch, EC2. ℂ 020/7613-4411. Tube: Old St.

The Library One of London's poshest drinking retreats, this deluxe bar boasts high ceilings, leather Chesterfields, respectable oil paintings, and grand windows. Its collection of ancient cognacs is unparalleled in London. In the Lanesborough Hotel, 1 Lanesborough Place, SW1. ℂ 020/7259-5599. Tube: Hyde Park Corner.

7 The Gay & Lesbian Scene

The most reliable source for information on gay clubs and activities is the **Lesbian and Gay Switchboard** (ℂ 020/7837-7324). The staff runs a 24-hour service for information on gay-friendly places and activities. *Time Out* also carries information on lesbian and gay-geared events and places. A good place for finding out what's hot and hip is **Prowler Soho,** 5–7 Brewer St., Soho, W1 (ℂ 020/7734-4031; Tube: Piccadilly Circus), the largest gay-lifestyle store in London. You can buy anything from jewelry to CDs, books, fashion, and sex toys here. It's open until midnight on Friday and Saturday.

Admiral Duncan Gay men and their friends go here to drink, to have a good time, and to make a political statement. British tabloids shocked the world in 1999 when they reported that this pub had been bombed, with three people dying in the attack. Within 6 weeks, the pub reopened its doors. We're happy to report that the bar is better than ever, now also attracting nongays who show up to show their support. 54 Old Compton St., W1. ℂ 020/7437-5300. No cover. Tube: Piccadilly Circus.

Barcode This is a very relaxed and friendly bar. Hosting everyone from skinheads to "pint-of-lager" types, it has much of a "local pub" atmosphere. The bar is fairly male-dominated, but does not object to women entering. Open daily from 1pm to 1am. 3–4 Archer St., W1. ℂ 020/7734-3342. No cover. Tube: Piccadilly Circus.

The Box Adjacent to one of Covent Garden's best-known junctions, Seven Dials, this sophisticated Mediterranean-style bar attracts all kinds of men. In the afternoon, it is primarily a restaurant, serving meal-size salads, club sandwiches, and soups. Food service ends abruptly at 5:30pm, after which the place reveals its core: a cheerful, popular rendezvous for London's gay and counterculture crowds. The Box considers itself a "summer bar," throwing open doors and windows to a cluster of outdoor tables at the slightest hint of sunshine. The bar is open Monday through Saturday from 11am to 11pm, and Sunday from noon to 10:30pm. The cafe is open Monday to Saturday 11am to 5:30pm, and Sunday noon to 6:30pm. 32–34 Monmouth St. (at Seven Dials), WC2. ℂ 020/7240-5828. No cover. Tube: Leicester Sq.

Candy Bar This is the most popular lesbian bar in London at the moment. It has an extremely mixed clientele, ranging from butch to femme and from young to old. There is a bar and a club downstairs. Design is simple, with bright colors and lots of mirrors upstairs, and darker, more flirtatious decor downstairs. Men are welcome as long as a woman escorts them. Open Monday through Thursday from 8pm to midnight, Friday and Saturday from 8pm to 2am, and Sunday from 7 to 11pm. 4 Carlisle St., W1. ℂ 020/7494-4041. Cover £5–£7 ($9.25–$13). Tube: Tottenham Court Rd.

The Edge Few bars in London can rival the tolerance, humor, and sexual sophistication found here. The first two floors are done up with decorations that, like an English garden, change with the seasons. Dance music can be found on the crowded, high-energy lower floors. Three menus are featured: a funky daytime menu, a cafe menu, and a late-night menu. Dancers hit the floors starting around 7:30pm. Clientele ranges from flamboyantly gay to hetero pub-crawlers. One downside: A reader claims the bartenders water down the drinks. Open Monday through Saturday from 11am to 1am, and Sunday from noon to 10:30pm. 11 Soho Sq., W1. ℂ 020/7439-1313. No cover. Tube: Tottenham Court Rd.

First Out First Out prides itself on being London's first (est. 1986) all-gay coffee shop. Set in a 19th-century building whose wood panels have been painted the colors of the gay-liberation rainbow, the bar and cafe are not particularly cruisy. Cappuccino and whiskey are the preferred libations; and an exclusively vegetarian menu includes curry dishes, potted pies in phyllo pastries, and salads. Don't expect a raucous atmosphere—some clients come here with their grandmothers. Look for the bulletin board with leaflets and business cards of gay and gay-friendly entrepreneurs. Open Monday through Saturday from 10am to 11pm, and Sunday from 11am to 10:30pm. 52 St. Giles High St., W1. ℂ 020/7240-8042. No cover. Tube: Tottenham Court Rd.

Friendly Society This is a Soho hot spot that bustles with young gay life, and there's even a rumor that Mrs. Guy Ritchie (Madonna) made a secret appearance here heavily disguised. "As what?" we asked, but no one knew. The action takes place in the basement of the building, which one patron called a "space-age lair." Perhaps the white-leather pod seating creates that aura. Come here for the drinks and the company—it's very cruisy. *Time Out London* describes the spot as a "gay, women-friendly venue with an alternative underground feel." Open daily noon to 11:30pm. In the basement of 79 Wardour St. (entrance is via a side street named Tisbury Court), W1. ℂ 020/ 7434-3805. No cover. Tube: Piccadilly Circus.

G.A.Y. Name notwithstanding, the clientele here is mixed, and on a Saturday night this could be the most rollicking club in London. You may not find love here, but you could discover a partner for the evening. Patrons have been known to strip down to their briefs or shorts. A mammoth place, this club draws a young crowd to dance beneath its mirrored disco balls. Open Monday through Friday from 10:30am to 4am, and Saturday from 10:30pm to 5am. London Astoria, 157 Charing Cross Rd., WC2. ℂ 020/7734-9592. Cover £10–£13 ($19–$24). Tube: Tottenham Court Rd.

Heaven This club, housed in the vaulted cellars of Charing Cross Railway Station, is a London landmark. Heaven is one of the biggest and best-established gay venues in Britain. Painted black and reminiscent of an air-raid shelter, the club is divided into at least four areas, connected by a labyrinth of catwalk stairs and hallways. Each room offers a different type of music, from hip-hop to rock. Heaven also has theme nights, which are frequented at different times by gays, lesbians, or a mostly heterosexual crowd. Thursday in particular seems open to anything, but on Saturday it's gays only. Call before you go. Open Monday and Wednesday from 10:30pm to 3am, Friday from 10:30pm to 6am, and Saturday from 10:30pm to

5am. The Arches, Villiers, and Craven sts., WC2. ⓒ **020/7930-2020.** Cover £5–£12 ($9.25–$22). Tube: Charing Cross or Embankment.

Ku Bar   The Happy Hour here lasts from noon to 9pm, and the bartenders assure us that their watering hole attracts "the tastiest men in London." Those bartenders serve up some of the tastiest drinks, including peach, melon, apple, lemon, and butterscotch schnapps. Come here for a fab time, to throw a bash, and to cruise. 75 Charing Cross Rd., WC2. ⓒ **020/7437-4303.** No cover. Tube: Leicester Sq.

Shadow Lounge   This is the current fave hot spot for gay men in Soho. "Our male patrons are fresh and sexy," a seasoned bartender told us. Shadow Lounge is in the vanguard of gay life in London, which, as the millennium deepens, is showing a tendency to shift from gargantuan dance palaces like Heaven to more intimate rendezvous points. Young men, who look like the cast of the British version of "Queer as Folk," meet here at 8pm for drinks. Some return after dinner to dance to raucous house music. Open Monday through Wednesday from 10pm to 3am, and Thursday through Saturday from 9pm to 3am. 5 Brewer St., W1. ⓒ **020/7287-7988.** Cover £3–£10 ($5.55–$19). Tube: Piccadilly Circus.

Index

See also Accommodations index below.

FROMMER'S® NATIONAL PARK GUIDES

Algonquin Provincial Park
Banff & Jasper
Family Vacations in the National
  Parks

Grand Canyon
National Parks of the American
  West
Rocky Mountain

Yellowstone & Grand Teton
Yosemite & Sequoia/Kings
  Canyon
Zion & Bryce Canyon

FROMMER'S® MEMORABLE WALKS

Chicago
London

New York
Paris

San Francisco

FROMMER'S® WITH KIDS GUIDES

Chicago
Las Vegas
New York City

Ottawa
San Francisco
Toronto

Vancouver
Walt Disney World® & Orlando
Washington, D.C.

SUZY GERSHMAN'S BORN TO SHOP GUIDES

Born to Shop: France
Born to Shop: Hong Kong,
  Shanghai & Beijing

Born to Shop: Italy
Born to Shop: London

Born to Shop: New York
Born to Shop: Paris

FROMMER'S® IRREVERENT GUIDES

Amsterdam
Boston
Chicago
Las Vegas
London

Los Angeles
Manhattan
New Orleans
Paris
Rome

San Francisco
Seattle & Portland
Vancouver
Walt Disney World®
Washington, D.C.

FROMMER'S® BEST-LOVED DRIVING TOURS

Austria
Britain
California
France

Germany
Ireland
Italy
New England

Northern Italy
Scotland
Spain
Tuscany & Umbria

THE UNOFFICIAL GUIDES®

Beyond Disney
California with Kids
Central Italy
Chicago
Cruises
Disneyland®
England
Florida
Florida with Kids
Inside Disney

Hawaii
Las Vegas
London
Maui
Mexico's Best Beach Resorts
Mini Las Vegas
Mini Mickey
New Orleans
New York City
Paris

San Francisco
Skiing & Snowboarding in the
  West
South Florida including Miami
  the Keys
Walt Disney World®
Walt Disney World® for
  Grown-ups
Walt Disney World® with Kids
Washington, D.C.

SPECIAL-INTEREST TITLES

Athens Past & Present
Cities Ranked & Rated
Frommer's Best Day Trips from London
Frommer's Best RV & Tent Campgrounds
  in the U.S.A.
Frommer's Caribbean Hideaways
Frommer's China: The 50 Most Memorable Trips
Frommer's Exploring America by RV
Frommer's Gay & Lesbian Europe
Frommer's NYC Free & Dirt Cheap

Frommer's Road Atlas Europe
Frommer's Road Atlas France
Frommer's Road Atlas Ireland
Frommer's Wonderful Weekends from
  New York City
The New York Times' Guide to Unforgettable
  Weekends
Retirement Places Rated
Rome Past & Present

Travel Tip: He who finds the best hotel deal has more to spend on facials involving knobbly vegetables.

Hello, the Roaming Gnome here. I've been nabbed from the garden and taken round the world. The people who took me are so terribly clever. They find the best offerings on Travelocity. For very little cha-ching. And that means I get to be pampered and exfoliated till I'm pink as a bunny's doodah.

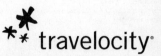

1-888-TRAVELOCITY / travelocity.com / America Online Keyword: Travel

Travel Tip: Make sure there's customer service for any change of plans — involving friendly natives, for example.

One can plan and plan, but if you don't book with the right people you can't seize le moment and canoodle with the poodle named Pansy. I, for one, am all for fraternizing with the locals. Better yet, if I need to extend my stay and my gnome nappers are willing, it can all be arranged through the 800 number at, oh look, how convenient, the lovely company coat of arms.

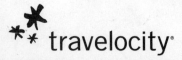